Options Trading

This Book Includes:

Beginners Guide + Crash Course for Start Now + Advanced Winning Strategies Guide, 3 Manuals for Generate Income Now and Learn Profitable, Start Investing Now.

Trading Club America

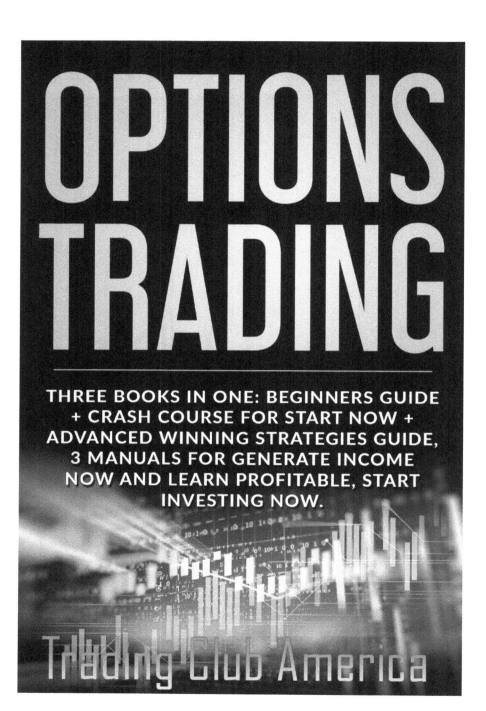

OPTIONS TRADING

THREE BOOKS IN ONE: BEGINNERS GUIDE
+ CRASH COURSE FOR START NOW +
ADVANCED WINNING STRATEGIES GUIDE,
3 MANUALS FOR GENERATE INCOME
NOW AND LEARN PROFITABLE, START
INVESTING NOW.

Trading Club America

Table of Contents

Options Trading for Beginners

The Latest Complete Guide 2021/22, All the Systems, Tips, and Strategies, Explained Step by Step in a Simple and Practical Way, Start Now and Invest in Options Trading.

Trading Club America

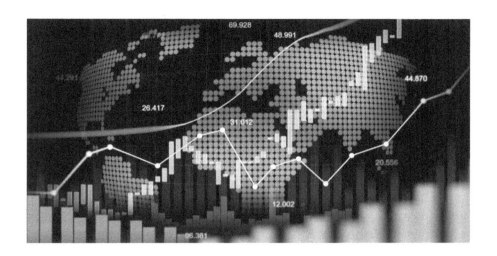

deemed liable in any fashion for any damages or hardships that may result from any of the information discussed herein.

Additionally, the information in the following pages is intended only for informational purposes and should thus be thought of as universal. As befitting its nature, it is presented without assurance regarding its prolonged validity or interim quality. Trademarks that are mentioned are done without written consent and can in no way be considered an endorsement from the trademark holder.

Chapter 1: The Basics of Options Trading

When you hear about investment what clicks right away for most people is stocks and bonds. The word options trading escapes unnoticed.

An option is a contract allowing the bearer (but not forcing the bearer) to either put or call the stated asset at a named price within a defined period of time. A call option allows the bearer to buy stock while a put option allows the bearer to sell the stock.

Investors' portfolios are usually made up with a number of asset classes. It could be stocks, currencies, bonds, ETFs or cash equivalents. Another type of asset class is options and when used in an appropriate manner they offer more advantages than stocks and ETFs combined.

Options can positively affect an individual`s portfolio through added income, protection and leverage depending on the situation. Another use is that they help in speculation purposes.

Options are a member of a group of securities called derivatives. From the perspective that, the price of options is dependent on the going price of other assets. Derivatives may include things like; futures, forwards, mortgage-backed securities, calls, and swaps.

Being an asset option can be purchased like any other asset. An investor needs a brokerage account to invest in the stocks they hope will turn their initial investment into a lifetime fortune.

It is important to find a broker that gives you access to all the kinds of different investments that are important to you. The key features to look in a good broker include;

- Low commissions
- Good research
- Great customer report

Options are best traded in the following platforms;

- **E*TRADE**

Best for options overall

E*TRADE offers quite expensive options trades but the magnitude held by this platform is great for options trading and the broker offers different mobile applications.

- **InteractiveBrokers- Lowest commissions**

  Interactive Brokers is not the best platform for relaxed or unplanned individuals but it propels the industry in international trading and minimum commissions desired by more planned and informed traders.

- **TD Ameritrade- Best option tools**

  The increased expenditure incurred when trading with TD Ameritrade does not go unaccounted for. The brokerage offers amazing platforms, research, mobile apps, education, and customer inquiries. No doubt it has the top-bar grade in all-round experience.

- **Trade Station- Well-rounded offering**

  Trade Station is a well-established trading technology and it is very supportive of its web-based platform and active traders through its awarding desktop platform.

- **Charles Schwab- Unique order types**

Talk about reduced costs, proper research, top-notch trade tools, and well-calculated future plans Charles Schwab will not let you down.

So how much do you need to have in your pocket to start this great investment journey?

Normally options trade in share blocks of 100, so a $1 option costs$100, commissions included. But also, options may be agreed on in any kind of named assets such as bonds, currencies or even commodities.

The upper hand in buying options is that an investor can take part in predicting the price moves of stock, without having liquid cash. Options trading is an almost high-risk area of the investment world. According to statistics conducted by CBOE just about 10% of options are carried out, 60% are closed out, and 30% goes to waste.

Where a broker is involved you should be notified that options never miss risks and are not for just anyone to venture in. Options trading is unpredictable and has a high-risk percentage of loss. The investor must be made aware of this before jumping into it.

Stocks and bonds have one thing in common with options and that is risks. Options trading takes more effort to do well than stock trading but it pays at the end of the game.

Chapter 2: The Types of Options Trading

The financial market has lots of ways of making money. Options trading happens to be one of these methods. Like any other money-making scheme, there is always a need for a prior understanding of the dynamics of the trade in the spotlight. Stock markets have their own ways and regulations. To fit in you have to align with the trade that favors you and feels right. The main types of options trade are calls and puts. They don't stop there, they can also be classified on the basis of time a contract can be put to work, expiration date, the security they are connected to and lastly the method of trade. Discussed are the various types of options trades to top up the option trade knowledge.

Calls are those financial contracts; agreements that offer the owner mandate to purchase an underlying asset in the future at a price that was agreed on. Buyers of these options will do so with speculation that the price of the security will go higher. They identify a time when the value of the option is high enough and make a sale which comes with a profit. Sometimes daring before the exercise date can get you more than what the market price was, so patience may help earn more cash. These buyers of options can also be referred to as holders while those that assist them in selling the options are called writers.

The underlying security is said to be the asset that holds the contract. An example would be you purchase a call based on some shares in this company Y, by purchasing them you obtain the powers to buy shares in the same company. A call has an expiration date and therefore it has to be sold off at a profit before or on the expiry date. Sellers in a call option have the obligation to sell off the stocks as long as they are assigned.

Put options are the trade whereby you make a purchase on the rights to make a sale on all stocks at a better price at any moment before the set and agreed on the date of expiry. The price is predetermined. Inputs, the holders believe the stock price will decrease with time. The sellers of a put option find themselves in a spot where they are obligated to buy the stock if only, they are assigned. You will buy a put I you believe that its price will fall. Puts are therefore perfect tools for leverage and also important as hedging; reducing any risks predictable at a reasonable cost, tool in financial markets. Puts mean that if by example you buy a put based stock, it comes with the right to make sales on shares in the given company at a price; strike price. The strike price is the price that an options trade can be exercised on.

American style options have no relations to where the contracts are to be bought or sold. Its focus is on the terms agreeable on a contract. A normal put or call contract requires the buyer (put options) or the seller (call option) to exercise their securities at that time before the expiration date. In the American style option, the owner who owns the contract has some privileges that include a right to exercise at any given moment as long as its time prior to the expiration date. It is however not mandatory to follow the expiry date as a holder. This type of trade has some risks that it poses to the option sellers.

A European style option has a close similarity to the American one only that they differ at the time of exercise of the trade. With the European style of option trading, you can only exercise the right to buy; if it's a call option, or sell; if it's a put option on the exact date of expiration and not any time before or after. This style is advantageous because it is less common which translates to lower cost of maintaining it and running it. This type of trade also does not focus on geographical regions. This trade type has reduced flexibility that can be noted since it has also an effect on the contracts and tends to make them even cheaper.

Exchange-traded options are common around the globe. An exchange-traded option is commonly known as a listed option and it's a standardized form of the option. It can be sold or bought by just anyone interested in the trade but under the guidance and help of a broker sometimes. This group of trade type holds any option contract that is listed on a public trade exchange.

Over the counter option is another type of options trading that focuses on the purchase and sale of options only on the OTC markets; over the counter. They are well-tailored and have a bunch of complicated terms than most contracts. They are not readily available to the general public. It is also known as dealers' option since it involves two private parties that come up with their well-customized contract to accommodate the needs of the parties involved.

Apart from those discussed, types of options can also be based on the underlying securities. You would not believe me if I told you there are, many underlying securities available in the market. They include the following.

Stock options stand for those contracts in the form of shares that are available in a specific company that is already publicly listed.

Index options use the index in place of stocks as the underlying security.

Currency options involve grants to the ownership rights to place a purchase and sale that particular currency at a rate of exchange that was agreed earlier on.

Futures options include futures contracts. They give the owner the right to exercise and enter into a futures contract.

Commodity options involve physical commodities or commodity futures contracts as the underlying assets.

Basket options involve a contract that is based on a number of securities that have the potential to make to stocks, currencies and other financial instruments.

Options can also be categorized along with a timeframe. They can be regular, weekly, quarterly, and long term expiration anticipation securities.

Chapter 3: The Advantages of Trading in Options

There are several people who have found it appealing to trade in stocks because of its popularity. This is because several people fear trading other financial instruments. This is not supposed to be the case since other financial instruments such as options have a myriad advantage in the financial markets. Despite several people trading stocks, the numbers of people who are trading options have increased tremendously over the years. The major trigger of this increase is the advantages possessed by options. These advantages include;

Capital Outlay and Cost Efficiency

There is one of the major reasons that is owned by the trading of options. The talked about reason is the potential of making huge amounts of profits. It is more advantageous because an individual does not need to have huge capital investment in the trade. This phenomenon has made it ideal for an investor to focus on options trading because they can be able to start small as they invest more as time goes by. It is an attraction to even investors who have huge budgets as well because it proves to be cost-effective. In simple terms, one can be able to use leverage so as to acquire more trading power.

It is an occurrence has been proved to be true in the financial market. It is in the sense that an option trader can be able to purchase options of similar stock. This will give him or her the power to purchase the stock by using a call option. Buying options and later buy shares, in the event he or she sells the shares in the present market situation, one can be in a position to make a huge amount of profits. The trade of options has certain positions an individual can take to make sure that he or she save his or her capita investment depending on the underlying asset.

Risk and Reward

The risk to reward advantage is often linked to the first advantage illustrated above. It is all narrows down to profits an individual is able to create in the options market. Traders and investors in the options markets are able to make proportionate gains with regards to the amount they have invested in the trade. A good depiction can be made from the potential an individual has to gunner from small investment which also has the potential of multiplying. The advantaged risk to reward ratio is achieved to its maximum potentials in the event that an individual uses the right strategies.

 It is important for an individual to constantly note that there will always be risks involved in options trading. This is because it is a characteristic of any form of investment or business done by any person. There are trading strategies that can be very risky when it comes to using them to base critical decisions such as those that are speculative. The general rule in options trading is that speculation with high potential returns tends to have high-risk involvement in it. On the other hand, options that have low-risk levels tend to have fewer amounts of gains. Options trading involves various types of options contracts. This makes it easy for an individual to limit risks in option trading depending on the contract he or she has settled on.

Flexibility and Versatility

Flexibility is one of the most appealing elements that options trading poses. It is often in contract to several forms that are resented as a passive investment while some are inactive forms. The common characterization here is that an individual is limited to making money or using other strategies. A good depiction can be used by an individual who buys stocks for the thought of building his or her portfolio so as to serve long term gains. Such an individual can be able to use two kinds of strategies. The first strategy will involve a trader focusing on the long term gains and purchasing a stock that has the potential to increase in value in the future. The second strategy will involve an options trader can choose to invest in stock that gives regular returns. Buy and hold is a strategy that has several techniques involved to help it to be a success. However, the flexibility and versatility offered by the trading of options mean that an option trader has the potential of opening more opportunities. This means that a trader or investor of options has the ability to make profits in any kind of market condition. One is able to speculate price movements of foreign currencies, indices, and commodities. What this means is that a range of option trading strategies plays higher roles to a trader in the identification of other profitable ventures and being successful in them.

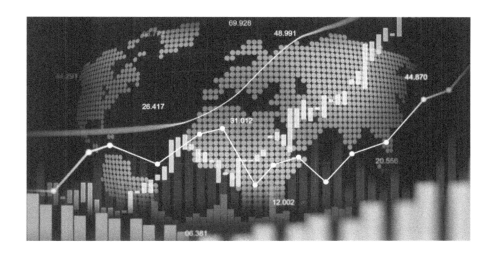

Chapter 4: The Components of an Option Contract

Underlying Asset

An underlying asset can be described as the financial assets in which prices of a derivative are based upon. In this case, the derivative will be options. It is a financial instrument that can price a specific asset. A good elucidation can be depicted by an option on a certain stock say XYZ. An options trader has the right to either sell or buy the option at an agreed strike option price which has a limited time. An underlying asset is able to spot the item being the aim of the contract. This helps an individual to be able to value the contract he or she is signing up for. The underlying asset tends to give participants of the security that is needed by both parties.

The price of the contract an individual is participating in is often determined by the type of asset being traded. The contract of an options trade is supposed to have two parties who are either buying or selling the underlying assets. Let's expound on the stock options as the underlying asset. If an individual has the potential of purchasing one hundred shares of a certain company at a price of one hundred American dollars, this will be the determinant of the value possessed by the option contract. An underlying asset can be a market index.

Type of Trading Option

The current financial market has seen numerous types of options being traded. The contract agreed by option trading parties is supposed to have a clear indication of which type of option is being traded. The types of options that are known in the current world tend to categorize and named depending on the varied features they pose. People across the globe are familiar with two types of options. Calls and puts options are popular in the financial markets.

Puts option gives a trader the ability to sell underlying assets. On the other hand, call options give an individual trading option the right to purchase an underlying asset. There are two common types of options that have been featured in the options contracts are known as the American and European options. Entering into a contract of American options allows a financial trader to be able to trade his or her underlying assets between the date e or she had purchased them to the date they are bound to be invalid. On the other hand, trade options contracts that contain European options bound an individual to perform his or her trades on the edge of the expiry time.

Strike Price

The presence of a strike price is a common phenomenon in the trade of options. It can be described as a major component when it narrows down to penning down of an option contract. Options such as calls and puts are heavily dependent on this factor. Its critical nature can be shown by an option trader who needs the call options. It is important because it determines the value possessed by the option. There are several people who have familiarized strike prices with a different name which is known as the exercise price.

The criticality of this component of the contract makes it one of the components that are discussed earlier between the contractual parties prior to them entering an agreement or contract. It is able to inform an investor or trader what the trader what in-the-value money is supposed to be achieved. The underlying price value of the traded assets is supposed to be lower than the strike price. In many cases, the strike price is always affected by the time frame of the contracts. One is supposed to remember that strike price operates on fixed amounts that can be converted to dollars. However, they vary depending on the contract and individual has.

Premium Price

The premium can be described as the price an option buyer in a contract pays the seller of the option. Terms of an option contract state that the amount is always paid upfront. It is always important for a trader to always remember that this component of a contract is not refundable. The rule extends itself to the side that one cannot be refunded his or her money even if the contract has been exercised. The premium quotation in a contract is always done in a certain way for efficiency. The most common way across the globe entails the quotation of option in the foundation of shares which is termed per share basis. The amount of premium is always affected by several variables before it is agreed on. The common determinants of premium prices are swayed by three major factors that are the volatility value of the option price, its timing, and the intrinsic value.

Expiration Date

One can easily understand the term expiration date of a contract as the last day he or she has the right to exercise either buying or selling the underlying financial instruments. A contract is termed worthless in moments the expiration date has passed. The expiration date tends to differ depending on the type of contract an individual has entered this despite the general principle of the contract being worthless after the last days. A contract using the American style of option trading gives an options trader the right to be able to trade his or her options from the date he or she purchased them to the day they expire. However, European sty trading fixes an individual to only performing his or her trades on the last days of contract expiration.

Settlement Option

The settlement of options can be described as the process by which the holder and writer of an options contract resolve and exercise the terms stated. The process entails the participation of two parties in the trade of options and it differs depending on the options one has decided to trade. It can be illustrated with both the calls and puts options. In calls options, it involves a holder paying the writer of the option. This is the reverse in the puts options since the holder of the options is the one selling them.

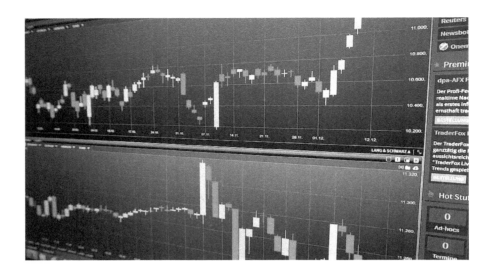

Chapter 5: The Fundamentals of the Pricing Options

Optional trading has grown significantly, even in the selling of stocks. The traders in this market care about the future growth of the business and not the present as opposed to the usual stock exchange. In this practice, one acquires the right to buy a stock but not the obligation. However, it should be before a certain maturation period. By the word obligation, it means that you are not mandated or forced to buy but is optional. This practice is a contract because it has the maturation period which the trader should follow.

You have to know the critical definition of some of the terms of this trading. These terms will prove significant in realizing the price trend of this trade. Remember that your main aim in the business is to have less value future contracts of buying an asset. You need to follow keenly on information regarding the assets to transact because their amount depends a lot on the premium you pay. The following are some of the terms found in this market.

There is a capped style option. This business is usually practiced when you are already aware of the asset's price. Therefore you can quickly evaluate the profit you will gain at the end of the maturation date. The risk of trading is also significantly reduced, and you can examine the right amount to use for the business.

Always remember that this business is related to forecasting of the future price and having the right to buy the assets with no obligation. However, you may wonder who facilitates such actions. It is not a broker as many of you may think but is an option writer. In simple, this person may be called the seller of an option. He or she is the mastermind of the whole process and will direct you on how to calculate the maturity value. The person also is in charge of receiving the premium. One extra thing with him is that he is obliged to buy the assets or the underlying security at the mandated price.

Sometimes due to the volatility of the market, you fear that the market will elapse significantly. There you make the right call by choosing the options trading. If you are that guy, who postpones the trading with the hope that it will maintain its worth at the expense of a volatile market, then you are wrong. Therefore, know that you are practicing the call options. This strategy is crucial if you anticipate that the market for the stocks is going to rise beyond your budget.

Another aspect is the put option which is vice versa of the call option. That involves the seller of the shares who fears that the stock market will recede. Therefore that seller will exercise the mandate to sell stocks at a particular price at a future date. In this case, the stock value falls below the next amount.

That future price is referred to as the strike price. It is thus the value that is realized at that scheduled times which the buyer or seller expects. More straightforward to say, is the value bought or sold over that specified period where you made either a call or put option. That price usually is exercised before the contract matures.

Everyone deserves the credit for their work even the option writer too. Therefore that credit is costly in terms of payments. You have to pay that individual an optional premium. That price is realized per the agreement between you and the optional writer. That right, you are buying or selling you have to secure it with the premiums paid. Otherwise, it will be reserved for somebody else.

You have to gauge the profit you will take in the optional trading. Therefore some terms like the intrinsic value should not escape your ears. This value is calculated by subtracting the value of the underlying stocks with the strike price. Remember that this trading is a derivative organ that depends on the amount of the fundamental asset. That fundamental has its market index, which must be less in case of call up or less in case of put up option.

Extrinsic value is another significant segment in this type of market. It is the value of that right against the intrinsic value. This trading is usually regarded as a time value fixture that has fewer profits.

Assumptions and Consideration of Optional Pricing

One assumption is that the underlying price of the stock is evenly distributed. That means the logarithm in working on its value is constant. By doing so, you can anticipate what will be the strike value or the expected value of the assets. In other terms, the volatility and the trend of the market are specific. Recognize that the volatility is the sharp increase and decrease in the price of a stock. The scheme also makes the mathematical calculation of the premium and the intrinsic value operational because of that constant function.

There are no transaction costs realized in this avenue. Moreover, there are no taxes evaluated which are calculated alongside the striking value. Otherwise, the tax and transaction costs will influence the intrinsic value reached. Therefore by including those in the final value, there will be a sensitivity of the change in the financial instruments. Value relative to the price of the underlying assets.

There are no dividends too in this security. The bonus would operate just like the taxes and the transaction costs. That is to mean if they are included, the final value will be different from the expected. They too have to be paid per year, and it is practical to remove the dividends so that one can reach the accurate results.

The risks free rate is assumed as constant. This rate is typically associated with government subsidies or incentives. If these aspects were included, they would manipulate the results of the outcomes negatively.

Stock trading is also thought to be continuous. For you to oversee that future settlement of trade, it means that the securities will continue even at a next date. If the stocks were not continuous, then it would pose a threat to those traders with buying shares at future expectations.

Chapter 6: How to Start Trading in Options

Would you agree that optional trading is exceptional? Some of you may not agree with this because you are fond of trading in the shares or the currencies which you consider less risky and volatile. How would you feel playing around with figure which future-oriented? Like a game of chess where you fill a puzzle of uncertainties, it is the same deal with optional trading where you do not know the future. Most of you discredit this trading because you think it is filled with uncertainties. However, with useful speculation of the trade, it will not earn you much of the risk. There are certain things you as the beginner you ought to follow. The following strategies to come up with the right option.

First is that you have to think of your investment objective. You do not go there in the trading aimlessly because you will lose a lot of money. Remember that options require that intelligent speculation because you are dealing with future gains. You have to establish realistic and measurable values that you expect. Such goals will give you a way to go and the route to follow. You may plan which type of optional trading you want. That is where you want the put off option or the call option. Moreover, do you want to speculate on the performance of the underlying asset or to hedge out their risks?

You have to examine the risks and the returns that the assets may bring you. Your biggest aim is always to harness sizeable gains while reducing the risks. You think that there are risks in the present and decide to buy them in the future. Or you with the put up option you predict that the shares will fall in the price and you award others right for protecting their expected depreciation. You have to be tolerant, optimistic, and persistent in your tasks. If you are a risk-taker, this is the right avenue for you. If you sense a volatile market exploit that opportunity to gain much.

Identify the different events of the market of the sector you are trading. Those events will institute the volatility of the occurrence. You can either experience a drift or a rise in the market. Those events can be grouped in two ways, where one is the market-wide, and the other is the stock specif. The market-wide are like those government jurisdictions that affect the economy of the whole sector. For example, the government banning or subsidizing some products. In the stock-specific one, they include issues like product launches and many others.

You have to derive the right strategies after knowing the stocks to trade and the returns you desire. These are distinctive tactics that you will apply to harness many gains. You must be that intelligent speculator who will read the patterns and try to realize the peak points and the volatility of the market. Moreover device some strategies like selling a call option against the stock. That is a tactic where you exercise a covered call approach on the security that you already own. You must sell the cover calls against your shares to identify the profitable spot. The other strategy is using the bullish or bearish strategy for call option and put option, respectively. Always buy puts options on significant stock platforms where you anticipate a substantial fallout of the top players in the industry.

Decide on the right parameter to facilitate your marketing. These are like the variables you will use to make a successful trading. Remember that for this trade, it requires one to know the trend, price analysis, and many other types.

Steps of Optional Trading for a Beginner

First is to identify the right brokerage account. You can do that by researching those that pay well and with the right features. You can still seek recommendations from the expert dealers. Check on their websites and create an account by keying in your correct details. Therefore, try to log in where you should remember your password vividly.

When you log in to that platform, you will be asked to select the right trade options you want. By now you should know the firm you want to buy from which you choose. It depends on the brokerage account because you should click on the odder or trade platform after identifying the shares to buy. This page should be clearly labeled, where click on to go to the next phase.

Search for the specific stock you want to buy. If you cannot find it in the list of the many securities, search for it in the search box. There will be multiple displays of the live quotes of share that re being traded, hence select the one you want to buy. Still, you can navigate on the quote table to identify the primary and the options ones. Chose those alternatives because they are the reasons you are doing the trading.

Then there is the maturation month option where you must identify the peak times. That expiry period is the point where your contract ends; thus, you should set it according to your potential. The month should be realized when you have studied how the market behaves. You may have discovered that in a particular month the selling of shares is relatively high while in another period they are low. Choose that month that looks productive on your strike index.

Selecting your strike is the second last step. That is the amount of an asset in the predetermined period. It should level up to what you can afford and oversee if it generates good revenue. You should not set the illogical or unrealistic figure just because you want to earn more. Know your potential and the size of your wallet.

Select the put or call options that are found at different columns of the table. Usually, calls are grouped on the left and the puts on the right. Recognize the side you want to venture. There is the platform for the quantity too. That is where you should fill the number of contracts you want to trade. Moreover set the price to pay for the option. Check and recheck the orders, when everything is clear now is right for you to confirm and send.

Chapter 7: The Platforms and Tools for Trading Options

You can never choose the right brokerage firm until you are assured that it contains the essential features. Many firms like to be distinct and unique so that they can have that competitive edge against their competitors. There are many different styles of portraying the features of the options trading that includes even their standard trading program. Some platforms have gone as far as offering the customized accounts which feature your specific styles and features that you prefer.

It is upon you to research the trade wisely about which brokerage accounts that would suit you. Optional trading needs seriousness because you need to learn how the shares will fair even in the future time. There are also the tools necessary to facilitate this trading and interpretation in the trading. They also help you to analyze the mathematical concept of that particular business. Some of the platforms found in those brokerage accounts include the following

You may have been told severally by your elementary teacher that 'practice, practice makes perfect. The same concept needed here because you cannot wake up one early morning and find yourself professional in this trading. Therefore you have to exercise until you graduate from being an amateur to a professional trader. In that regard, some sites offer paper trade platforms. That is the accounts where there is fake cash. Remember that alternative trading is volatile where if you are an amateur, you can suffer quite big losses. However, the demo accounts will help you to prevent such misfortunes. You play around with these accounts because you are losing nothing in the game. You also gain experience in trading and identify the trend which you will use when you stake the actual payment. It also sharpens the skills of interpretation and analysis in trading. You have to be aggressive and consistently trading to gain that experience.

The technicalities of the trading deem you to sometimes search for a website where you engage other traders. Remember that you and other traders share the same interests, and you help each other to trade. For that concern, you establish a social networking platform for all traders. In simple, you are batching the networking program and compose all your marketing need to your audiences in social marketing. You first create a profile files with your status so that other people may know you. Then you make several posts to your friends who may help you in your trading scheme.

There is also risk management orders. What makes people fear most in optional trading is the volatility in the business. Therefore in the processing of hedging out any risks, you may realize that you have suffered substantial losses. However, you need to reduce such losses. You use this site to learn the risk control orders such as the stop loss ones. For that reason, be vigilant in the trading and do no fear the risks, that moment you fail to stake your cash maybe the moment destined for your success.

There is also a personalized or customized layout in the trading. Some of the features found in brokerage accounts must correspond to your individual needs. Some of these brokers will contact you to detail them on which layout you prefer. That in particular concerns with the type of charts, the variable to use, and how they should be arranged in the layout. You always feel psyched to trade on a platform that you prefer. You even believe your chances of amercing good returns in the optional accounts are increased.

Which Are the Tools Known in the Optional Trading Is the Charts

The charts are some of the essential tools for optional binary trading. These charts are diagrams that exhibit trading schemes. They are featured with horizontal and vertical axis each with the independent and dependent variables respectively. In some firms, these charts are advanced in that they enable one to react to the fast-moving prices. They still have risk controller platforms. You have to analyze these charts to know how the options trade will fair. Recognize their marketing predictor's ability of the tables too. If you are an experienced reader, you will have just a glance at the chart and determine the trend the trade is following. Remember that you are making the future derivatives where the charts must also outline the value of the underlying assets and the staking price.

You need the indicators which show you the performance of the trading. This phenomenon shows you the direction and the trend of buying or selling. You also establish the volatile regions where the peak times and the recession point are also known. Check an indicator such as the MACD, where it measures the trend and the direction of the price. Here you quickly detect a high and a low trade.

The use of technical analysis tools is crucial in this subject because you will learn about the technicalities that make you succeed. This tool links the chart with the indicators. Is serves to predict the options trade price by checking at its past performance. Therefore you do not have to research for information on other sites or manuals. However, you can have that historical and trend data at the trading platform. By using this approach you can examine the type of indicators in measuring the trend. That is like the volume indicator which is located below the price pointer. It has a calibration like green and red. If the price moves upward, it is showed by green and if it moves down, it is shown by red.

Another technical analysis tool is the chart pattern. It mainly consists of the trend continuation patterns which shows that the correlation of the prices which are moving in the same direction. The trend reversal trend is another type in which its figures are moving in the opposite direction. Take an example of the rising wedge that is found in the trend continuation and the falling wedge in the reversal pattern. The one found in the rising contention has the bearish movement and the one falling has the bullish effect. Remember that for the bearish effect it is concerned with the put options and for the bullish is related to the call type. Therefore, these effects prompt the rising wedge to move in the same direction and the falling wedge moves in the opposite direction as you are operating with a call option.

Chapter 8: Leverage

Leverage is a term that is, in most cases, made use in financial management. It comes up from borrowing capital as a way of funding as well as expanding an investment. It will then generate some returns on the risk capital. It is a strategy to invest in using money that is borrowed. It increases the profits of the investment made. Leverage can as well be the debt amount that a company puts in use to finance its assets. When the leverage is high, that means that the investor has more debt that has accumulated than the equity. Leverage is known to boost the returns and hence, an increase in the profit.

It multiplies the potential returns from a particular investment. It will bring down the is likely to come up in case the investment you have made does not turn out as you had expected. The idea of leverage is put I use by investors as well as firms. An investor will use to make sure that there is an increase in returns on the investment. The investment will be levered using specific instruments, including margin accounts, options as well as futures. Companies will use leverage to finance their assets. Instead of issuing stock so that they can raise capital, they decide to use the debt to finance, aiming to increase the shareholder value.

Investors do not prefer to use leverage in a direct way they have their means to access it indirectly. They opt to invest in a company that they know uses force to fund as well as expand their investments. The company does not have to increase the outlay necessarily. Leverage is an excellent approach anyone can put in use to multiply the buying power in the trade out there. However, you can decide to use margin as a way of creating leverage.

Types of Leverages

There are several types of leverage, but they do not need to be combined with being productive. They instead form the entire process even though they are independent. They include;

Operating Leverage

Operating leverage is just concerned with the investment activities of an individual firm. It is about the incurrence of the fixed cost of operation in a company's income stream. The operating price can either be fixed, semi-fixed, variable as well as semi-variable. The fixed fee is contractual, and it is subject to time. It does not necessarily have to change when the sales change, and it is supposed to be paid despite the number of sales.

Variable cost t has a direct variation with the level of sales revenue. There will be no variable cost if there will be no any sales that are made in a certain period. Semi-variable, as well as semi-fixed, will vary partly with the number of purchases made and it will remain partially fixed. It is subject to be broken down into variable as well as fixed portions and is brought together according to the variable or the fixed cost. The fixed operating cost can be subject to be put in a lever, and hence the decisions of investment will go in favor of using assets that have a fixed price.

When a firm decides to use the fixed cost, it will increase the effect that a change will have on the sales when EBIT changes. The ability that a firm will have to put the fixed operating cost in use to increase its earnings before the interest as well as the taxes is what is known as operating leverage. The leverage will be concerning the variation of the sales as well as profit. When the percentage of the operating cost is high, then there will be a rise in the level of operating cost.

Financial Leverage

It is a relation to the combination of debts as well as equity in the capital format of a company. When there are financial charges in existence, the financial leverage will as well exist. The business costs should not depend on the operating profits in any way. The sources in which the funds that help to boost an investment come from can be put in categories. The funds can either be having a fixed charge, and some may not be having the fixed financial cost. Debentures, preference shares, bonds as well as long-term loans have a fixed financial burden. Equity shares are known to have no fixed charge at all.

The fixed financial charge is used as a lever, and hence, the business decisions will go in favor when you employ such funds. When there are fixed charges in a company's income stream, financial leverage will be an outcome. It is an excellent idea to make sure that the change that will be made in EBIT to affect EPS will be significant. The higher the level of fixed charges, the higher the probability that the degree of financial leverage will go up. When the fixed costs do down, the economic advantage will go down as well.

Combined Leverage

If you bring both the operating leverage and the financial leverage together, they will come up with the combined force. It is concerning the risk of one not being able to cover up for the total amount of the fixed charges. When a firm can cover fully on the operating as well as the financial burdens that is when the term combined leverage comes in. The higher the fixed operating cost as well as the financial charges, the higher the level of the combined force.

Working Capital Leverage

When there is a decrease in the investment of a particular asset, there will be an increase in profit. When there are many investors in the market and dealing with the same trade, there will be decreased profit. When there is a decrease in the investment of an asset, the risk associated with it will go high. That means that risks, as well as returns, have direct relations. When the probability of risk goes up, there is a likely hood that the profit will increase as well. The ability of an individual firm to increase the effect of the change in the current stock on the firm's returns is working capital leverage. It is so when there is an assumption that the liabilities are constant.

Chapter 9: Why Leverage can be Riskier

At some point, you will need to take some loans so that you can expand your investment. Debt financing is attractive since the lending entity will not in any way dictate how you will use the credit. When a firm has a lot of pending debts in comparison with the operating cash as well as equity, it is highly leveraged. When a company's leverage is high, it, in turn, becomes sensitive to the economic changes. They too are subject to the risk of being bankrupt. The reason why leverage is riskier is that they are subject to;

Limited Growth

When you have a loan, the lending company will expect that you will pay in the period that was agreed upon when you were getting the loan. They hope that you will be on time and no failures should come along the way. It is a problem when an investor borrows money for a long-term project that will not generate some income immediately. That will make them find an alternative to how they will pay the loan to avoid breaching the contract. If the payment period has come, and the investor has no returns, paying the mortgage can be a burden in one way or the other. When you decide to start paying the loan, it will mean that you use the money you borrowed to pay back. When that happens, you will have less money for financing your operations. You will not be in a position to implement full on the plan that you had. That means that you can have retardation, and you will not execute your plan fully. When investing, you need a plan and to set deadlines for the completion so that you will remain on your focus. When you have to pay the loan with the money that you borrowed, you will not be in a position to hit your deadlines. That will mean that you will experience limited growth, and you may not have the potential to continue as per the plan.

Losing Assets

When you are unable to pay loans, and you are highly leveraged, that can lead to a conspirator of the assets that you have. There is no way that a company should pay capital sourcing from equity. When that happens, and the lender expects that you will pay your loan in time, they can decide to take some of your assets to stand in for the loan. The assets can be of a similar value or a value higher than your investment. When in a loan, the company is supposed to pay the lender before any other deductions. Repossession of assets can happen if there is no money to pay the lender in time. It the lender has to be paid even before the employees of the company, it means that the employees may look for another option and quit working with you. That will make you lose assets of value, and you will be left stranded.

Inability to Get More Financing

Before a lender gives you money to invest in any trade, they will first check out whether you have any other loan. They will do that to establish how secure their payment is with you. If you are in debt, no lender will want to lend you more because they are not sure whether you will be in a position to clear their debt. They will access the risk that is associated in case the company goes down, meaning there will be no one to pay their loan. When a company goes down, it is declared bankrupt, and that means that the lender cannot claim their money even on a legal basis. No lender will agree to put them last on your loan list since they know they will be the last to be paid.

An Investor Will Not Be in a Position to Attract Equity

When a company has high leverage, they are not able to increase the equity capital amount. And it is rare for an investor to give money to a business that has bid records of unclear loans. In the same way, lenders will avoid providing more money to a company with high amounts of investments, and the same way investors avoid such business. You will lose the potential of attracting investors when you have a lot of pending debts. When a lender knows they are the last in your line to be paid their loan, they will not find it comfortable to lend you. If at with any chance you get an investor to give you, they will demand a significant percentage in terms of ownership in return of borrowing you the money.

Multiple as Well as Constant Losses

There is a risk in leverage in cases where you invest in a particular stock and the price of the stock takes a negative change when you least expect. You will end up suffering a lot of losses since you have to pay the loan back in time and you have other expenses to deduct. That will be hard on you since there is no profit made considering you made a loss. Taking a loan can begin with the increase in losses as well as end with the losses locking in within a short period. High amounts of debts can get out of hand and can lead to bankruptcy at a very high speed. When you are declared bankrupt, it comes with several consequences. There is no time that you will get any other loan no matter how you will have an enticing business plan. No investor will want to have an association with a bankrupt person. That will make any investor who has the potential to fund you to pull out.

Even though you need a lot of money to invest in a long-term plan, you need to have an idea of how to repay the loan. The project you have May not at times work in the way you would want it to and the need to have a back-up plan. If it is necessary, avoid late payment of loans and maintain the discipline of the highest level when the repayment period arrives. If you observe all the rules layout when taking the loan, you will not have a hard time with the lender. They will be willing to lend you more and more when you need it.

Chapter 10: The Advantage of Trading with Leverage

In trading, one opts for premises or rather a transaction that is profit-generating and one that plays a critical role in increasing the capital base of an investor. In other words, no one enters into any trade to suffer a loss. However, individuals, as well as premises, take time to think of the options that will help them solidify a marketing position and earn more profits in the long run. In Forex trading, the decision that one takes plays a critical role in determining whether one will earn profits or not. However, taking leverage options might be the best decision that one can make. Even though force is associated with several risks, it has the benefits that it carries as well. As outlined earlier, the higher the risk, the higher the probability of getting high profits. The advantages of trading with leverage include and not limited to. Take a look at some of the advantages of leverage options:

Increase in Profit

Leverage will earn you more benefits without necessarily having to put in more effort. Since it is borrowed money, you do not have to toil so much so that you can earn it; instead, you look for a lender. When you fulfill the requirements, the lender will finance you and you will have to repay back when the period lapses. When you inject more capital into a business, it is likely to give you more returns under favorable market conditions. It does not matter the amount that you are adding to the investment. You can stake a large or a small amount and your profits will not remain at the same level they were before you get the loan. It does not matter the kind of trade that you are in; what matters is that you have added more capital in it. There will be an overall growth when more financing is put in a business, meaning that there will be growing as well in the levels of profit. Leverage makes sure that you are one step ahead all the time and a step forward in terms of profit.

When you need to inject more capital into a business, the primary objective is to make more money out of it. That is why people go for leverage since there is no other way to raise funds in a fast way. When you take a loan, you need to have a commitment in the business you are doing and invest your time is that it will have positive yields. When you take a loan, and you forget about being zealous, you will suffer losses and the need to be active. Let your focus be to multiply the money is that you can get some to pay the loan with interest and you can achieve your aim for making a profit. Before you go for the loan, take a scan of the trade you want to invest in, and see the changes it has to make more money. Pick on the hot deal, and you will have good returns at the end of the day.

An Increase in Capital Efficiency

When you increase the amount of money in a particular transaction can lead to a rise in productivity on how you use your capital. You need to consider capital as an asset, and it can increase the level of yields. When you take a loan, you will increase the amount of money, and you will raise the level of efficiency. The amount you get when there is no loan in your trade will mean that it will rise when you add more capital. Reinvesting more times will make sure that more frequency, as well as efficiency, is arrived at. Leverage will not just increase the profit level, and it will as well give a considerable return on the investment within a short period.

Is a Tool that Mitigates Against Low Volatility

Leverage is a great approach that can be put in place to mitigate the effect brought about by low volatility. Volatile trade is known to deliver huge profits in the Forex trade. It can deliver good benefits from a small transaction and can shield against the effect that comes with low volatility. A small entity can become a big firm with the help of leverage. Leverage will help you to capitalize on the small significant levels of movement in the trading price.

Leverage is double-edged, and it will work for you in a great way. When things turn around you, it will be hard to get out of such a position. And so, the need to be extra careful when you are dealing with leverage since it can be a rescue tool for an investment that is going under. It is an alternative that you can seek when you need to boost your trade. When you are choosing leverage, choose the one that is in line with the trading strategy you have. Do not take much loan than you need since it will give you a hard time when repaying, and maybe you did not invest all in the business. You will struggle when paying, and no return is seen.

Low Cost of Entry

The arithmetic options that are used in leverage options are relatively cheap, but the resultant profits are relatively high. In other words, one is required to pay a relatively small amount to fit in the market. You can buy as low as 50 shares with a minimum of $1000. It is worth noting that the option is simple, but there are many chances of getting higher profits. The aspect is critical in the sense that the number of risks involved is relatively low than the benefits accrued to this option. The other element that makes it more straightforward is the fact that it is one of the most flexible options. Traders are given several options that allow them to earn well despite having used a minimal amount of capital used as the initial investment.

Chapter 11: The Disadvantages of Trading Leverage Options

Lower Liquidity

It is worth noting that a lot of individual stock options dint has many volumes. There are cases where one is forced to own very few stocks. The aspect that in all the options that one has will trade at different strikes of payments as well as expectations, the particular option will be forced to have a less volume unless it is one of the most popular stock index or stocks. However, the lower liquidity won`t affect smaller traders who would prefer working with manageable amounts of about ten contacts. Larger traders with more than 100 contracts will be forced to have other options or undergo an extra cost to increase their volume. Some are forced to take several options to compensate for fewer amounts. However, there are cases where such an opportunity doesn't work due to the rules and regulations that operate in different organizations. In most cases, the traders are forced to accept the lower volume and look for other options of investing. However, the art of being forced to take only the popular options or rather the stock indexes that have larger volumes causes them to suffer a massive loss in case the organizations fail to meet its target.

High Spreads

The art of lacking liquidity among these trading options causes higher spreads. The aspect is detrimental due to the fact that one is forced to pay more indirect costs while using thus trade option. The element is linked to the fact that when one is using the opportunity, they will be spreading the trade. It is worth noting that larger organizations of firms with higher operations power are forced to pay more indirect costs to compensate for this spread. The aspect becomes a fail when issues crop up, and the firm is forced to limit the art of range. In most cases, individual or rather organizations which had primarily invested in the premises are forced to suffer huge losses as the organizations look for ways of compensation. It is worth noting that there are cases where the firms with large contracts are forced to outline all the options of trade and use all of them as a means of compensating for the low liquidity. The art increases the spread, and more risks are attracted. The aspect is linked to the fact that the owner or the organization will have to pay all the indirect costs to compensate for the many spreads.

Higher Commissions

When one is operating with such organizations, one is forced to pay using commission terms. In other words, one has to pay a certain amount of commission for each dollar that is invested. The demerit is worsened by the fact that the option has very many options that forced one to have a lot of spreads. It is worth noting that for all the ranges that one is involved in, there is a certain amount of commission that one has to pay. The aspect is detrimental since the organization has low liquidity and attracts from more spreads. Thus, in case of any loss, the premises or rather individuals who have invested using such an option are forced to dig deeper in their pockets so as they can compensate for the commission required to fund or allow such possibilities of trade to be operational.

Complicated

One of the aspects that forced people or instead traders to ignore the options of trade in the fact that it is one of the most difficult choices. There comes a time where even those who have been investing with the option, fail to understand the processing of their trade. The aspect is more complicated among beginners. In other words, beginners fail to know the number of options they ought to take before they can think of investing. There are numerous cases where traders are confused about the number of spreads to be involved in. The other option that complicates everything is the fact that one has to pay in terms of commission. The aspect is challenging as these commissions aren't fixed. In other words, they keep changing from time to time. It is worth noting that the art of having complicated options causes traders to opt for other options that seem natural and command higher profits in the long run.

Time Decay

When you buy this option, one is forced to lose the value of time and money. In other words, as you hold these options, you lose their value in terms of time. The more you keep them, the more you lose their value. One of the most difficult and challenging aspects of this option is that there is no exception over this rule. In other words, so long as you take this opportunity, you will have to hold it for some time. The more you keep, the worse it becomes as their value reduces.

Less Information

The option is very painful when one is forced to accept whatever they receive. In other words, there are no options where one is given the complete information of what is happening with their accounts. In most cases, the choices don't provide analytical information about the organization. What happens is that the owners try to understand what they receive with the mind that their options lost their value as they were holding them.

Availability

It is worth noting that this option is not available for all the stocks. In other words, although the option is available for several shares, there are still limits over the capital that applies the option. The aspect is more complicated as one may not comprehend the kind of stock that takes this option. The limitation is detrimental in the sense that it puts the traders in jeopardy over the opportunity to choose. The aspect is linked to the fact that few options have such terms. In most cases, one is forced to consult brokers who end up charging other fees hence increasing the commissions that one has to pay for the option.

Chapter 12: How Much Leverage It Takes to Trade-In Options

Leveraging options can be compelling when it comes to the art of investing. In other words, if the season works out in the best way for you, you will enjoy the fruits of the option. The aspect is linked to the fact that the number of commissions might reduce as well as the expenses and the profits earned might rise with immeasurable value. There are cases where small amounts of capital are invested using this trade option, and in the long run, the premises earn a lot of profits. The profits earned are then channeled to the various traders who opted to take the leverage option. When one is having different financial instruments such as stock, one may take advantage of the possibilities and borrow funds that take the position forever. In other words, with such devices, the art of investing using leverage options becomes available. One of the best choices about this contract is the fact that the leverage option contracts them. The aspect causes a great multiplication that increases the amount that one had invested.

The Much It Takes

When one is buying contracts, one is allowed to control more considerable amounts of underlying security such as stock. The aspect is critical in the sense that such options trade by themselves. In other words, one doesn't have to be in the market and do the trading. However, the option contracts the leverage themselves and multiplies the amount of capital that was initially invested. In the long run, more profits are generated to the winners in these accounts. In other words, if you have some capital and want to invest using these options, you can buy a stock that uses leverage and earn in the long run.

For instance, if you wanted to invest $ 1000and wish to use a company that is well known in the nation. One of the aspects that emerge from such an option is that you expect the organization to increase the investment and turn it into a profit-making opportunity. However, this is not what happens always. There are situations where the organization misses the mark and loses are channeled to the owners of these options. If the organization or rather the company of choice trade its shares $20, you will be forced to buy at least 50 shares with your $1000 investment. In case the organization does well in terms of its operation, and a profit is generated, the shares will be sold at a higher price. For instance, if the shares trade at $25 each, when all the shares are resold, the owner of the option will earn $5 in each stock and amass a profit of about $250.

When it comes to leverage option, let`s assume you want to invest $1000 in the same company trading at $2 with a strike price of about $20. If the contract size is, let's say 100, you will be in a position of buying five contracts at $200 each. The aspect means that you will be in a good option of controlling over 500 shared in the organization. The element is different from the first option, where one is forced to buy only 50 shares directly. In other words, leverage options provide opportunities for taking contracts instead of buying shares directly from the organization. In the long run, a lot of profits are generated to the owners of the leverage option.

The aspect illustrates the basic principle of how leverage works. One of the merits of the leverage option is that it can command a lot of funds or instead profits with very little starting capital. In most cases, the organization or stock with leverage options encourages even small traders who might be having a small amount of money, to begin with. However, with time and with a favorite season, the organization can generate a lot of profits that are in turn made to the owners of these options.

Thus, one can earn as much as they can invest. In other words, the amount received depends on the option that one takes, as well as the funds spent. However, with as low as $100, one can enter into a few contacts with the origination offering the option at a relatively low price. The aspect is critical in the sense that the organization does well, and it doesn't depend on the possibilities one had taken. All the profits are channeled to the owners of these leverage options depending on the number of contracts that one had.

It is worth noting that the price option that one takes moves as a fraction of the entire amount. The other aspect worth noting is that if you have a choice of $5, it is not a must that the earning be $5 more. Depending on the opportunity as well as the season of the organization, one can command higher or fewer profits. The aspect depends on the calculations as well as the commissions that one is forced to pay. However, in most cases, individuals, as well as an organization, can command higher profits, and there are cases where their ama9unt of investment doubles. The aspect indicates that there are no limits over what you can earn provided the organization is generating profits and channeling them your way.

In a nutshell, the ability to use leverage to multiply the profits is a massive advantage to various trading options. In other words, with the right timing and the best trading options, organizations, as well as traders, can earn a lot of profits. However, increased earning attracts several risks on the premises. Thus, before you opt over any investment plan or instead leverage option, it is wise to consider the options available as well as the risks therein. The aspect is linked to the fact that you may earn a lot of profits but end up suffering losses due to the risks involved. It is wise to be aware of the role of money in your leverage contact.

Chapter 13: How You Can Manage Risk in Options Trading

Appropriate risk management in options trading may sound like an outdated idea to some people but the truth is that effective risk management is the number one recipe for success in options trading. Being able to efficiently manage your risk exposure as well as your capital is key when trading options. In as much as risk is basically unavoidable in any business venture, the exposure to risk should not be a problem. The key solution is to take measures that will successfully manage the finances that are at risk. Always make sure that you consent to the degree of risk you are exposing your trade to and that you do not expose yourself to untenable loses.

In this chapter, we take a look at some of the measures you can put in place to manage your risk exposure.

Use Your Trading Master Plan

It is crucial to be in possession of a comprehensive trading master plan that designs the parameters as well as guidelines for the trade. The most practical uses of this kind of plan include money management and most importantly, in this case, managing your exposure to risk. Your trading plan should be inclusive of detailed information on the degree of risk that you are at ease with as well as the amount of capital you intend to invest with.

When you follow your plan to the letter and strictly use the funds that have been categorically set aside for the purpose of options trading, it becomes easy to fend off some of the greatest blunders that traders and investors make, such as, investing using funds that are "scared".

The moment you opt to trade using finances that you should have allocated to other uses or finances that you simply cannot afford to divest, chances are that you will not make logical decisions in your trading activities. Whereas it is hard to entirely do away with emotions that come forth in options trading, you desperately need to focus as much as possible on your trading activities. Why?

As soon as emotions overwhelm you, chances are that you will begin losing your focus and consequently behave in an irrational manner. For example, you can be driven to carry out transactions that you would otherwise not have made in normal circumstances. However, if you strictly work in accordance with the design of your trading plan and strictly use the resources you allocated to investment, then chances are that you will take control of your emotions.

You should also strictly abide by the degree of risk that is stated in the trading plan. Giving your consent to trades that are low risk means that you should refrain from putting yourself in positions that will expose you to higher risks. Usually, it is tempting to put yourself in vulnerable positions by exposing yourself to risk if you make a couple of losses and yet you are in the quest to make things right, or perhaps you have performed exceptionally well with a number of low-risk trades and you have the desire to revamp your gains at a much quicker faster. If your choice was to settle for minimal risk investment, there is definitely no need to go out of your safe zone by falling prey to the emotions we discussed earlier on.

Using Option Spreads to Manage Risks

Option spreads can be termed as powerful and necessary instruments whenever you are trading in options. Options spreads are basically whenever you integrate more than one position on options agreements in reference to similar fundamental security to efficiently come up with a general position of trade.

An example would be, making a purchase in the money calls on a certain stock then going ahead to write out of money calls that are cheaper on that stock. Doing this means that you will have come up with a type of spread that is usually referred to as the bull spread. Purchasing calls insinuates that you are in a position to make gains if the value of the basic stock upsurges. However, you will lose a section of or all the funds used to purchase them if it happens that the stock's price failed to rise. When you opt to write calls based on that same stock, you will have the ability to take control of a number of costs you incurred initially and consequently cut down the total amount of funds you could have lost.

Virtually all the strategies of options trading call for spreads to be used and these spreads are a representation of a very efficient way to mitigate risk. They can also be used to cut down the upfront costs of getting into a position and lessening the number of finances you are in a position to lose, just like in the bull spread example we have discussed above. This basically means that you probably cut down the profits you should have made but eventually managing the general risk. Spreads are equally important when somebody seeks to reduce the risks that come whenever you enter a position that is short. It is possible to get into positions that present you with a chance to gain profits if the prices move in your favor, however, you can effectively minimize any losses you would have incurred if the movement of prices did not favor you. This explains why very many options traders use spreads; they are magnificent tools for risk management.

There is a wide range of spreads that have the ability to take control of virtually any condition that the market brings forth.

Risk Management Through Diversification

Being diversified is an instrument used to manage risks by traders who are creating a collection of stocks through a strategy of buying and holding. The underlying criterion of being diversified for this kind of traders is the dissemination of trades to a range of different sectors and companies and building up a portfolio that is balanced instead of having a lot of funds stacked up together in one sector or company. A portfolio that is diversified is broadly considered to have minimal exposure to risk in comparison to a portfolio that is composed of mainly one particular kind of investment.

In matters related to options trading, being diversified is not really important in a manner similar to the one discussed above. Nonetheless, it still has a variety of uses that you can use to carry out diversification in a number of dissimilar ways. In as much as the principle mostly remains unchanged, you should not have a lot of capital tied to one specific type of investment.

Diversification can be carried out using selected and varying strategies by executing trading options that are dependent on a series of fundamental securities, as well as ensuring that you trade in a variety of options. Basically, the goal behind being diversified is that you have the potential to make profits in different ways and that you do not completely rely on one specific outcome for the success of all your trading ventures.

Risk Management Using Option Orders

A comparatively easy way to mitigate risk is to make use of the various orders that you have the potential to place. To add to the four key order types that are used in close and open positions, there are a series of extra orders that can be placed, and the majority of these can be instrumental in managing risks.

For instance, a normal order in the market will be completely full upon the availability of the finest price during risk implementation. It is an excellently basic method of selling as well as buying options, however, in turbulent markets, chances are that your order might get full at either lower or higher price than how you expected it turn out.

In addition, there are orders that can be used in making the process of exiting a position automatically. This is irrespective of whether it aims at locking in profit that has been made or cutting losses on trading activities whose outcomes were not favorable. Making use of orders like the trailing stop order or market stop order, you acquire the ability to easily determine the point to leave a position.

This process will be crucial in helping you avoid situations where you do not get profits because you stuck in one position for a relatively long period of time or suffer losses because you did not close out on an unfavorable position fast enough. When you use option orders in the right way, you can minimize the risk you get exposed to any time you trade.

The Bottom Line

Very many people who are new to the field of options trading make a gruesome mistake of blindly investing a lot of their money in their business ventures. This exposes them to a series of risks, including the loss of significant amounts of hard-earned money. Therefore, determining the right amount of funds to use as capita and how to use it in options trading gives the investor the ability to unlock the potential of leverage. The main solution to handling being exposed to risk is to ask yourself a number of "what if" questions, and as you do so make sure that you use risk tolerance as the guiding factor.

Chapter 14: How You Can Trade Options Intelligently

Even with its numerous benefits, options trading exposes the trader to the risk of losing their capital, and it is known to be naturally speculative. Not everybody has the ability to become an intelligent options trader. This is because smart options trading requires a trader to have a specific set of skills, attitude as well as personality type.

Here, we will discuss some of the ways you can trade-in options intelligently.

Exercise Active Learning

A report from the Chicago board of trade indicated that 90% of traders who venture into options trading incur significant losses. What barricades the intelligent traders from the average ones is that smart options traders ensure that they learn from their misdoings and consequently the lessons they acquire in their trading strategies. Smart options traders have practiced, and practiced even more over time until they fully understood the lessons behind every loss they incurred, they grasped the economics that steers the market, as well as how the market behaves on different occasions.

Financial markets are in a state of continuous change and evolution; a smart trader has to clearly comprehend what is taking place and how the entire system works. By exercising active learning, you will not only have the ability to execute your current strategies but you will equally have the ability to spot opportunities that other people may bypass or not see.

Consider the Key Elements in an Options Trade

When you decide to take out an option, you are acquiring a contract to sell or buy a stock, normally one hundred shares of the stock for every contract, at a pre-arranged price by a given date. You must make three critical choices before you place the trade:

Determining What Direction You Think the Stock Will Move

This greatly affects the kind of options contract you adopt. If you feel like the stock prices will go up, you will choose to buy a call option. A call option refers to a contract that allows you to buy but does not obligate you to purchase a stock at a prearranged price (usually referred to as the strike price) in a given period.

If you are of the idea that the price of stocks will decrease you will purchase a put option. This kind of option allows you but does not obligate you to trade in shares at a stated amount of money before the expiry of the contract.

Foresee How Low or High the Price of the Stock Will Move from Its Price at the Moment

It is advisable to purchase an option that will show where you expect the stock will be located during the lifetime of the option.

For instance, if you feel like the price of shares of a company that is presently trading at $100 will go up to $ 120 sometime in the future, you will purchase a call option that has a price that is lower than $120.In this scenario, you will hypothetically opt for a strike price that is not greater than $120 subtracted from the option's cost, in that the option still rakes in profits at $120.If it happens that the stock actually rises beyond the strike price, then your option is in the funds.

In the same way, if you are of the belief that the share price of the company will go down to $80, you would opt to purchase a put option (allowing you to sell shares) at a strike price that is higher than $80 (preferably a strike price that is not below $80 in addition to the option's cost in such a way that the option still rakes in profit at $80). If the stock dips under the strike price, your option lies in the money.

It is important to note that you cannot just choose whichever strike price you want. Option quotes, professionally referred to as option chains have a variety of strike prices within easy reach. The accretion in the midst of strike prices are regulated throughout the industry and usually depend on the price of the stock.

The amount that you pay for an option, usually referred to as the premium, contains two elements: time value and intrinsic value. Time Value refers to whatever remains, and it includes how turbulent the stock is, interest rates, the time left before it expires among other components. On the other hand, intrinsic value refers to the disparity between the share price and the strike price, on condition that the stock price is higher than that of the strike. For instance, let us say you have a call option worth $100 whereas the price of the stocks is $110. Let us make an assumption that the option is at a premium of $15.Ths time value will be $5 whereas the intrinsic value amounts to $10 ($110 subtracted from 100).

Predict the Time Frame Within Which the Stock Is Expected to Move

All the options contract that you purchase have an expiry date that shows the final day you can use the option. It is also important to note that in this case, you cannot simply generate a date out of nowhere. The choice of a date is determined by the ones that are given whenever you bring forward an options chain.

Expiry dates range from years to months or even days. Weekly and daily options have a tendency to be extremely risky and are set aside for experienced traders. For investors who have been in the trade for a long time, annual and monthly expiry dates are preferred. prolonged dates of expiry give the stock ample time to move and wait for your investment proposition to play out.

A prolonged expiry date is also important because it gives the option enough time to add value, regardless of whether the prices of stocks is lower than the strike price. The time value of an option decays as the expiry date comes closer, and option purchasers do not desire to see the options they bought reduce in value, possibly expiring without any value if the stock turns out to be below the strike price at the end of the period.

Chapter 15: Technical Analysis

Technical analysis is increasingly becoming a favored viewpoint to trading, gratitude in part to the development in trading platforms as well as charting package. Nonetheless, a new trader comprehending technical analysis as well as how it can assist in foreseeing market trends can be challenging and daunting.

Technical analysis basically involves studying the manner in which prices move within a market, in such a way that traders use patterns from historic charts and indicators to foresee the impending market trends. It is a visual reflection of the present and past performance of a given market and it enables traders to make use of this information in the fashion of indicators, patterns, as well as price action, inform and guide forthcoming trends before getting into a trade.

Here, we focus on the basics of technical analysis and consequently how it can be put into use in trading.

Comprehending Technical Analysis

The technical analysis mainly involves interpreting patterns in charts. Traders use historic data that solely depends on volume and price and consequently use the information they acquire to spot lucrative opportunities to trade based on familiar or habitual patterns in the market. Charts are exposed to a variety of indicators to establish points of entry and exit to enable traders to maximize the potential of a trade at a ratio of good risk to rewards.

In as much as the people who support fundamental analysis have a belief that economic factor mainly contributes to market movements, technical analysis traders insist that olden trends are helpful in foreseeing price movements in the future. In as much as these styles of trade vary, comprehending the disparity between technical and fundamental analysis as well as how to collaborate them can be very advantageous in the long run.

How Technical Analysis Can Help Traders

Numerous trades have approved technical analysis as an instrument for managing risks, which can be a major setback. As soon as a trader comprehends the principles and concepts of technical analysis, he/she can use it in virtually any market, thus making it an adjustable analytical instrument. As fundamental analysis seeks to identify a market's intrinsic value, the technical analysis seeks to spot trends that can suitably be caused by basic fundamentals.

- Technical analysis has the following benefits:
- It can be used as an independent method.
- It is applicable to any market using any timespan.
- Technical analysis enables traders to spot patterns in the market.

Using Charts in Technical Analysis

Technical analysis is centered around charts. This is simply because the only way to gauge a market's past and current performance is by analysis the price; this is where you kick off the process of analyzing the ability of a trade. It is possible to represent price action on a chart because it is the most uncensorable indicator of the impacts of the price.

Charts are useful in finding the general trend, regardless of whether there is a downward or upward trend over a short or long term or to discover rage bound circumstances. The most known types of technical analysis charts include candlestick charts, line charts, and bar charts.

Whenever you use a bar or candlestick chart, every period will feed the technical analyst with information on the high and low of the period, the price where it started and also the close. Candlestick analysis is preferable the patterns as well as how they are interconnected can help in predicting the direction of the price in the future.

As soon as a trader comprehends the fundamentals of charting, they can use indicators to help in predicting the trend.

Technical Analysis Indicators

Technical traders use indicators whenever they are looking for windows of opportunity in the market. In as much as there are very many indicators, price, and volume-based indicators. These are useful in finding out the levels of resistance and support are, how they are breached or maintained as well as determining how long a trend is.

A trader has the ability to see the price as well as any other indicator by doing an analysis of numerous time frames ranging from a second to a month. This, in turn, gives the trader a different view of the price action.

The most known indicators in regard to technical analysis are:

- The corresponding strength indexes
- Moving averages
- Moving average divergence as well convergence

The last two indicators in the list above are usually used to spot market trends whereas the corresponding strength index is basically employed in finding out probable points of exit and entry. Indicators help traders in conducting an analysis of the market, finding entry points and doing validation of how trades have been set up.

Limitations of Technical Analysis

The major setback to the authenticity of technical analysis is the economic aspect of the efficient markets hypothesis (EMH). EMH asserts that market prices are a reflection of all past and current information, therefore, there is no way to exploit mispricing or patterns to get more profits. Fundamental analysts and economists who have a belief in efficient markets have no belief that any sort of information that can be acted on is contained in volume data and historical price, and in addition, that history does not repeat itself, instead, prices shift like an unplanned walk.

Technical analysis is also under criticism because it is applicable in some cases only because it contains a self-actualization prophecy. For instance, most traders will position their order to stop loss under the two-hundred-day motion average of a given company. Considering that a variety of traders have done that and it happens that the stock gets to this price, then the number of sell orders will be enormous and it will shove the stock downwards, approving the movement that traders were anticipating.

Thereafter, other traders will notice the reduction in price and also opt to put their positions up for sale, consequently improving the robustness of the trend. This selling pressure that is generally short-term can be regarded as self-fulfilling, however, it will have very minimal direction on where the price of assets will be a couple of weeks or months to come. To sum it up, if people employ similar signals, it could result in movements foreseen by the signal, but eventually, this main group of traders become incapable of steering price.

Chapter 16: The Supports and Resistances

The chart patterns in any kind of trade calls for support and resistance. Whether you are dealing with fired trading, commodities, stocks, futures or options. In any world of trading, it is the basis of the chart patterns. To understand better what support and resistance mean in the options trade, you can relate to the most common type of trade that is easily accessed by almost everyone because everyone is involved in at least one type of trade in the market.

Let's take an example of a situation where you go to the market to purchase a commodity that you've been using frequently. In this case, you are the bull. This is a product that you like so much and to encourage the seller to restock this product, there's that price that you will support so hard that you don't want it to fall. This is what we refer to as 'Support.' The buyer takes control of the prices and protects it so that it doesn't go down. The reason as to why the buyer would want to prevent the price from going down to the extreme is because of the fear that the seller would stop bringing the commodity on the market because they won't see its value. This is the concept of support that can be easily understood by anyone. For resistance, it's the other way round. Here the seller now takes control of the price and prevents it from rising higher. For trading to carry on successfully, the buyer and the seller must agree on a specific price. Raising the price too high may make the bull to reconsider an alternative commodity with a lower price depending on the amount of money they would want to spend. On the other hand, the seller would not consider trading at an extremely lower price than what they expect. This is because no one easily accepts a loss. Selling at weird spoils the motive that someone had for participating in the market.

Investors trade depending on the price levels. For instance, someone would prefer to purchase a good when the price of commodities is at a level where it is more likely to shoot after some time. When it happens as per their expectations, then it's a favor on their side because they are going to record again when they resell the commodity. This level where a large number of investors tend to believe that the prices will rise higher is what is known as the support level. It is what determines the decisions made by the majority of investors. When a support level is broken, it changes its worth and becomes the new resistance level.

At the resistance level, the investors always assume that the prices will fall lower. This makes the major investors think otherwise. Those who purchase commodities in bulk when the price is lower and is expected to move higher would not want to proceed to purchase the same commodity when they know that the price is more likely to drop so low that if they go ahead and sell it at that price, they would record a huge loss. Also, when the resistance level is broken, it changes and becomes the new support level.

On many occasions in the market, you will realize what is referred to as 'Noise'. This is when there are errors in pricing making them go beyond limits. The tops and bases of pricing are exceeded which may lead to misunderstanding between the bulls and the bears. However, this is a normal activity in the market and the traders always take care of it to ensure that trade moves on, even though it always brings some disagreements in most cases.

Beginner traders must always understand the concept of support and resistance to enable them to trade successfully without having diverted minds on what they are doing. When they get to understand how the market prices fluctuate with different seasons, they will be in a position to decide which commodity to trade with during what season. The errors associated with market pricing should be clearly understood by the beginner trades to prevent them from getting stranded when the price levels change from time to time.

Someone who is new to the trading market is sometimes made to believe that when the commodity prices are low, they are definitely meant to rise higher after some time and this is where they normally get disappointed when the prices fall lower. It is normal that the prices go extremely down and this is always assumed to occur when new goods arrive in the market and replace the old ones. Many people would prefer going for the latest commodity instead of the previous one.

Buyers and sellers must always come to an agreement for the prices of every commodity. This is because the investors' plans are always different from the plans of any other normal trader. Understanding the level prices is not always easy for beginner traders but once they get used to it, trading becomes easy for them and they find it more comfortable dealing with different clients. Maintaining support levels and resistance levels helps both the bulls and bears to maintain good trading relationship and remain positive about the results of the trade.

A good support level encourages the investors to invest more in the commodity with the belief that when they will be exchanging this particular commodity at a later date, the market prices will be fair on their side making them earn a reasonable profit. At this time, the previous buyer now becomes the seller and they have the task of controlling the prices of goods to ensure that it doesn't rise higher making it difficult for others to purchase. Everyone has a different preference when it comes to trading. Setting a higher resistance level can sometimes make it difficult for the seller to earn the expected profit. This normally happens when the buyers shift to a lower price commodity and let go of yours because it is not affordable to them. This only leads to you

Chapter 17: The Main Features of Technical Analysis

Technical analysis of options trading always shows how successful options trading has become and what normally leads to its success. It lists the number of successful trade on the option and what contributed to the success of these traders. Definitely, there are guides and trading techniques that a trader should always consider for them to achieve success. The analysis of options trade has always shown different features and the main feature we are going to discuss below.

First and foremost, we are going to talk about discipline. This is the key to any successful trade or even a project. As a trader, you need to be highly disciplined about what you are doing. It is however not so easy being disciplined up to a certain point in options trading but still for you to be successful, you must always exercise discipline in your field. You need to be highly committed to what you are doing for you to achieve the best that you need. You don't necessarily have to concentrate on one thing the whole day but the commitment that you show is very important.

You also need to learn from the losses that you encountered in the past. It is normal for all traders to record a loss at some point during the trading session. This does not mean that trading should stop. You learn from the loss, pick up and move on. No shortcut. You should be in a position to accept the losses and carry on with trade because of everyone's losses and if everyone was to panic and quit there would be no trading that would be proceeding until success is recorded. If you trade, lose and give up, there is no progress.

You should also be ready to learn. You are new in the market and you don't have a full idea about what you are doing. You just allow yourself to take lessons from the experts and be ready to apply the same tactics for you to carry on successfully. Watch what others do. How they carry out trade and respond to different matters is very important. You will realize you are gaining more and being well prepared to go for what you want. Technical analysis shows that if you are not well experienced in the field of options trading, you are only subjected to making mire errors than you work to succeed.

Be the decision-maker in your trading. Don't wait for others to decide for you what to do. Being your own decision maker allows you to carry out your trade successfully without putting blames on anyone. Learning for yourself is very important as much as you feel you need to take lessons from what is happening where you are. Nothing should influence you and dictate the decisions that you make. Take lessons but be independent in selecting what is best for you. This is the only way you can keep moving forward. Following what someone else is doing only leads you to a destination that was never meant for you.

A trading plan is another important feature of technical analysis of options trading. You should always have a trading plan of your own. Plan yourself well and decide what is best for you. You know exactly what you can handle and what you cannot handle and this means if you let someone plan for you, you risk straining to do something that is not within your level capacity. This only makes trading boring for you and that's why most traders quit and divert their attention to something else or blame someone for making them fail.

Watch how you react. Don't just react because you are supposed to react. The careless reaction is the number one cause of failure in any world of trading. You may face losses in your trade or some difficulties that come unplanned. How you react to them is what is more important. How do you handle losses? How do you respond to your client when something is not right? Being proactive helps you build good customer relationship with your clients and also help you to remain positive to keep moving on despite the challenges. Understand the market and making decisions based on your trading plans. Letting emotions take over you and control how you react will only interfere with how you participate in the market.

Develop a broad scope of learning. Don't just stick to one idea and think you are good to go. Everything needs a wide view so that you know how to attack everything from a different angle. When you have more ideas on what you are doing, you will find it easy switching to another plan when one fails. Being in a position to have several options helps you as a trader to be at room temperature with all types of trades. Open up your mind to convince different ideas in different fields.

Do not be in a hurry. Everything needs time so be patient. Take your time to balance ideas before you come to a final decision. Analyze every plan you have carefully and know the possible results of every decision you make. This will help you when it comes to arriving at safe decisions. Any decision made in a hurry has always led to the failure of most traders. Rushed decisions are always a result of panic so be relaxed and follow your trade plans carefully.

Lay aside your ego. Nothing can be successful if the ego takes the center stage. Avoid unnecessary ego and open up your mind to work with your clients at their level. Be ready to listen to them and deliver according to their interests. Your interests are not your client's interests and it is important to note that. Putting your ego before everything will only push away clients painting you a failure. For you to be successful, you have to let go of your ego and remain humble and respectful throughout the business session.

Having the above features in your mind and putting each of them to practice is what will move you to the next level. Play safe.

Chapter 18: The Different Types of Graphs that Exist in Technical Analysis

Graphs that are used to analyze technical analysis are commonly referred to as charts. The technical analysis charts that are used in the financial markets tend to aim in identification two major components in trading. They narrow down to depicting the trends and patterns that are being experienced in foreign exchange markets. There are other chart functions that are used in the process of an individual trying to understand the financial markets. It can be a hard task to interpret the graphs for an individual who is a beginner in the financial markets.

There several forms of graphs that are used in the current world to analyze financial markets technically. However, there are three common graphs that are heavily relied on by traders in this sector of trading. These charts include candlesticks, line charts, and graphs. There is a common similarity that is shared across the three graphs. They are all created by the use of the same price data. However, the difference crops in when it comes to it come to displaying of data. All three graphs have a different way in which they display the data.

The difference between the three major types of graphs makes a trader have varied forms of technical analysis. However, the graphs have various advantages that they present to a trader investing his or her time and resources in financial markets. They help a trader to make informed decisions about the market. The advantages and uses of technical analysis graphs can be effectively used in the trade of options. These analyzing graphs include;

Line Charts

This form of type of graphs is common in financial markets. It is common for people who are known for trading stock. However, the fame and advantage of this analysis graph have led it to be used in the trade of options. It this sector of financial trading, it has proved to also be effective in the roles it is tasked with. People who are beginners in options trading and other forms of financial trading are always encouraged to use this graph because one can easily understand it. It is easy for someone to interpret this graph because it focuses on the market holistically. This helps to eliminate the shifts in data that proves to be a heavy task for various people. Emotions are always put aside because this form of analysis uses factual figures presented to it.

What this graph simply does is illustrating the display are the closing prices. There is nothing else that is portrayed in the line charts. Each of the portrayed closing prices tends to be linked to the closing price that was seen in the previous trading session. This makes a continuous line that flows easily. This type of graph has places that easily depict it. They are popular in several web articles, newspapers and television programs. It is because they can be easily digested by several people. The graph provides an individual with less amount of information to handle. This is completely different from those bar charts or candlesticks. One can describe the graph as having a simplistic view of the market with just a simple glance.

There is something intriguing when it comes to the advantage of this graph helping an individual to manage his or her emotions. The process of trading is done by humans who are characterized by having feelings attached to what they do. These emotions are drawn away by the usage of neutral colors. Several choppy movements have easily eliminated the usage of several colors

.

Bar Graphs (OHLC)

Individuals who commonly trade options that involve commodities as the underlying assets are commonly known to use this graph. It is very popular because of its effectiveness in the financial markets and its success is vastly experienced in trading stock options and foreign exchange markets. An individual who is at the intermediate level of options trading will be advantaged to using this graph while studying the market. There is a unique way by which this graph analyses the trends in the market. The data collected on the prices of financial instruments help to sport the trend in the market. They help in the identification of the entry and support or resistance points in the trade of options. The advantage with this graph is it's detailed hence giving added information to a trader.

This bar graph is able to display closing, opening, high and low prices for specific periods that are designated in the bar. The high and low prices in the graph create the vertical line of the graph. There are always two dashes that are present in the graph. The one of the left always signifies the signals of closings price while the one on the right signifies the signals of opening prices. There is a similarity that is presented between this kind of graph and candlestick. Both graphs are easily viewed on the sides though the bar graph tends to have a clearer view.

Candle Sticks Charts

There are individuals who are used to trade in the financial markets tend to use this graph to analyze the options markets. They can be equated to the bar graphs since they are commonly preferred by intermediate traders in the trade of options. Candlestick can look easier in a trader's eye compared to bar graphs because of their full nature.

A candlestick graph does a function of displaying the opening, closing (OHLC), low and high prices in the for the period that is designated for each candle. The candle body of each stick represents the opening and closing prices. On the other side, the candle wicks tend to signify the high and low prices for each specific period. There are several colors that are used in this graph which are green and red. The green color represents the prices closing high than when they were opened. On another hand, the red color signifies the prices closed low than when they were opened.

Chapter 19: The Possible Advantages of Applying Technical Analysis

There are several advantages that are accompanied by the usage of technical analysis. The most common users of these forms of analysis are the short term traders. It has seen a success story in markets such as options trading. These advantages include;

Provision of Current Information

The current price tends to reflect the present information about a specific price of an asset. There are certain moments that rumors have the potential of consistently swirling the price causing a surge in the market. However, a balancing point is always achieved when the current price is depicted in the markets. The options market is characterized by the movement of traders and investors swaying most of the time. These two groups of a participant in the financial market can sway to becoming buyers or sellers. This situation occurs through the speculation of the value of the option being traded.

There are moments during trading that a tricky situation can present itself. Traders and investors tend to rely on the price charts because of a solid reason. It is because the charts tend to contain all perceptions and information about the value of an option or other underlying assets. The used information about an asset's value is recorded in charts using the gyration form. A trader in the financial market tends not to concentrate on why prices irrespective of if they rise or fall. This is despite them being able to show a trader when buying interests in more than selling interests and vice versa.

This has the potential of making trading of options to be much simpler to several participants. It is because the technical analysis focuses on the price charts. It is easy because an individual does not have to spend much of his time reading the latest financial news or analyzing the financial statements.

Depicts the Trend of Price Movements

There are moments that traders can have a difficult time to make gains in the financial markets. One of these moments is when the prices of options are gyrating. During the moments of wild gyrations, the overall prices of options tend to sway greatly with the experienced trends. Directional bias is a common occurrence which proves to be advantageous to several traders in the financial markets. There are several ways that technical analysis proves its wits on this issue. It is able to determine when the market trend is in place when is not being experienced and moments it is reversing.

Strategies that use the trend to base their trading methods tend to be very profitable. There is a common way that individuals can use technical analysis to achieve this phenomenon. An options trader begins by first by isolating the trend. He or she then goes ahead to finding the viable opportunities that are going in the same direction as the current market trends. This helps an options trader to be able to capitalize on the price movements that are biased. There are various degrees that this trend can occur. The upward trend can go on for several weeks or days which are accurately depicted in the charts. The downtrends are always depicted on the left side of the charts.

Depiction of History

Technical analysis is hugely based on unearthing the common patterns that are seen day in day out during options trading. These patterns are used several times in options after being uncovered by traders. However, one is not supposed to be brainwashed by this kind of reasoning. It is because one is prone to thinking that history is bound to repeating itself. A good depiction of this advantage possessed by technical analysis is portrayed by the chart known as the triangle. The common constructs tend to be similar, however; there are moments the constructed triangle can either be larger or smaller than the initial triangle. It means that the results can be able to pop out differently from the prior construct thus the odds of history repeating itself has very low odds.

One is supposed to realize what the essence of human psychology plays in this case. It is prone to not shifting most of the time. Technical analysis is prone to revealing that that options market is commonly characterized by several rise and fall in price value of options. Therefore, an individual is able to know how to deal with emotions of greed and fear when they are triggered during the process of trading. Emotions can also be patterned by the use of technical analysis when it comes to the values of the underlying financial assets. The history depicted by these factors plays a crucial role in making a major decision in the market since they act as a bearing.

Timing Provision

Technical analysis has time provision as one of its major advantages. It provides an options trader with accurate timing of his or her trades in the financial markets. There are several findings an individual can be able to dig out in moments he or she uses the fundamental approach as his or her strategy. The findings can make individual trading options to speculate of gains in the value of options that are being traded. However, this is not the same case that a trader using technical analysis will be subjected to. A technical analyst is able to find leverage of waiting till the prices are able to inform him or her that the prices of options are about to rise.

Provision to Be Used in Any Market

The concept of technical analysis can be used to variedly numerous fields. This has seen its application in several markets such as binary options, stocks, forex, futures, and CDFs. The pattern of human psychology and market trends has a high potential of being depicted in several markets. There are several moments this knowledge can be useful to an options trader. It is because; some options can be used to trade other underlying financial assets. These moments can prove to be the best points in trade and options trader can use this concept.

Chapter 20: The Strategies and Tricks That Can Be Applied with Technical Analysis

Several investors in the finical market are known for analyzing options they own based on the fundamentals they possess. This includes looking at an option's valuation and revenue. However, fundamentals have low odds when it narrows down to portraying the current market prices of options as the underlying financial assets. It is where technical analysis comes to save an options trader in the financial markets. It is because it is it helps an individual to maneuver through the gap that is created between market prices and the intrinsic value of options. The action is made to be simple because of fundamental analysis has a way of leveraging behavioral economics and statistical analysis. This has seen the rise of numbers in traders and investors using technical analysis.

There are major approaches that are used by participants of options trading when it comes to technical analysis. These major approaches are two and they include a top-down approach and bottom-up technical forms. The top-down approach has several traders who prefer it. Most of the traders that are characterized by using the top-down approach in the options market are the short term traders. The long-term trader and investors are prone to using the bottom-up approach because it favors them.

- **Top-Down Approach**; it involves an options trader or investor screening for particular options. The intended options are supposed to be able to fit certain forms of stocks that fit the intended criteria. A good depiction can be sourced from a trader looking from options that have their moving averages at fifty days.

- **Bottom-Up Approach**; this entails an options trader analyzing options that have an appearance that is fundamentally interesting. These stocks tend to give an individual an added advantage in knowing the exit and entry points in the trade of options. An easy illustration can be used for those options that have a downtrend. With the use of technical analysis, a trader in the options trading can be able to identify entry and exit points. These points are critical in moments the options are swaying in the market.

The current world has millions of options traders who prefer to use different forms of technical analysis. Options traders who perform day trading tend to prefer simple volume and trade indicators in moments they make trading decisions. On the other hand, swing traders tend to have a preferential of using the chart patterns and other technical indicators. The trade of options has seen several technological advancements in it. It has to lead to several traders developing algorithms that are highly automated. They tend to anchor their analysis on volume and technical indicators to base their decisions in the options markets.

Steps to The Strategies Used in Analyzing Options

There are five steps that are core in realizing the strategies used to analyzing options using technical analysis. These steps include;

Identification of a Technical Analysis Strategy

This is the first step and it can also be referred to as the development of a trading system. We can use a situation of a beginner in this case who is participating in the options market. He or she is supposed to follow the strategy that involves the usage of moving averages. The option trader is supposed to track two moving averages in a specific option market. The two moving averages can be those of fifty or two hundred days. The fifty-day moving average can be used for the basis of supporting the short term trading options. On the other hand, options traders aiming for the long term trading of options can use the two hundred moving averages. A buying signal is always portrayed when the trends in a price move upward while the signal of trader to sell his or her options is realized in moments the prices of options have a downward trend.

Identification of Tradable Options That Fit with the Technical Strategy

The common knowledge in option trading is that not all kinds of options have similar strategies that are applied to them. Most of the techniques stated above tend to favor options that are highly gyrating in nature than those that are not volatile. This case might favor the usage of moving averages that are characterized by fifty days. However, an individual can use the two hundred days if the option he or she is trading is not volatile in the options market.

Finding of a Brokerage Account for Existing Trades

An options trader is supposed to be in apposition that he or she has found the right brokerage account to be able to conduct his or her trade. The account is supposed to have a certain minimum requirement for its success. An account used by a trader in options trading is supposed to be an able function to the utmost best in being able to track and monitor the technical tools used in technical analysis. A good account is supposed to do this function with the reduction of costs involved in accessing this data. One will be on a very good side of options trading if his or her account can be able to incorporate candlesticks.

Selection of a Good Interface to Track and Monitor Trade

Options traders can differ on the level of functionality which is dependent on the functionality of the strategy he or she is using. A good depiction can be made of a trader who requires a margin account that provides information about the market. On the other hand, several people prefer basic accounts because they have low-cost options in them.

Identification of Other Applications That Can be Implemented on the Settled Strategy

There might be other options that might need extra happening for a trader to realize maximum gains from them. There are options traders who have gone to the extent of receiving mobile notifications about any changes that can be experienced in the options markets. There are options traders who have automated their accounts to an extent they perform automated functions for them.

Chapter 21: How to Control Emotions: Have a Right Mental Approach

When most people start trading, they are so eager to make money, and most of their decisions are emotional. Instead of being strategic and strictly follow their plan, they rely on their emotions to make trade decisions. Often, a trader will find himself making pushing trades when it's not the right time in the market to trade. Other times, due to motions, the trader will make losses without making stops and even take profits too soon in fear that waiting for the profits might result in losing it. Most of these emotions come when a trader thinks that they are missing profits easily made by other traders. In the eagerness to catch up, they will end up making emotional decisions instead of following through their plans.

The solution to avoid emotion trading is to start treating the trading market seriously, even if you are trading for yourself. Treat the trading as if it was your own business by creating a business plan with achievable goals and a daily routine. By doing this, you are sure that you have your emotions to the side, and you are now doing the business with the right mental state. What a business plan is to help a trader remove any sorts of emotion greed that may come long and also eliminate the emotions of fear. It also helps a trader stop forcing trade whenever they are feeling bored or even when they are going through the internal pressure of production.

Understanding trading psychology, therefore, becomes very important so that a trader is able to separate emotions from trading. Psychology involves understanding the mind and behavior that follows; in this case, therefore, we are trying to understand how the mind is involved in the trade. Trading involves controlling the figures, but controlling the trader's emotions is what will lead to reasonable control of the statistics. Some traders may argue that there is no way emotions are involved in trading, but there are so many losses that happen every day, not because of bad traders. It is because good traders let emotions get in their way of good trading judgment. The decisions made out of emotions quite often ignore the basics of trading and do not follow a trader's trading plan. The end result for a trader who lets emotions take over is never good. Therefore a trader having the right mindset free of emotions is what trading psychology is all about.

Trading psychology helps a trader reduce mistakes made on the impulsive judgment. The trader learns how to assess his reactions when trading and therefore, able to identify emotions that could help him to make bad decisions. Usually, bad decisions are a result of fear after losing trade severally. A trader will then react by holding on to a position for so long expecting things to make a turnaround. But a trader who is in their right state of mind knows that by doing the hold-up, it will result in further loss and it is always a great idea to close the position.

Steps to Help Improve Your Trading Psychology

- Setting your mind right and freeing yourself from emotional trading is only achievable if a trader is continuously motivating himself. Encourage yourself to accept the fact that you do not need to pressure yourself too much. That other trader's success does not need to give you panic attacks. The trader needs to allow himself time to grow on his own and learn from the mistakes. Allowing fear to take over is what will cost a trader and make him trade from emotions of another failure. Every day before starting a trade, the trader should take time to meditate on the day ahead. This will make him more mentally prepared for all the risks and challenges ahead of you. When the mind is mentally prepared, the trader gets calmness and therefore eliminates the possibilities of quick emotional decisions. Meditating on the day helps you reduce all types of emotions that may affect your performance. Plus you have already allowed yourself time to accept that if any loss occurs during the day, it won't change your trading life.

- Another way to control your emotions is by increasing your overall knowledge of the market. When you are knowledgeable about what you are expected to do, you will not be afraid of taking risks. When you know what to do as a trader, you will rely on your knowledge rather than your emotions to make decisions. No matter how much tempted you to feel to follow your emotions or what an emotional trader would call instincts, you will do what is right. Being knowledgeable means that you know how much every decision counts, and therefore, you will try to get rid of the emotions. Knowledge about the market gives you some sense of calmness that you need to make decisions. Without calmness, it means you are making decisions without clearly thinking about the consequences. Patience allows you to think ahead in terms of what you can do when faced with all the market risks.

- As a trader, sometimes your emotions will tell you that you are not good enough and that you will make losses.

Start allowing positive emotions by thinking of how strong you are. When you think of yourself as someone who can achieve anything, you will win the day. Thinking of yourself positively will help you always see the bigger picture at all times, and you will feel more encouraged. Positivity eliminates negative emotions.

- It's also important to think of what failing would mean to you. This will motivate you to do the best you can to eliminate emotions that may lead you to that failure.

- Remind yourself always what will be at stake if you allow negative emotions to take over you. Think of how much you stand to lose should you make decisions based on your emotions.

- Observe what other traders do because sometimes you continue making the same mistakes because your guts fail you. There is always something to borrow from others that will help you make better trading judgments.

- The best way to boost your emotions is to look back at your journey. This will encourage you to keep pushing on when you see the achievements you have made and also how the failures made you strong.

Chapter 22: The Basics of Psychology in Trading

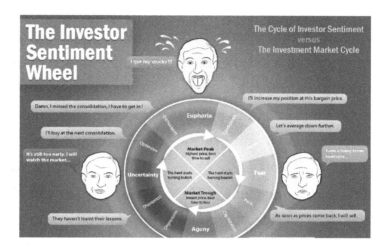

Despite the many risks involved in trading, people don't seem to give up on entering and staying in the market. The chances of loss in this market are so high, and many traders have lost so much money. However, for the traders that have achieved, trading is by far the most rewarding way to make money. Trading gives trader independence because they do not need to be employed anymore; they can employ themselves as traders. It also provides a person with a financial breakthrough if their trading works for them. Trading is like having your business, and therefore you become a sole proprietor, managing your own money and time.

Challenges of Trading

There are so many challenges involved in the market for a trader, especially for the newcomers in the market. For this reason, not many people are able to stick around the market for long. When a trader lasts long, it is usually an expensive experience for the trader. Statistics show that not many traders continue in the market for more than four weeks for short-term traders. While for long-term traders, not many people make it past five years. This is quite shocking that a trader would put money in an investment and opt-out after a month. However, it is not impossible in trading because trading can be expensive. It is costly because if you put too much money into the trade and lose it all within the first month, you are unlikely to have the will to add more money. The entering capital can also be very expensive because to make a lot of profits you need a substantial capital. However, small capital can also produce significant profits, but it takes a lot of time that most traders are unwilling to wait on. Someone may want quick money, and trading is not the place for fast cash, you need a lot of patience. Therefore for a person who is the breadwinner, it becomes hard to wait until the earnings start feeding the family. However, with patience and a lot of practice and significant decisions in trading, trade is the most fulfilling career.

Emotional Trading

A trader's psychological behavior has a lot to do with their success or losses. Being able to handle your emotions as a trader is what will determine your achievements in the market. Every decision needs-controlled emotion because failure to that the decisions will be wrong and damaging for the trader. The two most damaging emotions involved in trading include fear of failure and greed to overachieve. When a trader allows these two emotions to take over his trading experiences, he is unlikely to make it for long in the market. Therefore, these two need to be handled with care because they are emotions in every human being, and they do not necessarily need to eliminate but to be controlled. The following is an outlook of how the two emotions affect a trader.

Fear or panic – Fear is reasonable; it makes a trader careful about making bad decisions that could lead him to lose significant in the market. Fear in trading, when done in the right state of mind, can lead to great success because you will use that emotion to help prevent you from making hasty or delayed decisions in trade. Fear can be looked at in two different ways to distinguish the right kind and the wrong kind.

Fear of failing- This type of fear is when a trader is continuously worrying about a possible loss in the trading market because they feel that failure will define them. For this reason, a trader will always put himself under pressure to perform because they do not want to lose. Any sign of an upcoming loss will throw them off balance to the point that they will make a rushed decision to avoid it.

Fear of succeeding- this type of fear involves a trade being so afraid to make it significant that they let opportunities slide away from them. A trader will have the right opportunity to make a close that could be his great blessing but will be afraid to do so because he is afraid he is not ready for that kind of success. The trader will, therefore, wait for things to come a little down before making a close.

When fear is involved when making trades, a trader is likely to have panic attacks and also be extremely stressed. Stress will make a trader very exhausted that they will not enjoy the trading process. It is therefore important that a trader lets go of this emotion because failure to it will make a trader exit the market.

Greed

For a trader to be considered a good trader, it is not only because he is strategic. Being a successful trader means that your account can back you up, therefore most people are so eager to have so much money in their account. Greed will most times result in a trader wanting to overtrade. The trade will tend to go against all the odds to overtrade in order to get more money. This will make even the trader will also take unreasonable risks that cannot be controlled in the long run. While taking risks is good for a trader, it is highly damaging when you are taking risks that are beyond you as a trader. Greed will often lead to overconfidence which will, in the long run, lead to a downfall. Overconfidence makes a person ignore all the trading basics, and therefore in the long term, the trader will be forced out.

Most traders make the mistake of being in the trading market without a proper plan. Trading is a business; without a plan, there is no success. Traders also the mistake of not knowing how to handle their money correctly, a trader may make a lot of money, but without proper management, you will lose it all. Sometimes traders will rely significantly on tip-offs before making the decision. This will not work out all the time, and it is damaging because as a trader, you don't give yourself enough opportunities to grow.

All traders need to have a proper goal as that is what will keep them on their toes and encourage them to stick in the market for long. A well-defined goal wills you the calmness and the right state of mind to keep fighting even when things get tough.

Chapter 23: Why Those with the Right Mindset Become Successful Traders

Making it in the trading market does not require you to be highly educated with a college degree. A successful trader also does not need to spend all their day working to achieve it in the market. What makes a trader successful in their state of mind? In trade, you need to combine a great strategy with an excellent state of mind as this will help a trader gain confidence in all their transactions. Mindset is how your emotions and thoughts make you respond to issues. We generally react to problems due to how our mind is set up, and that's why it is essential to have the right mindset to be able to make great decisions. That is why to achieve anything, all we truly need is the right mindset that will encourage us to push on despite the many challenges we are likely to encounter along the way. The right state of mind gives calmness that later results in a trader being able to make decisions that are free of any emotions. Without emotions, a trader is able to look at the market at all angles without being forced to fall on one side. You appreciate the wins and all the profits you get as a trader you are aware you earned it by putting your hard work into it. You also take the losses positively to be a lesson for you so that you know what to do and what not to do in the future. Therefore as a trader, you can take responsibility for all the decisions you make.

Successful traders understand why it is essential to keep away their emotions from trading. Trading can be taught, and anyone can make it in the market, but who stays in the market is determined by their ability to separate the two. Being an emotionless trader means that not only do you make stable decisions, but you are also very accountable as a trader. You will never place blame on anyone or anything for your mistakes because you know you did your best it's only the circumstances that weren't favorable.

When the trader has the right mindset, it also means that they make the right realistic goals. A trader does not become too over-ambitious, making rational decisions that will not yield any results. Having set realistic goals means that your strategies as a trader are practical; therefore, there will be no time wasting trying to figure out the market. You already know what to expect from the market, and the market is also ready for you to make you a successful trader. Your expectations as a trader are also very realistic. You only take risks that you are aware of as a trader you can handle. A person who is not in their right state of mind will take risks that are way beyond him and then lose his mind when things don't work out.

Having the right state of mind makes a trader successful because they then get to understand how unique they are. This means there will be no comparison with other traders because this is often a way to failing. When you always compare your success with other traders, you are likely to be discouraged because each one has different levels of success. A successful trader will believe so much in themselves that there will be no room for this type of comparison. When you believe in yourself, it means that you believe in every single decision you make and therefore you will approach every trade with so much confidence.

A successful trader has patience which is only achieved when you have the right state of mind that gives calmness. Traders become successful when they can wait for the markets to show them when it is time to make various positions. A trader will have the patience to wait for profits to generate without feeling like they are pressured to take whatever comes along. A successful trader also has the patience to accept the losses; their right state of mind tells them to grab the loss as a learning lesson. Therefore the trader will use the endurance to overcome all the hard market situations.

The right state of mind enables a trader to overcome the emotion of greed. He can identify when he is a good trader who wants to make the right money and when he is just a greedy trader. A greedy trader makes closes on trades when it is too soon because they want to make profits regardless of how small the amount is. They, therefore, make many closes instead of being patient for the earnings to grow before making the close. A successful trader accepts that there is power in letting go of a loss. However, a greedy trader will overwork trying to make up for past failures and forgetting to focus on the present.

The right state of mind helps a trader become successful because it eliminates the fear of taking risks. While other traders are trying to be careful thinking they taking risks will put them at a losing end, a trader with the right state of mind will go for it. The right state of mind helps a trader knows that to make it in the market, there have to be huge risks that one has to face. There is no fear of failure for a person with the right state of mind because the trader knows that part of the trading process.

The right state of mind makes a person a successful trader because it gives a person the ability to let go of the past. Most people fail as traders because they are stuck in the past, always trying to mend the past when what they should be doing is dealing with the present. A right state of mind enables a trader to focus on what they can do to improve their present and also on how to prepare for the future.

Successful traders are traders whose right state of mind encouraged them to keep learning no matter how excellent they felt. This is what distinguishes successful long-term traders and successful short-term traders. While short-term traders achieved for a while and relaxed, the long term trader continued learning and therefore got to their current successful state.

Chapter 24: Mistakes to Avoid on the Expiration Day

Options trading only gives you the freedom to sell or buy securities before the expiration of the options. Options usually lose their value as they approach their expiration day. This kind of trade is sometimes very volatile and its expiration date may be very hard to be predetermined. This, therefore, makes options traders commit some mistakes on the expiration day of the trade that makes them make losses. There are various mistakes that a vigilant trader should at all cost try to avoid on their trade's expiration day. These mistakes are discussed below;

- **Forgetting when the trade is set to expire**
  Different options trades have different rules that determine their expiration day. On opening a trade, one's main aim is usually to make a profit. Some individuals once they make profits, tend to forget to exit the trade yet it has approached its expiration day. On the other hand, if one had made losses, they may tend to leave the trade open as they try to get some of their money back which might never happen. As the trade approaches its expiration date, it is a fact that it loses its value faster. Therefore, the chances of one making

more profit from the trade are very few. To avoid losing your trading capital, it is safer to close your options trade and claim your losses or profits before the trade close.

- **Exercising your options**

  In case you own options and the expiration day is approaching, then you should never dare to exercise them. It is advisable not to own stocks whenever you purchase options unless if you are taking on an options strategy or a stock. If you have a strong urge to own stock as you buy options, then you should plan earlier. Failure to do so then you will be making losses and it will have no difference with throwing it away into thrash. Several options traders, especially beginners, purchasing options are not the best approach to owning shares.

  In case the prices of stock increases by a good margin that is enough to recover the premiums paid, then you will have made a profit. This does not matter when it comes to a person who purchases options intending to own shares at a later time. There are many exceptions but it is advisable not to exercise your options on the expiration day. Instead, you should sell the options if you do not feel like owning again. Exercising options on their expiration day will not make you any profit but instead, you might lose it all.

- **Margin calls on the expiration day**

  Beginners in options trading, especially those owning small accounts, usually fall into the purchase of options. The purchase of options is not an issue but they fail to understand the trading rules thus fail to sell out their options before the expiration day. If an options trader owns five August 40 calls and does not make an effort to sell them, it would be fine for the person to let them expire worthless. On the other hand, if a trader does not closely watch out and allows the trade to close at $40.02 on its expiration, then the trader will now own 500 shares. If the trade closes with more money by a penny or more on its expiration day, then the options are usually exercised automatically.

  On the next Monday after expiration day, the 500 shares the trader now owns will come with a margin call. Since the trader did not know that he or she was going to purchase stock, they will lack enough money in their accounts to pay the shares. They will, therefore, be forced to sell the shares. It is thus very important to avoid this mistake of failing to sell long options before the expiration day.

- **Fear of Assignment notice**

  As an options trader, you should never fear when assigned to an exercise notice for an option that you sold. If you are prepared then you should never fear provided it does not result in a margin call. On selling an option, you should be able to understand that the owner of the option can exercise it any time before its expiration day at will. This should, therefore, be neither surprised nor a problem when it happens. Writing a covered call, you are assigned guarantees to the trade's maximum profit.

  In case you make a sale of options that has got no position in the stock, then you should be sure to meet margin calls if you are assigned an exercise notice. It will be the work of your broker to supply an answer if you are not able to personally figure it out. This case should not, however, freak you out. It is very beneficial to get an assignment notice before expiration day as it reduces the risks associated with the trade. Fear of assignment notice is, therefore, one of the mistakes that should be avoided before the expiration day.

- **Failure to differentiate how European-Style Options expire**

  Unlike any other type of option, European-style options usually expire on the third Thursday of every month as compared to other options that expire on each third Friday. This is the most common mistake that is committed especially by new options traders. If you have a plan of closing your trade on its expiration day then fail to consider the time difference, then your options might expire without your knowledge. This might result in big losses to options traders. You might never know that your options expired until the time when the settlement price shall be determined. The settlement price is usually determined either in the early Thursday afternoon or Friday morning. You should, therefore, avoid this kind of mistake by closing your trades on Thursdays before their expiration. It is very vital to create a reminder if you doubt that you can remember to do so in time. The reminder would alert you and thus be able to close the European options trade on time before it expires.

Chapter 25: Other Strategies for Beginners in Option Trading

Before venturing into options trading, it is vital to have a plan of action. Options trading has of late become very popular since it gives individuals a chance to make money fast. This does not mean that no losses occur but one can also lose large amounts of money fast. Options trading strategies range from simple to complex ones with a variety of odd names and payoffs. The simple strategies already discussed include long call, covered call, long put, short put and married put. These strategies had been earlier discussed thus we will discuss other different strategies for beginners in options trading. These strategies are more complex as compared to the previous ones and are discussed below;

Long Straddle Strategy

This options strategy is where an options trader purchases both long put and long call for the same asset having a similar strike price and expiration date. This strategy entails benefitting from unpredictable and big moves. This strategy is said to be complex due to the sophisticated calculations that are done by options traders. This strategy aims at making profits from any outcome but also has challenges just like any other investment. Risks associated with this strategy is that the market might not react to the event generated by it strongly enough. This, therefore, makes this strategy expensive since it entails investing in two approaches.

This strategy can alternatively be used in capturing the expected increase in the trade's volatility. Implied volatility is very influential when determining the prices of options. An increase in the volatility, therefore, means that there is an increase in all options' prices. This strategy is characterized by limited risks and unlimited profits. In case the prices of the stock increase continually, then the advantages expected are limited. On the other hand, if the prices of the stock become zero, then the profit is the difference between the strike price and the premiums that were paid for the purchased options.

Buy-Write Strategy

This strategy is also referred to as the covered call strategy. This strategy is majorly employed on stocks. An example of this strategy is the sales of covered calls. This strategy entails the purchase of stocks then the investor sells the stock's call options. The main purpose of this strategy is the generation of income from the premiums paid for options. This strategy works by making assumptions that the security's market price would change and might rise before its expiration day. On the other hand, if the option's price declines, the investor would then write a call to keep premiums from the sale of options. This strategy may be used to increase returns by periodically repeating it when the time for the options is lackluster.

To implement this strategy accurately, the option's strike price should always be higher as compared to the price of the stock. This, therefore, needs well-executed judgment as the strike price should be higher but not as to make the premium price insignificant. If the expiration period is set to be prolonged then this means that the premiums will also be high. This strategy might lose its position in case the price of options rises rapidly.

Married Put Strategy

This strategy is also referred to as a synthetic long call. Married put strategy is an options trading strategy that entails the trader purchasing put options together with shares equivalent to the purchased stock. This strategy is commonly employed in cases where the investor acts bullish on certain stocks and might want to benefit from the stock. Its profit potential is unlimited and is similar to that of the long call. This strategy also has got a limited risk which is usually calculated by the addition of the premium paid to the commissions paid. The break-even point of this strategy is achieved by determining the underlying price. The break-even point is determined by adding the premium paid to the price of underlying securities. This strategy works similarly as an insurance cover having certain strike-price and is against the short-term losses. At the same time frame, the options trader would the very call options at an increased strike price.

Protective Collar Strategy

This strategy is where an options trader purchase shares of a given option then sell a short call option and simultaneously purchases a long put to limit downside risks. This strategy majorly aims at the protection of stocks that have got a low market price. Protective collar strategy employs call options upon its sale and puts options upon purchase. In this case, both put options and call options should have a similar number of shares and expiration date.

This strategy entails the integration of short call, long put options, and long stocks. In options trading, a long stock refers to where a trader purchased underlying assets hoping to earn from them in the future. When employing this strategy, it is advisable to take a long put option if the market price might continuously fall and you want to prevent further loss of money and limit risks.

An advantage of this strategy is that it is cheap as compared to the purchase of protective put in instances where you will have to sell out your money from your shares. On the other hand, this strategy might be disadvantageous since the profits are limited in instances where the price of stock increases. The protective collar strategy works well with the protection of profits obtained from stock.

Long Strangle Strategy

This strategy is neutral and it entails simultaneously purchasing an out-of-the-money call and out-of-the-money put having a similar expiration date and the underlying stock. This strategy is characterized by limited risks and unlimited profits gained from the stocks. This is obtained where the options trader believes that the stock would experience significant volatility. This strategy is a debit spread since debit is usually taken so that one can enter this trade. The large profits for this strategy are usually obtained in cases where the price of an underlying stock fluctuates at expiration day. The maximum loss for this strategy is obtained by adding the total premiums paid to the commissions paid.

Chapter 26: The Best Strategies to Invest with Call and Put Options Trading

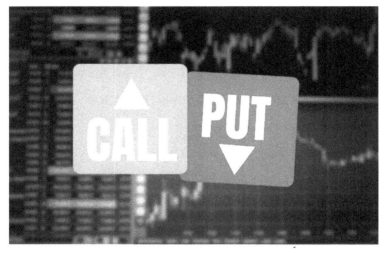

An option is a contract that provides an opportunity to an investor either to purchase or sell an underlying commodity as security at a particular price over a given time period. There is a market where the purchasing and selling of these options, which is options trading, is carried out. This market is referred to as the options market. Options trading basically involves trading in options and are particularly involved with securities of stock or even bond market. These options are classified into two, namely, call option and put option. A call option is when a buyer of a contract holds the right to buy purchase an underlying asset at a price predetermined for the future. On the other hand, a put option is when a buyer purchases the right to allow him or her sell an underlying asset at a price predetermined for a future time. It is also important to note that the trade options are better preferred compared to the direct assets. This is because there exist some advantages to trading options. These advantages include providing increased cost efficiency, they are of less risk to direct assets such as stocks and most importantly they provide some strategic alternatives. The right to buy or sell options is viable to an investor throughout until the date of expiration. There are very many strategies that an investor can use when participating in options trading. These strategies vary depending on the reward, risk among other factors. Below are some strategies to invest with call and put options trading;

- **Go for a covered call**

  This strategy involves purchasing a call option that is referred to as naked. This strategy lowers some of the risks that could result in the investor becoming alone long stock. It also generates income for the investor. The compromise to this particular strategy is that an investor must be willing to sell the shares at a price that is a short strike. In order to carry out the strategy, you have to buy an underlying stock as you would normally, and at the same time sell the same shares on the call option.

- **Married put**

  Here the investor buys an asset, for example, stock shares, while at the same time purchasing an equal number of put options involving shares. This strategy safeguards an investor's downside risk at the time they are holding stock shares, thus any investor prefers to use it. If it happens that the price of a stock begins falling sharply, this strategy creates a base price. Basically, for this strategy it is appealing to an investor since it offers protection from the downside should there be any negative occurring event. Likewise, if there be any upside from stocks gaining value at any time, the investor benefits fully from it. This strategy, however, has one disadvantage, whereby the investor will lose the amount paid as premium for put option if the value of the stock does not reduce.

- **Bull Call Spread**

  A bull call spread is our third strategy to invest with call and put options trading. Under this strategy, an investor simultaneously purchases calls at a certain price and sell the equivalent quantity of calls at a strike price that is higher than the amount he or she used for buying them. The underlying asset is the same for the two call options as is the expiration. This type of strategy is referred to as being vertically spread. It is used when there is a bullish investor who also is expecting that any rise in the asset price should be moderate.

- **Bear put spread**

  This strategy of a bear put spread is actually the opposite of the bull call spread in terms of explanation but involves the put options. An investor will buy put options at a certain strike price and simultaneously sell that same amount of puts at a price that is lower than the buying strike price. Similarly, to the bull call spread, both of the options will be having the same underlying assets and expiration dates. This is a strategy used by a trader or an investor who expects a decline in price for the underlying asset and at the same time is bearish. It provides gains and losses that are both limited.

- **Long Call Butterfly spread**

  In this strategy, it combines two other strategies, which are the bear spread and bull spread strategies. However, it uses three strike prices that are completely different from each other. The underlying asset and date of expiration are the same for all options. An investor ends up using this strategy when he or she thinks that the expiration for the stock will most definitely not experience a big move change. Maximum loss under this strategy happens when the stock is either below or at a lower strike, or if it settles above or at the strike call that is highest. Both the upside and downside of this strategy are limited.

- **Long call strategy**

  Here a person purchases a call option. This strategy stakes at the price of an underlying stock rising by expiration above the set strike price. This strategy is used by an investor who is not bothered about losing an entire premium by staking on the rising of stock such that he or she could receive greater profit than if they directly owned the stock.

- **Long put strategy**

  This strategy is very similar to the sixth above only that for this case one wagers on the decline of stock rather than a rise. An investor purchases a put option, counting on the stock to fall by expiration below the strike price. Under this strategy the investor sacrifices to lose the full premium, waging that the stock will decline. If it happens that stock decline, an investor ends earning much by owning puts than he or she would have by selling the stock.

Chapter 27: Describe Examples of Trade

There are many types of trades in a financial market that one can choose from. These trades require an intensified prior research and in-depth understanding before setting your foot into any of them. However, one is advised to try to master one specific trade that they are comfortable with. It is, however, advisable to be proficient in other trades as well. This is to enable you to find that specific trade that best suits your specific interests and one that you find having a higher probability to provide you more profits. This provides you with the opportunity to analyze them and make the right decisions on which type of trade you will invest in. These different types of trade focus on the sale of securities, stocks, etc. In this chapter, the five main types of trade are explained in depth.

Position Trading

It simply means taking a position in an asset with the anticipation of joining a larger market trend or rather expecting that the asset may increase in value over a given period of time. Position trading does not put much emphasis on the minor price fluctuation or market corrections that have the tendency of reversing the price trend temporarily. The long term performance of the various assets in the market is the positional trader's main concern. Their main aim while in the market is to analyze that specific trend in the price of securities that can relatively go for a long period. Position trading can provide very high returns amidst the high transaction costs involved. It also has the advantage that it does not require a lot of the trader's time, once the trade has been made and necessary market strategies put in place, then once you only require to wait for the outcome. However, it is also associated with substantive risk especially in cases where there is an unforeseen trend reversal or rather in cases of low liquidity. Generally, positional trading revolves around the utilization of fundamental and technical analysis. An options trader is usually at liberty to use both methods to ensure that he/she makes sound decisions.

Day Trading

This involves the sale and purchase of securities in just a single day. This trade can go for hours or even minutes. Day trading is most of the time characterized by an easy way of getting rich, however, day traders suffer great losses within a day. They usually make short term strategies to benefit from small fluctuations in prices. Day traders usually exit the market before the market closes to avoid getting risks. This method of trading can be applied in any type of trade through it is quite common in the foreign exchange market. It is a requirement that you be well updated on the current news so as to benefit from day trading. This is because these emerging issues are the reason for the small price movements. They include various announcements such as corporate earnings, interest rates or economic statistics among others. The technique used in this trade is the intraday strategy. These strategies include scalping which tends to make small profits based on small price fluctuations throughout the day. Range trading which usually uses resistance levels to determine they buy or sell decisions, New based trading basically captures trading opportunities from market volatilities resulting from news events. The high-frequency trading strategies which basically use algorithms to identify short term market inefficiencies.

Scalping

This involves obtaining very small profits repeatedly. This type of trading usually takes advantage of accruing small profits based on very small price fluctuations. Scalping trade is usually based on the anticipation that the majority of the stocks will complete the first stage of the movement. Its movement after the first step is however uncertain. The traders who carry out this type of trade are characterized by making numerous types of trades within a day. They work from the basis that these small shifts in prices are the easiest to capture as compared to the larger price fluctuations. This trade requires strict exits strategies however since the loses that one could incur might be huge enough to eliminate all the small gains that you may have accrued over some time. It may be so easy to lure people into this type of trade due to the thinking that it has returned, for beginners, it is not recommended as one may risk making very huge losses. This trade requires some kind of expertise and skills to succeed in it.

Momentum Trading

In this trade, the traded focuses on making their buy or sell based on the strength of the recent price trends. The trader ensures that he/she makes the trade at the point where there is maximum momentum on either the upstream or the downstream. Most of the times they put more focus on that stock which follows one direction on a high volume. This type of trade usually lasts from several hours to a few days based on how swiftly the stock moves and at what instance it changes direction. The strategies employed in this trade are usually both short and long term. While investing in momentum trading, one holds the belief that a particular trend persists until its conclusion and that it is possible to profit from as long as you stay with the trend.

Swing Trading

This type of trade involves holding a tradable asset for a period of one to several weeks with the aim of making profits from the price changes. Swing traders can use both technical and fundamental analysis to capture trade opportunities as well as in analyzing the trends of market prices and patterns. Usually, the main goal is to capture a high potential price move and then move on to the next opportunity. This type of trade has the tendency to expose the trader with the risk of making huge losses in cases where a closed session opens up with a substantially different price. Usually, the swing traders use a set of mathematically based rules for making trades to eliminate various technicalities when making the buy or sell decisions. Other strategies used include the Alexander Elder's strategy. This strategy measures the behavior of an asset price trend using three different moving averages.

Chapter 28. Probable Tips and Suggestions to Try to Succeed with Options Trading

Becoming an options trader who consistently enjoys success in his endeavors is not just something that you find yourself achieving overnight. You require to spice the process by bringing in new ideas and concepts that may seem probable. When these tips are incorporated in the right way you will surely find yourself up the ladder of success with a lot of ease. This article will equip you with some of these tips that you may use to your advantage.

One of the key tips is in ensuring that you focus on the prices of the options. You realize that options grow more and more worthless as time goes by simply because at the end of it all they will finally expire. This is a characteristic shared by all the options, no exception. The majority of the option traders make the mistake of laying so much emphasis on studying the market as well as the stock. They usually make their decisions on whether to buy or sell their options based on this. They often forget the prices of these options. You should always focus on buying low-priced options and sell the high-priced options. Being able to differentiate the low-priced options from the cheap options in the market is one of the steps towards success in options trading. A low-priced option usually provides a very high return. Failure to consider this factor of options prices may just make you end up accumulating losses. When the options are well thought of and analyzed properly they can be very rewarding.

Another tip is to ensure that you have the necessary tools to stay in the market. Your risk management strategies should be well outlined. Your option trade can turn out to be the most successful if you manage your risks appropriately. However, the majority of the option traders usually focus on the amount of money they plan on getting and forget the loses they risk accumulating. You realize that most of the decisions that you make in option trading will be influenced by this factor. As for the case of the amount of capital that you would invest, you would only risk investing that amount that you would bear to lose in case things worked against you. Most of the option trading strategies, however, are quite risky. But you can try out various risk management strategies so as to minimize loses as much as possible. Enormous loses have the potential of affecting you for even a whole month or even make you exit the trade.

Creating a good game plan that is quite quantifiable is a major tip in ensuring success in options trading. Make sure that the goals outlined in the strategy are quite clear and realistic. They should not set the bar too high or rather appear in achievable in any way. With a clear strategy, you are able to focus on the latter. Your strategy should also be strict in a way that asses all the aspects of your options trading. Ensure that you also exercise the virtue of discipline to your course so as you reap success in an options trade. Your game plan should also be quite flexible to accommodate the changing market patterns.

It is quite advisable to trade with a well-known stock or rather one that you are quite familiar with. By this, you are able to even predict the price movements of stock. This is usually a very crucial exercise that can reap you maximum benefits. You also do not have to go through a lot of struggles on analyzing the stock as you are already familiar with them. However, there is a need to ensure that you consistently do a lot of market research on the same to keep up with the changing trends. For well-known stock, the majority of them enjoy huge volumes and have the tendency to remain in the market for longer periods.

The other tip is on the choice of an options trade broker. It is wise to ensure that they offer you with quite affordable or rather user-friendly commissions. High commissions will affect your profitability as well as your strategy. Nonetheless, do not go for the low fee brokers if they are not in a position to offer you reliable services like better trading opportunities as well as saving you time. Failure to which you may end up losing much of your dollars due to their inefficiency. For online brokers, ensure that they have convenient methods or platforms that can enable easy transfer of money. This decision on the choice of a broker is a decision worth spending a lot of time on. The success of your trade highly depends on the broker you chose.

It is quite possible to think that your psychology does not play a key role in the options trade. Many options traders overlook this and end up making decisions that ruin their trades completely. This is quite common especially when you make huge losses and become emotional. This is very normal and expected but you should learn that any decision you make while in this state of mind may completely work against you. It is therefore advisable to learn how to react to such losses. Moreover, try as much as possible to combat the fear of losing. This may refrain you from enjoying huge profits that you could have earned in case you entered the trade.

Ensure that you take advantage of market volatility. Many new traders have the tendency to overlook this critical factor. They do forget that it is not always that options will reflect the move that a particular stock will take. It is advisable to understand how market volatility affects the implied price of the option. In the case where there are susceptible high market volatility and consecutive huge moves. It is quite advisable to use the straddle strategy. This refers to the buying of the call and the put option at a particular strike price for a given period of time. It usually has the advantage of providing limited risks.

Chapter 29: Possible Errors to Avoid That Can Be Committed in Option Trading

When trading options, it is possible to lose money that you have invested and it is therefore important to be aware of errors that can be made when trading. They include lack of a strategy in exiting the market, trading in options that are not liquid among other mistakes that will be comprehensively discussed below.

Buying into the Option of the Out-Of-The-Money Call Options

In the options market, buying into the out-of-money options is one of the most difficult means of making money. Such call options are always inviting to new traders for in most cases they are always less expensive than other options. What most new traders do that make them lose money is enacting this strategy only, which does not give successful, consistent gains.

Lack of a Strategy in Trading

When a trader does not have a strategy in entering and exiting the market, there is a high possibility to make losses. Without a strategy, a trader will not know when to make a trade, and with what amount of money. A chance may, therefore, pass you when you've got no plan for your trading. Before buying or selling an option, make a clear cut and concise plan, to avoid making mistakes when trading, that would have otherwise been avoided.

Lack of a Strategy in Exiting the Market

Some traders lack an exit plan suitable for when they are making losses and conversely when they are making profits. An exit plan is to provide a solution when you want to close a trade. Without one, you will not know the appropriate time to close down a trade, which may leave you open to making huge losses in the market, when you don't close the trade early enough and reversed profits to losses when the markets reverse.

Not Putting into Consideration, the Expiry Date

Not have a prediction made on the time frame that a trade will go may prove to be loss-making. In trading options, making a prediction on how long trade of an option will take is a key aspect. Factors such as reports on earnings are crucial in determining the expiry date. Traders may fail to make decisions on the correct expiry dates that correlate with the factor events, that makes their strategy to be useless at this point.

Having so Much Leverage on the Trades Made

Traders who are mostly used to trading in the stocks market make the mistake of buying options with way too much money that is needed for options. Options are classified as derivatives and they do not, therefore, cost as much as the options. Large sums of leverage are therefore not needed in this category in the market, a mistake that many traders from the stock market are susceptible to doing. This opens up their trade to many losses, stemming from the unnecessarily high amount of leverage on the trades, such that when a trade does not go as intended, their whole strategy crumbles.

Trading with the Less Expensive Options

Cheap options in the market, which some traders may prefer, turn out to be no money-making options. The mistake in trading in the cheap options is that they have low premiums, whose strike price will always be way above the cost going in the market or as well below the market costs. To counter such a difference in the prices, the trader is therefore forced to create a more drastic strategy to salvage the options traded. It is not a wise decision to always buy cheap options.

Indecision on Early Options

The indecision that plagues some traders on the early options is always uncalled for. On an early option, some traders do not buy and sell the options in the right manner, according to the rights that they are accorded by the buyers. The indecision is always rooted in a panic on what to do with the options. They do not know at what appropriate time to close their losing trades and let the gaining ones remain open, without panicking over the possibility of the market reversing and them making losses thereafter.

Trading with the Wrong Size of a Trade

The portfolios that some traders have do not always go hand in hand with the size of the trades that they make. In one case scenario, they can be risking too much in trading risky options, whereby if they make losses, their portfolios cannot cover them. On the other hand, they can be making a trade that is way too risky, where they lose on trades that would've made gains, and the portfolios are well capable of covering that, the most common case under this mistake is the traders risking all of their portfolios. They do not think about the question of whether they can afford to risk the amount of money traded if the trades made losses.

Maximizing on a Losing Trade

Maintaining a losing trade for a long period of time is one of the mistakes that traders are highly susceptible to making. Riding on a losing trade that will just result in losses is of no good. When the indicator shows high levels of losses, traders do not exit the trade, with prospects that the trade will reverse. They do not distinguish between losing trades that do not reverse and the ones that can have the possibility of reversing from proper analysis.

Trading in Options That Are Not Liquid

This is a mistake that costs traders when they want to close a losing trade and at the same time much money than if the option would have been liquid. An illiquid option does not give the leeway to buy and sell options in a quick manner, therefore exiting the market when the trader's desires become difficult. Most of the traders who trade in options that are not liquid do not often check on the opening interest on the option. Most of the options that are illiquid will have less interest, thus less flexible that these with larger interests, usually the larger companies.

Chapter 30: The Conclusion on What Was Written and the Goodness of the Book

You are at the end of the book: *Options Trading for Beginners Book Outline* and thank you for reading through it and making it to the end. Let's be hopeful that it has been helpful enough to provide the knowledge and skills that are needed to start trading in options as a newbie in the market. And as not everything might have been covered in this book outline, it would also be great if you would seek to enrich yourself with such knowledge from other sources apart from this book. The book has nonetheless covered great subjects on the introduction of the options market to a new and a beginner trader that seeks to apprentice the reader to the market. Written in this outline, as you've read, is a comprehensive guide to starting trading in options.

As the main subject of the book is, the basics of options trading have been greatly discussed, offering the reader a clear picture of what options reading in general is. The points outlined at the opening chapter break down the options market in chunks that a beginner can well relate to. It also piques up your interest to find more about options trading and how they operate in making money. You are also encouraged to start on trading options by the book outlining the advantages of the trade that leaves you motivated to start on it already. You are made aware of the fundamentals of the trade and the components of it, further expanding your knowledge of the options market, which will prove to be very helpful to a beginner in the market, for they are well aware of what options trading comprises of.

The highlight of the book to the reader is talking about how to get started in trading the options. This part offers you the practical skills and gears you up to take the first step in making your beginner trade. The knowledge written in this book would be to naught if you, the reader, who is a beginner trader, would not make the first trade, following care guidelines. And this book has just done that. Written down great and helpful tactics to kick you off as you start your journey in the options trading world. After gaining such skills, employ them in the real market world and get to experience the highs and the lows, but as stated in the book, nonetheless great strategies.

As a beginner in trading, you have also benefited from other aspects written in the book such as risk and risk management; very crucial, leverage, and others such as technical analysis. These aspects will be vital in trading, for in most cases that determine the profitability of the trades that you have made. Let's hope that you have gone through these aspects carefully and taken away the key points that will be crucial when you are trading. Factors such as leverage will distinguish you from becoming a professional trader in no time and a trader who makes mistakes and errors that would have otherwise been avoided. Technical analysis in the book has been discussed extensively as one of the key issues to dwell on when you begin trading. As observed in the book, it can be termed as the backbone that holds the trading. It is the most important takeaway you can take. Without the analysis, your takeoff as a beginner trader would be baseless, for you would be making assumptions on the market without any reference, which is a suicidal thing to do in the market.

Of great import to traders in this book outline as they progress from being beginners is the subject of psychology in trading. The book has delved deeper into the emotional outplay in options trading, where the thoughts in this chapter seek to elevate you to a higher state of emotional approach towards trading in options. We are hopeful that you will be able to learn from this outline the importance of trading with your emotions kept in check, as the book advertises, for successful trading. Apply this knowledge in real-time trading and approach the market in the right mental state, this being one of the skills that were mentioned in the psychology of options trading. It will do you good to be well conversant in this section as a beginner.

As a beginner, probably the most exciting part of the book was where tips on succeeding in options trading were extensively written down. This should buoy your beginner trading spirits up and gear you up for being successful in this field, which you'll be, after following the tips outlined here and from many other sources. To be fully confident in your trading capacities and abilities, this outline had also provided in text form of the mistakes that are to be avoided when you are trading.

All this said, it remains up to you, the beginner reader of trading in options to make the most crucial move; and that is making your first trade. This should not be procrastinated as the book has prepared you enough for the market, and you should be confident to make trades, and also make it a learning experience from your gains and losses, which are a sure thing to make in trading. Also, be sure to get useful information from enlightening sources to keep you on top-notch. We hope the skills that you've gathered from this awesome book will prove to be helpful as you start trading and making your way in options trading. We wish you the best of luck as you start on this enthralling endeavor in your life, packed with all the information you need. May you make the best trades and predictions with this outline as your guiding ray.

Thank you for taking your time to go through this outline and if you found the contents of this book to be helpful in any way, please do a review of it in any platform, which will be highly appreciated.

Description

What could be the basics options of trading? What are the types of options trading? What are the advantages of trading in option? What are the components of an option contract? What are the fundamentals of the pricing options? How do you start trading in options? What are some of the tools required for trading? What are some of the risks of leverage? What are the advantages and disadvantages of trading leverage options? How much does it take to trade-in option? How can one trade intelligently? What are some of the features of technical analysis? What are the different types of graphs that could exist? What are some of the strategies that could be applied with technical analysis? How do one control emotions? What are some of the basics of psychology in trading options? What are some of the examples of trade? What could be the possible tips and suggestions that could be borrowed for success? What are some of the possible errors that can be avoided in options trading?

Options trading is meant to direct one on when there is more profit in the market and when the market is not making any progress at all. It will act as a tool that will provide leverage and will give possible accounts of how the market of the commodities is fairing on the outside. The option trading is supposed to be the contract between two parties who have sat and have to discuss what is entailed in the contract document and are now reading on the same script or have agreed on the terms of the contract. We have two types of options trading they are puts and calls.

Some of the reasons why we have trading options are that it acts as a form of insurance. You cannot put all your eggs in one basket. That is why it is recommended that you get the insurance that will protect what you have invested in. the other reason is that it will bring income to you. This happens when there is some sort of selling to other individuals you will be making some income. The other reason is that you will have limited some of the risks that you may encounter because you will have put in place several strategies to curb any type of risk.

The goal of this book is to ensure you understand the various options of trading. This book will give guidelines on how to go about the options trading.

In this book, you will learn:

- The Basics of Options Trading
- Types of Trading Option
- Advantages of Trading in Option
- Components of Trading in Option Contract
- Fundamentals of the Pricing Option
- Starting Trading in Options
- Platforms and Tools for Trading Options Leverage
- Why Leverage Can be Riskier
- The Advantages and Disadvantages of Trading Leverage Option
- How Much Leverage it Takes to Trade in Options
- How You Can Manage Risk in Options Trading.
- How You Can Trade Options Intelligently.
- The Support and Resistances
- The Different Features of Technical Analysis
- The Different Types of Graphs Used for Technical Analysis
- Strategies and Risk That Can be Applied in the Technical Analysis
- How to Control Emotions and Have the Right Mindset
- Describe Examples of Trade
- The Probable Tips and Suggestions to Succeed with the Option
- Possible Errors to Avoid that Can be Committed in Option Trading

Would you like to Know More?

Buy it Now and let you Customer get addicted ti this Amazing Book !

Options Trading Strategies

Advanced Guide with All the Latest Winning Strategies, Practical Tips, and Suggestions That Will Make the Difference in Your Trading. Start Generating Income Now.

Trading Club America

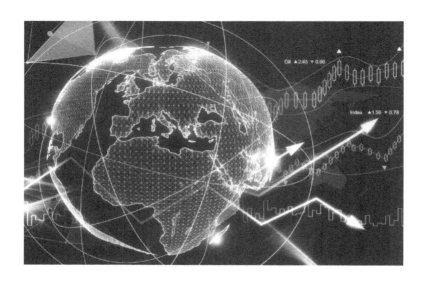

Introduction

Congratulations on purchasing *Options Trading Strategies: Advanced Guide with All the Latest Winning Strategies, Practical Tips, and Suggestions That Will Make the Difference in Your Trading. Start Generating Income Now,* and thank you for doing so. Most traders keep off options trading in the fear that options are too complicated or that they present too many risks, but I am glad you chose this path. Yes, options' trading is relatively complicated, but as you get more acquainted with the terms, strategies, techniques, and positions of trading, you will see that it is worth the hustle.

There is a lot of misinformation and myths surrounding options trading. Some perceive options trading to be as demanding as other investment crafts like day trading. The fact that options often come with an attached expiry date also puts many off. They are afraid that they might not sell their options in time. Others feel that options do not have many returns to offer, presuming other trades to have more returns. However, all these beliefs and many others are born out of fear and incorrect information.

The information in the following pages is broadly considered a truthful and accurate account of facts and as such, any inattention, use, or misuse of the information in question by the reader will render any resulting actions solely under their purview. There are no scenarios in which the publisher or the original author of this work can be in any fashion deemed liable for any hardship or damages that may befall them after undertaking information described herein.

Additionally, the information in the following pages is intended only for informational purposes and should thus be thought of as universal. As befitting its nature, it is presented without assurance regarding its prolonged validity or interim quality. Trademarks that are mentioned are done without written consent and can in no way be considered an endorsement from the trademark holder.

The truth is that no market can exist without sellers and buyers. Just as there are sellers and buyers in other investment types, there are writers and buyers of options in the options market. You do not have to worry about what will be bought and what won't. An expiry date doesn't necessitate immediate execution either; some may require execution, and for others, traders will just release to expire. When it comes to options trading, there is not much to worry about, and with a book as resourceful as this one, you will be well on your way to making tidy returns.

The following chapters will discuss options and options trading in depth. You will learn what options are, the types of options they are, and how traders make money. You will also get to know about brokers and the role they play, and we'll guide you on how to find one that will accommodate your investment needs. This book also lets you in on the secrets of success in options trading, and point you to some case studies that will prove to you the effectiveness of options trading over other investment methods.

There are abundant books on this topic on the market, thanks a lot yet again for picking this one! Every effort was made to guarantee it is full of as much useful material as possible. Please enjoy!

Chapter 1: Introduction to Options Trading

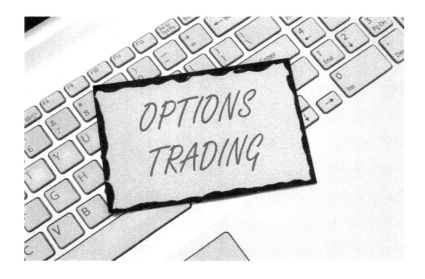

Calls, puts, derivatives, premiums, the strike price - the entire jargon options trading a rather complicated investment option. It doesn't compare to other investment forms like real estate or buying stocks, which are almost common knowledge. For this reason, many people do not like to get involved. However, although there is much to learn before you can dip your feet, and a lot of effort needed too, options trading may end up being one of the most rewarding investment decisions for you, in the end.

Well, the fact that there is much to learn does not mean that it is difficult; there is just a lot for you to grasp and keep in mind. However, once you gain an understanding of the basic concepts involved, such as what options contracts are, and how options trading is conducted, the more complex issues will be very easy for you to understand. Without further delay, let's now get into the basics so that we can get you market-ready, already enjoying the proceeds of your trade.

What Are Options?

An option is a contract to buy or sell the stock at a pre-negotiated price, within a select window or before a particular date. Usually, each contract holds 100 shares of stock.

Options take the nature of investment where people buy low and sell high. You would buy a stock if you determined that the price of the stock would go up, and sell the stock if you determined that the price would go down. With an option, you would not be buying the actual asset but would be betting on the direction that the stock is likely to take.

Although options follow other assets, they are an asset in their own right. Options are one of the derivatives, the kind that derives their value from other underlying instruments. The asset from which they derive value is called underlying security or an underlying asset. As such, an option is just a contract that follows future transactions of the underlying asset.

Each option contract must indicate particular details concerning the future transaction on which the contract is based. It indicates what the prospective transaction will be, the underlying asset, the price, whether it will be sold or purchased, and the point in time by which it will be transacted.

Whenever you purchase an options contract, you are allowed, though not obliged, to do several things. First, you get the opportunity to buy or sell shares of a stock at the agreed-upon price within a limited period. Second, you get the right to sell the contract to another investor. Third, you have the option of allowing your contract to expire and then walk away without any financial obligations to any party.

So far, options may appear to be short-term investment custom-made for people who fear commitment and are only looking to capitalize on the short-term price movements by going in and out of contracts. However, that isn't the best way with which to take on options trading. Options are best suited for investors looking to make long-term investments.

Types of Options

There are two types of options from which you can choose. They are:

Put Options

Put options are premiums paid to hedge against the risk of a possible market downturn. They are similar to an insurance policy, but for your investment. With a put option, if the price of your stock falls, you will still have the privilege to sell the shares at the exercise price. However, if the market swings upward or remains stagnant, and you decide not to sell, you will only lose the premium you paid when you purchased the contract.

Call Options

A call option is a deposit right to purchase a stock at a preset date in the upcoming future. In case the call option is not exercised before the contract expires, the investor loses his or her investment and the right to purchase the stock at the strike price.

The holders of call and put options contracts are the owners of the contracts and are not obliged to sell or buy, regardless of the market performance. They are free to exercise the option whenever they see it fit.

Conversely, call and put writers are the sellers of the options contracts, and they are exposed to risks because they must follow through on their promise to sell or buy their option.

Buying or Selling Put and Call Options

In the case of trading options, you can do any of the four things. You can buy puts, sell puts, buy calls, or even sell calls.

You are in a long position at any time you buy stock. As such, when you buy a call option, you are put in a potentially long position to the underlying stock. Short-selling a stock puts you in a short position in the underlying stock, and so does selling an uncovered or naked call.

Buying a put option places you in a short position with the underlying stock. Selling uncovered or naked puts places you in a potential long position in the underlying stock.

Remember that people who sell options are called the writers of options, while those who buy options are the holders. Call and put holders, the buyers, do not have an obligation to sell or buy, but they can choose to exercise their rights. This limits their risks to the premiums they have spent.

Call and put writers and the sellers, have the obligation to sell or buy, but only when the option expires when in-the-money. This is to say that a seller has to make good of his promise to sell or buy the stock. It also means that the option seller is exposed to much more (sometimes limited) risk. As such, writers stand to lose much more than the options premium.

Why Options?

There are many reasons and benefits of using options for investment. They include:

Investing in Options Requires a Significantly Smaller Capital Outlay Compared to Purchasing the Stocks Themselves

Options are a preferred investment vehicle because they allow you to make significant profits without necessarily having to dish out large amounts of money. This makes them ideal for investors who have very little capital and for big investors with large budgets. The reason small investments produce big profits is simple; leverage gives you more trading power with the little you got, and this does not compare to the shareholder power you would have had bought stocks.

Let's consider an example. Suppose you had $4,000 to invest, and the company whose stock you wanted to buy, Company X, has its stocks currently trading at $20. You expect that the company's shares will rise in value. If you choose to purchase stocks, your $4,000 investment capital will get you just 200 shares. If the stock price increases to $25, you would make a profit of $5 for each share, which would add up to $800. You would receive a 20% return on your investment.

On the other hand, if you purchased call options on the same stock, and the call price for each share was $2, your $4,000 investment budget would allow you to acquire 2,000 options, which will have enabled you to buy 2,000 shares. If the price of the stock went up, rising to $25, you could exercise your option to buy 2,000 shares, then sell them immediately at $25, for a $10,000 income. This profit would be a 150% return on your investment.

The example above illustrates to you how you can generate sizeable returns, whichever investment level you are at. Options will give this one significant advantage over any other financial instrument. As you see, you can save quite a lot of money when you take a particular position on the underlying security because it enables you to make cost-effective trades and investments.

With Options, the Investor Is Protected from the Downsides Risk Because the Contract Locks in the Price and Does Not Place an Obligation to Buy

This benefit is called the risk versus reward advantage. As you can see in the example given above, with options, large amounts of capital and profits can be obtained from an amount that would have given less, had you invested in the actual underlying asset. This makes options a cost-efficient investment option. In addition, if the trader employs the proper trading strategies, the risks versus rewards ratio will be relatively lower.

The fact that risks are low does not mean that there are no significant risks involved; any investment type will have them. The reality is that trading strategies that are speculative, such as options, can be very risky. The general rule, however, is that the higher the potential returns, the higher the risks involved. The good thing, though, is that you have the liberty to choose the level of risk you are willing to take and then do all you can to minimize it.

Risks are also more spread out for options because there is a wide range of options contracts and different orders you can take in, which makes it easier to limit the risk you expose yourself to than it would be if you were buying and selling stock.

Options can also be a tool for limiting the exposure to risks on the stock options you have already. For example, if you already own stock for a particular company and have concerns about the short-term volatility of the stocks because it could wipe out your gains, you can hedge against these possible losses. To hedge against these losses, buy a 'put' option because it will give you the right to sell a given number of shares at a specified price. If the share price goes down, the options contract will limit your losses and the gains you will get when you sell the contract will help to offset some of the losses.

As you go further in learning about options and the way they are traded, you will see just what an incredible tool they are when it comes to managing risks.

Options Buy the Investor Time to See How the Market Plays Out.

If you have been eyeing a company and you believe that its stock price will rise, you will opt for a call option because it will give you the right to purchase shares at a predetermined price at a specific date in the future. If it happens as you had predicted, you will buy your stock for less than it would sell in the open market. If the situation doesn't play out as you had hoped, your financial losses will be limited to the price you paid for your contract.

Options Are Flexible and Adaptable

One of the biggest pros of options is the flexibility options offer. This is unlike most passive income investments and some active ones too that have limited strategies and techniques for making money.

If you were to take the conventional buy and hold approach that involves merely buying stocks and building a portfolio in the long-term, only two investment strategies would be available to you. You may choose to buy stocks that will appreciate with time and cash in on this long-term growth, or you may want to buy stocks whose companies offer regular dividend payouts, and you will enjoy the regular returns. Some people even diversify their portfolio and use a combination of the two.

When using the traditional buy and hold strategies discussed above, the investor has to choose between whether to make very safe investments that give little returns or whether to endure more risks but have the potential for large profits. That said, with only two possible strategies, there isn't much scope as to how far your advanced strategies can go. There are not many options to increase your profits, as you would have trading options.

The flexibility and versatility of options mean that there will be very many investment opportunities in spite of the market conditions prevailing. In addition, options can be traded based on a wide range of underlying assets. Also, just as you can speculate on the movement of the price of stocks, you can speculate on the movement of the price of indices, foreign currencies, and commodities. As you can see, there are a vast number of opportunities that you can turn into potential trades and reap some profits out of them.

Take, for example, a person who is good at predicting changes in the forex market also has a deep understanding of some specific industry. The individual could use his prediction skill to navigate the forex market to trade options and will use his fundamental knowledge of the particular industry to trade options based on the available stock. The potential for finding your niche in options trading is almost limitless.

The number of trading strategies from which a trader would choose is also significant. Spreads, in particular, give you the flexibility of choosing the way to trade, whether you want to limit the risk of taking up a position, want to profit from price movements in either direction, or want to reduce the upfront costs of taking up a particular position.

The spread is what allows you to have true versatility. You can use it to hedge for existing positions during times of economic uncertainty and to profit from a stagnant market. Both of these uses are impossible when trading stocks.

Disadvantages of Options

As we mentioned in the beginning, mastering all there is to do with options trading is an uphill task. There is just so much to learn and understand, and for that reason, many investors choose to avoid it. There is no straightforward path to it, and to understand what it is all about, an investor needs to invest a lot of time and commitment. However, eventually, he or she will have the opportunity to make money in different market conditions, with a variety of underlying assets.

Another disadvantage of options trading is brought by the risks involved. Options trading can be particularly risky for beginner traders for their lack of experience. You need to understand each strategy required and to understand the risks that each carries before dipping your toes.

What Are Options Used For?

As you may have guessed from the sections above, options serve two primary functions: speculation and hedging.

Speculation is simply a gamble on the future price. In a case where a speculator predicts that the price of some stock will rise up, based on a technical or important investigation, the speculator will buy the stock or buy the call option on the specific stock. Speculation using a call option, rather than buying the stock outright, is useful to traders because the options contract gives them some leverage. For example, an out-of-money call option lets the speculator risk only a few cents or dollars, compared to if he would have purchased the stock itself at a high price.

The second reason, hedging, is the primary reason options were invented. Hedging is a sort of insurance policy that insures your other investments in stock or whatever asset, against a possible downturn. Hedging reduces risks down to a reasonable cost. For example, if you had bought stock and wished to bring down potential losses, you could do this using put options. The options would allow you to enjoy all the upside benefits while limiting the downside risks.

Chapter 2: Finding a Broker and a Platform

When it comes to finding the right broker and platform, the cheapest option is not always the best. You will find that spending some time evaluating brokers will guide you to the right choice, one that will give you quality services. With experience, you will also see that a diligent and reliable broker serves better, even if its fees are high compared to a cheap brokerage.

This chapter evaluates some of the factors you ought to consider when trying to find the right brokerage for your options investment needs.

What to Look for in a Broker

Discount Versus Full-Service Broker

Before going any further, you must first know that there are two kinds of brokers in the market: the self-directed discount brokerage and the full-service brokerage

The self-directed discount brokerage is the type that is built specifically to suit the needs of the self-directed or independent trader. In this case, the brokerage does not offer any investment advice but leaves the clients to make their own financial decisions. These brokerages only execute the clients' orders. For this reason, discount brokerages charge so much less than their full-service counterparts do.
The full-service brokers, the traditional brokers, are brokerages that provide a range of services at a fee. Among other services, these brokers give professional advice to their clients on the best investment opportunities.

Some brokerages offer a combination of full-service and self-directed services. Their services are ranked relative to the help that each investor category needs and the clients only have to choose, depending on the quality of services they need.

Most investors opt for the discount brokerages, and I presume that it is because anyone that gets into options trading must already have been running different investment instruments in the past and are knowledgeable in finance and investment matters, enough not to need a broker's help. They do this particularly when the broker's fee is measured by the number of trades performed rather than on the soundness of the advice a broker provides.

Fees and Commissions

One of the edges of competition for brokers is the cost of their services. Brokerages come up with creative ways to make money out of the activities of the traders, and you need to carefully examine the charges imposed before you settle for any single brokerage. Look at the contract fee and the per-trade fee.

The per-contract fee is the fee charged for every option contract signed in each trade, while the per trade is the minimum fee charged per transaction regardless of the number of contracts involved in each trade.

The total commission costs for each transaction is calculated using the following formula:

- Total Commission = $X for each trade + $Y per contract
- Here's another formula brokerages have taken up:
- Total Commission = Whichever is higher ($X for each trade or $Y for each contract)

- **Volume Discount**

Some brokerages offer discounts by charging a lower fee for a trading frequency that goes beyond a particular threshold. Therefore, if you plan to make numerous trades within the month, it makes sense to scout for a brokerage firm that has this discount scheme.

- **Limit or Market Order**

Some brokerages have differentiated fees for different kinds of orders; ensure that you take note of the charges for limit orders. Traders rarely make market orders.

- **Broker-Assisted vs. Internet Trading**

If you choose to trade with the help or guidance of your broker, it may cost you as much, or several times more than the independent internet trades. Therefore, to save on your costs, only choose broker-assisted trading when you know you will have no access to the internet because then, an excellent opportunity could come up, and you would need to take it up.

- **Disguised Fees**

Some brokerages charge low fees, but they make up for the low rates with some hidden charges. Therefore, if you come across a brokerage that charges unusually low fees in comparison to its competition, ensure that you look around to see whether the brokerage has placed some disguised fees.

Some of the hidden fees you ought to look out for include:

- *Minimum Balance Fee:* This is a periodical fee levied (every month or after every quarter) if your account goes below a set threshold.
- *Account Inactivity Fee:* Is the fee that some brokerages charge if the trader has not made any trade in a particular period of time.
- *Annual Maintenance Fee:* Is the fee that brokerages charge every year you hold an account with them, whether you have been making trades or not.

It is crucial that you give careful consideration to the commissions and fees charged because they have a significant impact on the profits or the losses you make, especially if your trading capital places a cap on the number of contracts you can make for each trade. For example, some brokers limit you to only having 1 or 2 contracts for each trade while others set the win/loss ratio to 6:4, or less. You need to know that a low-commissions broker is important because it can boost your earnings by up to 50%.

Quality of Service

 While making consideration of the fees and commissions charged affects the profitability of your trading, this ought not to be the only consideration. Other factors such as the ease of use, execution speed, and site availability matter, particularly in the case of self-directed online trading, also determine the quality of services a broker provides.

Here's a brief description of why you should consider each of the factors mentioned above.

- **Ease of Use**

By themselves, options are already a complicated lot, and using a complicated platform or brokerage would only make things worse. However, an easy-to-use interface helps to make your activities smoother and to minimize errors. If the interface is not right, trading mistakes that would follow will cause the loss of large sums of money because money in the options market changes hands every day. Therefore, when looking for a trading platform, opt for one that offers all its resources on a single screen for easy access.

- **Quality of Execution**

The SEC, through the National Best Bid or Offer (NBBO), requires brokers to offer the customers the finest obtainable asking price in the market when they buy securities and the finest possible proposal price to traders seeking to sell securities. Ensure that your broker guarantees trade execution prices that meet or even exceed the SEC requirements.

- **Availability and Speed of Execution**

Perhaps the most important factors to consider when selecting a brokerage are the availability of the site and its responsiveness. Options trading is time-sensitive, and you need to execute your trades immediately an opportunity comes up. However low the commission, and the fees are, if you cannot make the trades, or the site takes too long to load and execute commands, taking up this site will only cause you to waste your resources. The amount you save in commissions and fees will not be worth it.

A responsive site ensures that your price quotes are timely. In this information age, information moves fast, across the globe, day, and night. As such, traders should be able to react to breaking news very fast. You will not want to be the trader that lags behind and only hears of opportunities when other traders have taken them up.

Kindly note that the speed of your internet determines the speed of execution. Therefore, ensure that you take up a package that guarantees speed. A broadband connection is faster than dialup. Before you get on to the brokerage site, ensure that your connectivity is good.

Free Education

If you are a newbie or a seasoned trader that wants to expand his knowledge of options trading strategies, education should be at the forefront of your considerations for possible brokerages. You must get a broker that offers educational resources in the form of live or recorded webinars, online options trading courses, face-to-face meetings with a mentor, and one-on-one guidance via phone or through online means.

You see, options trading is complex, and you may want to spend the first few months, or even years, on the student-teacher learning mode. Get as much education and training as you can. If you come across a broker who offers a simulated, virtual, trial version of the options trading platform, take up the opportunity and test-drive with the dummy account before you can place any real money on the line.

Quality of Customer Service

Customer service matters greatly. You wouldn't want to be stuck with a broker that does not respond to you, or if you make a request or inquiry, the broker responds days or weeks later. Reliable customer service is a priority item, especially for those that are new to options trading. Experienced traders conducting complex trades also need all the help they can get.

As you choose between brokers, think of the means of communication you would wish to have with the broker. Would you like to speak with them on the phone, via email or to meet them in person for a live chat? Is the trading desk on call during the stipulated hours? If you are not sure of this, make several test calls to potential brokers to gauge their availability and responsiveness. Are they available 24 hours 7 days a week, or are they only available during the week? Are the representatives with whom you speak knowledgeably about options and options trading?

Before you settle for any trading platform or broker, ensure that you reach out and ask a few critical questions. See the quality of answers you get, and the time it takes to get them. If the answers are satisfactory, having considered other factors discussed above, make your choice of brokerage.

Recommended Options Brokerages and Platforms

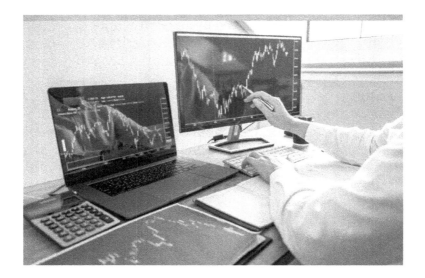

Below is a list of brokerages and platforms that offer the best options trading services. Read through this list to see the platform that is best suited for your options trading needs.

TD Ameritrade

TD Ameritrade is at the helm of the ranks thanks to its combination of desirable factors like having excellent education resources, and easy to use platform suited for traders of all levels, and reasonably priced services.

For each trade, TD Ameritrade requires its users to pay $6.95 and $0.75 for each contract involved in the trade. Traders also get to enjoy 60 days commission-free ETF, equity, and options trades to traders who place a deposit of $3,000 or more. The commission-free offer is available periodically, and you need to check whether it is currently available. Besides these benefits, TD Ameritrade offers a few more bonuses for clients with larger opening deposits.

Interactive Brokers

The Interactive Brokers platform has long been famed for its low-cost services. For a long time, this platform was thought to have a complex interface, and its customer service somewhat unreliable. Only hyperactive traders could use this platform.

Today, the situation has changed, and Interactive Brokers now extends its services to the less sophisticated and the less active traders. The company's trading platform, called the Trader Workstation platform, is now friendlier, easier to customize, and available either as a website or an app. The mobile app, in particular, does not need much typing because users can use voice commands and wheels to navigate the screen.

Interactive Brokers has also introduced a new feature called the iBOT to its platform. This application allows you to ask questions in English and get a direct answer rather than having to go through different features on the platform to get a response. For example, if you wanted to view the strike price and the expiry date of a particular option, you only have to say, "Show options chain for Company-X for the next two expirations."

Using the iBOT platform, traders can also set up a spread very quickly, and then extrapolate it into the future. The IB Probability Lab allows them to simulate possible trades before they can lay down real money.

Unfortunately, the IB platform only allows the streaming of its platform in one device at a time. This means that if you are using your mobile app to stream quotes, and you open the same on your computer, one of the platforms will automatically close, and you can no longer view the snapshot quotes. When it comes to fees and commissions, account holders with less than $100,000 deposit have to pay a minimum of $10 each month and may also have to pay additional fees to view real-time data. Traders also pay a fee of $0.0005 per share. Another downside of the platform is that its app form lacks some features.

Despite the disadvantages, Interactive Brokers remains one of the best options trading platforms because of its meager margin rates, numerous educational resources, and the fact that anyone can use it to trade. There is no set minimum account balance or the annoying per-leg base fee.

Robinhood

The Robinson trading platform is highly ranked because amazingly, it does not charge any commission. To a trader seeking to reap profits, it doesn't get better than free. Robinhood is an excellent app for beginner traders because it limits the risks to which they are exposed. This is because if you do not have to pay any trading fees, you only risk the money you set aside for your initial investment, and nothing more.

Although Robinhood does not offer much when it comes to research and educational material, if you had a rich educational resource, such as this book, you could refer to the knowledge in your book then practice your trading on the platform itself. This would be ideal for people who are starting options trading as a hobby.

For traders who have taken up other investment vehicles like ETFs, stock trades, cryptocurrencies, and ADRs (American Depository Receipts), Robinhood offers commission-free trades.

Lastly, since Robinhood is a web-first platform, traders get real-time notifications about the condition of the market, and this knowledge, they use to make trades and investments in their platform.

Lightspeed

This is a broker whose setup, the Livevol X, is designed to meet the needs of experienced very active options traders. The platform also offers a number of analytical tools like Skews Data and historical options Greeks, that other platforms do not provide. It also provides an array of analytical tools that scan the market to get a hold of different trading opportunities. In addition, its charting features are advanced and easy to customize to your needs and liking.

Once you get onto this platform, you can analyze your portfolio by grouping your positions under particular icons and symbols to determine the strategies that are currently active.

The Lightspeed platform also comes with a profit-and-loss risk graph to help you gauge the success of the strategies you have taken up. During trading surges, this broker was reported to perform very well, and to make trading very easy.

Since Lightspeed is a somewhat complicated platform, options trading newbies are advised to keep off it. Those who use it should also note that Lightspeed does not allow direct market access or futures trading in its platforms, both the web-based and the mobile app.

Overall, Lightspeed is an excellent app because of its terrific speed order execution software that also generates graphs to indicate price movement. The per-contract commissions are also very low, and there are no monthly or per-leg base charges.

Charles Schwab

The Charles Schwab brokerage runs a platform called the StreetSmart Edge. This platform can be accessed either by downloading it on your desktop or by simply accessing it in your browser. The StreetSmart Edge has numerous tools and content that help the user to build a spread by choosing the type of trade they need to place from its down-drop menu. Users can also choose the legs from the options chain exhibition feature on the platform.

The Idea Hub allows users to look for possible contracts going by their potential profitability and market activity, then arranges them into four options-specific categories. The categories include covered calls, big movers, premium harvesting, and earnings. Once you see the idea presented on display, click on it, and if favorable, click on Trade to fill your order ticket. If your option is low priced, you get to close it for free on this platform.

The Charles Schwab brokerage and its platform are best suited for the emerging options trader. You will only need to go through lots of education and support from the Schwab experts. You also will enjoy the low fees too.

Overall, Charles Schwab stands out because of its Idea Hub feature that gives you clues regarding actionable trading options in the market. It also offers trading lessons that advance as you grow in your trading. In addition, the options available are based on a wide array of asset classes.

The Charles Schwab brokerage and platform is one of the best trading platforms for beginner traders.

Chapter 3: Transaction Fees and Slippage

Transaction Costs

Transaction costs, also called transaction fees, are the charges related to the execution of a trade or the expression of an intention to maintain a position. As such, in options, the exchange gees, brokerage commissions and the Securities and Exchange Commission (SEC) fees count as the transaction costs.

Typically, brokerage commission is paid on a per-contract basis, and it pays for the services the trading platform renders like customer service and the execution of orders. The SEC fees are destined to take care of regulatory functions by the governing body. The exchange fees are a special fee to compensate markets for running a reliable and robust marketplace. If the investor wants to use his margin interest to complete a transaction, he must pay some margin interest. This makes margin interest the money that is charged for borrowing money from the brokerage.

Before you go ahead placing your order, ensure that you understand, and account for all the transaction costs that have to do with attaining and maintaining the position you have taken. The transaction cots affect much more besides the premiums you have paid or have received after the purchase or the sale of an option. Therefore, if you want to break even every time, ensure that you consider all variables involved in the trade, including the premium you paid at first, the option contract's strike price, and the transaction costs the brokerage firm charges.

Slippage

Slippage is the difference between a trade's expected price and the actual price at which the trade is executed. Slippage happens at any time in the year, but it is most prevalent in times of high volatility because that is when market orders are used. It is at that time that markets are highly volatile and susceptible to unexpected quick turns in a particular trend.

Slippage can also happen after a large order has been executed, although there is usually not enough volume at the time, and at that price, to maintain the current ask and bid spreads.

The change in price during a slippage is either negative or positive because it all depends on the direction the price has taken. It matters whether you are going short or long and whether you are closing or opening a position. As such, a slippage is any deviation from your trade strategy. Whichever direction the deviation heads, the slippage lowers the trader's confidence in the strategy's intended outcome.

If slippage is not well modeled, even a theoretically sound strategy could yield negative returns. If a seemingly positive winning strategy produces negative results, it means that the trader is yet to attain the best execution, and he may need to perform some auditing to determine the best execution policy. As such, proactively managing the slippage is likely to produce greater confidence in the overall trading strategy.

An example of slippage would be if you were closing a long position with the intended sale order placed at $100.20. If the order is executed at $100.15, you get a negative $0.05 slip. If the same order is completed at $100.25, it will have gotten a $0.05 positive slip.

If the slippage affects your positions, you still might be lucky to find some brokers who would be willing to fill your orders, but they can only do so at the worse price. However, the best trading platforms' execution practices ensure that once the price has shifted outside of your tolerance level, any time between when you placed your order and the time of execution, the order will be rejected. Their reason for doing this is to protect you from the adverse effects of slippage as you open and close your position. However, if the situation changes and the price moves to a better position, your brokerage would fill your order at the better, more favorable price.

Other ways to protect yourself from the effects of slippage is to install limits or some stop losses on your active positions. The limits help to avoid slippage as you enter or close your position because a limit order only fills at the price you have stipulated prior. On the other hand, the stop loss closes out your trade immediately; your asset's price hits the particular level you had specified. If the asset price is triggered, you are required to pay a premium.

When Does A Slippage Occur?

We have established that slippage occurs when there is high market volatility or low market liquidity. In a low liquidity market, the market participants are often very few, and this means that there are not many traders on the other end of a trade. In this case, it takes much longer to execute a trade because the seller often has to wait for a long time to get a buyer. In the course of the delay, asset prices change, and in a volatile market, this could happen in a split second; sometimes, in the few seconds, a trader will take to fill his order.

Slippages are most prevalent around the time when major news events are happening, such as when a major bank is announcing changes regarding its monetary policies or its interest rates. A major company announcing significant changes, such as when it presents its earnings reports or announces changes in its leadership, often produces the same result. Events like these increase market volatility and increase the possibility of experiencing a slippage.

Unfortunately, many of these significant events, like a company announcing a change in its leadership, are not often predictable. However, others like the reading of company financial reports, announcements by the central bank on different monetary policies, and major meetings like those of the Federal Reserve are scheduled, and traders can speculate what is to be talked about in those meetings. These predictions are not always right.

How to Avoid Slippage

Whenever it comes to managing slippage, consider taking only the best practices to limit the slippage risk. For example, now that liquidity leads to slippage, the best strategy is to counteract that liquidity. Come up with a strategy that accounts for the changing positions during the troughs and the spikes of the volatility. The strategy might involve limiting the number of market orders you place during periods of high-volume trading and increasing the number and sizes of the orders when the liquidity is low. This strategy will effectively reduce slips.

Another way to reduce slippage is to take up a more procedural and quantitative option that allows you to model for slippage. As you do this, you will iteratively improve the cost model with backtesting, which eventually limits your exposure to slippage.

Backtesting is a strategy that involves applying a particular trading strategy to historical data to see whether the strategy will produce accurate results. Backtesting is done to gauge the accuracy of any particular strategy. Many people use backtesting to gauge the profitability of the strategy using trading ratios like the risk-reward ratio and the win rate. They also rely on backtesting to unveil the underlying transaction costs in each strategy. As such, backtesting can effectively discern slippage because it is considered as part of the costs of doing business, just as it is used to discern other fees and commissions.

Backtesting is particularly common taken up when evaluating trading strategies used in the fields of production and development. Once a new strategy is developed, historical trade data is used to test the new strategy's slippage tolerance and the projected impact that slippage can have on the company's profitability. What's more, backtesting a currently running production or trading strategy, with the help of some adequate dataset, will also help to expose the strategy used to uncover some unrealized profits and to troubleshoot any underperformance. In either of these cases, the goal is to model the source of the slippage and to measure its impact, more accurately.

Overall, pinpointing the reasons and the trends that cause repeated slippage and inputting measures to minimize the errors and trends will minimize the slippage.

Other Strategies to Help Avoid Slippage

There are three other smart ways to minimize slippage and its effects on your trading.

Set up Some Limit Orders and Guaranteed Stops to Your Order Positions

Guaranteed stops, unlike other kinds of stops, are not subject to slippage, and will, therefore, ensure that your trade closes at the exact point you have set. This makes the guaranteed stops the ultimate way to manage risks when a market is moving against you. Keep in mind, however, that a guaranteed stop, unlike other stops, will require that you pay a premium once it is triggered.

Limit orders are also useful for mitigating risks that come with slippage as you enter a trade, and when you want to make a profit from a winning trade. When you have a limit order, your order will only be occupied at your predetermined price, even if the limit order is triggered.

Limit Your Trading Activity to Markets with High Liquidity and Low Volatility

If you keep to markets with low volatility and high liquidity, you will have avoided the primary causes of slippage: high volatility and low liquidity. Low volatility means that the price will not be changing too quickly, while a high liquidity market is one where there are many active participants on either side of the trades.

In the same way, you can also reduce the possibility of slippage if you limit your trading to the hours when there is the highest market activity because that is when the market is liquid. At this time, your orders stand a higher chance of being executed at your requested price, unlike when the market is less liquid.

The time when the US market is most liquid is when exchanges like the New York Stock Exchange and the NASDAQ are open. At this time, the trading volume is very high. The same is the case for the forex market because even though the market runs 24 hours every day, the best time to trade is when the London Stock Exchange is open.

If you ignore this rule and decide to hold positions when the markets are closed, such as during the weekend or at night, you are likely to suffer slippage. Slippage happens when the market reopens, and the prices have changed. The news, events of the night or morning, and other announcements will have had an effect on the financial market.

See How Your Broker Treats Slippage

If, when opening or closing a position, the price moves against you, some brokers might still execute your orders. However, this is not the proper thing to do because your broker should never fill your orders at a worse level than the one you have requested because it might be rejected.

A good broker sets a tolerance level on either side of your predetermined closing price, and if the market remains within this range at the time when the broker receives your order, your trade will be executed as the level you have requested. However, if the price steps out of this range, the brokerage does one of two things.

If the market shifts and the price is better, the broker will ensure your order closes at that better price so you can enjoy some additional profit. If, on the other hand, the market moves against you, beyond the brokerage's tolerance, the brokers ought to reject that order then ask you to resubmit your order it at the current level.

Chapter 4: Developing A Trading Strategy

The primary reason anyone invests is to 'make money,' but any seasoned options trader will tell you that there are other considerations to make. However, when it comes to options, there are other reasons, besides the desire to make a buck, for investing.

Investors use options to hedge against risks. Hedging is sort of like protecting or reducing the risks that the position you have taken attracts. While you may want to minimize losses, some of the strategies will also limit your profits, but others will not.

Traders also invest in options to manage risks. Managing is not the same as hedging. You see, hedging is protecting your investments from risks that could arise while managing is working to minimize the risks that already exist. This is the main reason traders turn to options trading.

Yes, you will get into financial trading with the intention of reaping profits, but options ensure that the risk of losing your investment capital is lessened. The strategy you choose will allow you to set a maximum loss limit for any trade, something that other investment vehicles might not allow you to do.

A stop-loss, for example, might be installed to control losses, but the losses can still fall further down, beyond the stop-loss price. The likelihood of earning more profits and the benefit of having your losses capped is what many traders appreciate about various options trading strategies.

Another reason for investing in options is to protect your investments against stock market surprises. Although the surprises do not happen very often, when they do, some are quite volatile and can be disastrous to the earnings of various stock market investors.

Lastly, investing in options is also meant to tweak the predictions made in regards to the stock market. This is particularly critical for experienced traders. For example, if a trader wants to adopt a bullish position relative to a particular index or stock, investing in options will allow you to reach your expectations.

Take Caution When Picking Using Trading Strategies

Before we get to the subject matter, it is important that I offer a word of caution to option traders, particularly the rookie traders. You should never place your hard-earned money at risk unless you are certain that you understand all the risks involved, and that you can see all the curves and corners of the strategy you want to take up.

Don't just take up the advice of those around you; do your part and study to see if the trade is suitable and that you can handle the risks that come with it. Understand all that it takes to make money using your chosen strategy, also know all the ways through which you can lose money, and when you are satisfied with your assessment, make the trade.

As you take up any options strategy, ensure that you firmly understand how that strategy works and have a clear understanding of the outcome or results, you hope to derive from managing the trade efficiently.

When dealing with options, put away the buy-and-hold mentality. Options should be traded, though not actively, but the expiry date should determine and hasten your exit. As an effective trade manager, or with the help of your broker, you ought to discern when a particular trade or a strategy is not working, and when you ought to walk out of that position. If you must suffer a loss, so be it. It would be negligent of you to hold a losing trade, one that would cost you your entire investment, in the anticipation that the trade will turn around and allow you to break even.

Developing a Trading Strategy

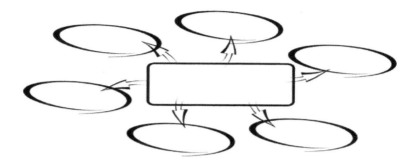

Most traders prefer using the already existing trading strategies because they are already proven, and you can already tell what the outcome will be if you apply the trading strategy appropriately. However, others like to take a different direction of creating their own trading strategies before they enter a position or on the go.

The good news is that coming up with a strategy is easy, but the challenge is to ensure that it is profitable. You will not, however, enter a new market and start making rules; you need to have studied and understood what works and what doesn't. Go over all the existing strategies, understand the indicators too, then use the knowledge you gather to charter your own path.

While starting out with high expectations is encouraged, thinking that the first trading strategy you come up with will bring supernormal profits and make you rich is unrealistic. Rarely do people get it right the first time, even with proven strategies. In addition, you will realize that profitable trading goes beyond the strategy you take up.

To develop your trading strategy, follow the following steps:

Build Your Trading Ideology

Before you put the clay in your hands, you must first have a good idea about what you are trying to make. Before you develop a strategy, you must first understand how the market itself works. The most critical of the questions you can ask yourself at this stage is, "What makes me think that I can make money from trading in the markets?" Think about why the financial market, and the options market, in particular, would be your suitable niche for your activities in comparison to other money-making activities.

The one secret to building wealth, one that I have come to treasure, is not to have a get-rich-quick mentality or to make plans in that regard. Do not believe any theories or claims that people make perfectly rational decisions.

Once you have worked on your ideology, everything else will be easier. You will make better decisions. Give them their due attention and ensure that you keep things as simple as possible. You do not want to come up with a strategy that will become too complex that it confuses you. Minimize the moving parts because the more they are, the harder it will be to manage or to make changes.

Identify Your Market

Of course, you want to trade options, which means that you will head for the options market. However, there are many kinds of options. Some are stock-based, others are index-based, and there are many more kinds. Which type do you want to trade-in? Go on and read about each and see the one that is best suited for you.

Assess Your Skills

How ready are you to trade? What do you know about trading? Do you have all the equipment needed? Have you figured out what you would do in each of the possible scenarios? Do you know how to use and read the indicators? Are you able to follow the signals? Are you confident that the knowledge you now have is enough to help you find your way through the market?

Trading is a give-and-take game. Do you know what is expected of you when you enter a particular position? Do you know what will be taken from you? Do you understand all the ways a situation could play out? Have you noted all the risks involved?

A wise trader will ensure that he has all these factors figured out and be prepared with the answers to each of these situations. Not having a plan will only amount to giving away your hard-earned money in the name of trading.

Choose a Suitable Trading Period

Before you head on to the market, you must decide on the most suitable time to do it. Are you available to trade? Will you have time to watch the market for an extended period? Will you be an active trader, or will you do trade occasionally? Choose to trade when you are available so that you pay keen attention to your trade. After doing this, some people actually realize that options trading is not for them.

Make Preparations in Your Mind

Is your mind prepared to take on the trading challenge? Are you ready? Are you physically, mentally, and emotionally ready for the battle in the market? If you are not ready, it is better to take some time off and resume trading later. If you don't, you risk losing your entire investment.

Mental preparation is essential because it ensures that you set away anger, resentment, the desire for revenge, preoccupation with other things, and other distractions are set aside so that you focus on the task at hand.

Once you start trading, the issues you face will not cease; you will still experience disappoints, losses, anger, and other distractions that would take your mind off the important issues of trading. When this happens, a mantra might help to get your mind in the right frame. Most seasoned financial traders have a market mantra they repeat before they begin their trading so that they can get their minds into what they're doing.

As you go into trading, come up with a mantra that will get you right in the trading zone. Also, ensure that your trading area does not have any distractions. Distractions could cost you greatly.

Set a Maximum Risk Level

As you get into trading options, how much of your capital will you be willing to risk at any given time? The amount of risk you can tolerate will depend on the trading style you have taken up and your risk tolerance. On any given trading day, ensure that your risk strictly stays within the 1% and 5% of your portfolio range. This means that if you lose that percentage amount in the morning, you get out and stay out the rest of the day. You do not go back to trading. It is better to retreat so that you live to fight another day.

Have Clear Goals

Your lack of goals would have you beaten and packing the day after you start options training. This is because, without goals, you will have no clarity regarding what you want, the minimum rewards or risks you are willing to take, or the profitability targets you want to reach.

Most traders set a target that they will not take a trade unless the potential profit they can reap from it is three times greater than the risk they will be taking up. Therefore, if you have placed your stop loss at 2 dollars per share, you ought not to make a profit of less than 6 dollars.

The per deal, weekly, monthly, quarterly, or annual profit goals you set will be a guiding light to help you assess how you are well or badly you are doing. Therefore, return to them regularly to see where you stand.

Conduct Some In-Depth Research

There is an unspoken rule that you ought to know everything that is happening in the field you specialize in. For example, when you take up options trading, you ought to know all that is happening in the options market, and by extension, the rest of the financial market. What is going on in the local financial market? What is the buzz in the overseas market? Is the market up or down? How is your underlying asset performing in the market? Gather all the relevant information available and use it to gauge the mood of the market, particularly before it opens.

If you come across some meaningful financial information, use it to determine the position you will hold in the market. If you find out that some important financial announcement or report is about to be released, think about whether it would be beneficial or not to trade ahead of the important report. Most traders prefer to wait for the report or announcement out and to see the effect it will have on the market before they take up any unnecessary risk.

Being a pro-trader does not mean that you should gamble. Lean towards probabilities and only take up the opportunities that are likely to bring you good returns.

Have Some Trade Exit Rules

Unfortunately, most traders focus their attention, up to 90%, on buy signals but do not give much thought to where, when, or how to exit a trade. When down, especially, the traders fear to exit because they do not want to take losses. However, if you cannot get over losses and move past a trade, you will likely not survive as a trader.

If your stop-loss is hit, it means that you were wrong in your prediction of the trend's likely direction. When this happens, do not take the loss personally. The reality on the ground is that the majority of the professional traders lose more trades than they win. However, by properly managing their portfolios and limiting their losses, they still end up making profits.

Before you enter a position, first take note of the trade that exists. Each trade should have at least two. The first is the stop loss to use in the event the trade turns against you. At what point will you put the stop? Put that information down instead of relying on some mental notes. Secondly, each trade ought to have a profit target such that once you get there, you will immediately sell a portion of your position, and your stop loss can be moved onto the rest of your position so that you breakeven whenever you wish.

What Are the Rules Governing Your Entry?

It is no coincidence that we talk about the exit before the entry because, as you will discover in the course of your trading, it matters more how a trader exits a position than how he enters it. Exits serve a much more important role than entries.

A sample entry rule is that if a particular indicator signals in regards to some options or other kind of asset, and you stand to make three times as much profit as the value of the stop loss, provided you are in support, you should go ahead and buy some contracts or shares.

Chapter 5: The Techniques to Control the Risk

Soon after getting into trading, most traders painfully learn that it only takes one or two mistakes or a few unexpected events for an entire portfolio to be destroyed. The key to avoiding that is to learn and to install measures that can control the risks to which you are exposed. It is also paramount that you understand how to manage your money properly so that you do not engage in trading habits that could bring you down.

Here are a number of techniques and practices to help you manage risk effectively:

Ease into Trading

On landing an opportunity that is so revitalizing, one that could usher you towards new levels of profitability while still protecting your current investments, 'ease into trade' is not the advice you would want to hear. However, although it sort of puts you down, it is one of the best pieces of advice because it reminds you to take caution as you take up the opportunity. You need to start slowly, then build your skills as you continue to interact with different factors in the field.

The learning period ensures that you do not risk so much that you would be thrown out of the trade. Also, since you will not be risking too much, you have the opportunity to test various strategies (all of them will be new to you anyway), so you can figure out the process of investment rather than only weighing the strategies by their potential results.

You must remember that in options trading, just like in any other craft, it takes time to make considerable profits. The beginning might be quite shaky, with a few mistakes here and there, but if you stay focused and work on perfecting your trade analytical skills and execution, the basics of options trading will become second nature to you. You will easily navigate the market, securing the winning trades, increasing your returns, and building your portfolio.

Although sticking to the basics at first could seem boring, keep in mind that every great champion or person that has achieved anything meaningful in life became successful because he or she first dwelt on the basics and made that knowledge the foundation of everything else that they know. Options trading is no exception.

To that end, I recommend that you start your trading with a virtual account. Most brokers have them. The simulation allows you to use the strategies and techniques you would use when operating a real account. You will be happy when you make successful trades and will beat yourself up when you make losing deals. Luckily, the money used in a dummy account is not real, which is good because you will get to learn and make mistakes without drilling a hole through your pockets. It allows you to go through the emotions and thrills that come with making live trades, and with that, you will be simulated into the training environment.

Get to see how well options trading might work for you. Some people get into it and realize that they need more training before they can venture into the real market, while others realize that options trading is not for them at all. Therefore, get started with a dummy account to see just how well you would work and survive in the options trading market before you enter with both feet.

Once you have been successful in conducting simulated trades, you will have built the confidence you need to make real trades. With only a few successful trades, the outlook of your portfolio will be changing. Your assets will grow.

Plan Your Trades

The famous Chinese military general, Sun Tzu, said that every battle is won even before it is fought. By this, he meant that it is the preparation, the planning, and the strategies took up that determine the winning team, but not the fighting. You might have also heard successful investors saying that you ought to plan the trade, then sell the plan. It would seem that in life, planning ahead makes the difference between failure and success.

Top among your priorities should be to investigate whether your chosen broker is down for frequent trading. Some brokers only attend to the needs of traders who do not trade frequently. If you do not intend to trade frequently, the broker would be good for you, but if you plan to be thoroughly engaged, getting with this broker would be a total mismatch. You see, the majority of the brokers who deal with irregular clients charge very high commissions, and for a regular trader, this would turn out to be too expensive. In addition, this type of broker does not offer any analytical tools.

Another angle to planning is to mark the stop-loss and the take-profit points of a trade. A trader should have determined how far he is willing to go in regards to the price, whether buying or selling. The reason is that they approach a trade having determined the possible returns from a trade, having weighed it out against the tendencies of the market. If the trader perceives that the returns will be high, he or she goes ahead and executes the trade.

In contrast, traders who do not take time to prepare and conduct research often end up unsuccessful. They get into trades without first identifying the points at which they will sell at a profit or a loss. Like a gambler who is on a lucky or unlucky streak, the trader's emotions begin to rise and take over, and trading decisions are made in a whim.

If the trader is making wins, he will be provoked to keep making more trades, and down this path, he could lose all that he has won. If the trader is making losses, the desire to make up for the losses with more trades overtakes, and this could just be the downward spiral that pushes him out of options trading.

Setting the Stop-Loss and the Take-Profit Points

The take-profit point is the price point at which a trader will sell his stock and take the profit. This happens when the trader perceives that given the risks, the chances of making more profits from the position he is holding are bleak. For example, when the stock price is approaching a resistance level, one that it cannot breakthrough, the trader may see it wiser to sell his options contract before the contract expires.

The stop-loss point is the point at which an options trader is willing to sell his contract and take in all the loss that comes with the decision. He does this when he perceives that the trade will not pan out as he had hoped. The stop-loss point keeps him from maintaining this position in the hope that the trade will turn around because, in most cases, this attitude often leads to many more losses. Therefore, when the trader checks out of the trade, he also avoids all the future losses he would have endured had he maintained his position.

As you may have guessed, the trader does not set the take-profit and stop-loss points out of guesswork; he has to have conducted in-depth technical analysis. The analysis also helps the trader get it right on the issue of timing to ensure that he does not lock out any possible benefits.

The moving averages are some of the most useful tools to help you determine your stop-loss and take-profit points. They are easy to calculate, too, in addition to being widely followed in the investment market. The key moving average is 5-, 9-, 20-, 50-, 100-, and 200-. If you set them against a stock's chart, you will be able to see how the stock price has reacted to them, whether they have been treated as support or resistance levels.

The take-profit and stop-loss points also fit well on the resistance and support trend lines. You can draw these trend lines by drawing a line that connects the previous highs or the previous lows, especially those that are above or below the average. Just as when you use the moving average, the key is to determine the level at which the stock price reacts to the trend lines when on high volume.

Using Options Spreads

An options spread is the combination of two or more positions on options contracts, using the same underlying security, to come up with one major trading position. Suppose you purchased money calls on particular stock but went ahead to also buy cheaper out-of-the-money calls on the same underlying stock, you will have created a spread, commonly called a bull spread.

When you buy both calls and create a spread, it means that you stand to gain if the value of the underlying stock were to go up, but that you would lose the money with which you bought the calls, some, or all of it, if the stock price failed to go up. The advantage of doing it, however, is that since you have written calls on the same stock, you get to control some, if not all, of the initial costs, and therefore, you can reduce the amount of money you spend trading.

All options trading strategies we discussed earlier make the use of spreads, and these spreads make for a very effective way of managing risk. For this reason, the strategies tend to be useful for reducing the costs that it takes to enter a position and for reducing the amount that a trader stands to lose. Unfortunately, while the trader gets to limit the risk to which he is exposed, he ends up limiting the profits they could make also.

All the benefits of the spreads we have covered above have to do with entering a long position. However, the spread is also good for reducing the risks involved when entering a short position. For example, writing your put options while it is in-the-money, you would receive a premium for these options. However, this would expose you to possible losses you would suffer in the event the stock's value declined. On the other hand, if you purchased out-of-money put options because they were cheap, you would have to make payment upfront. However, with your options contract, you would have prevented any further revenue losses that come with the fall of the stock price. A spread like this is called a bull put spread.

In both the in-the-money and the out-of-money scenarios described above, you can enter positions that will allow you to earn an income in the event the price moves away from you. However, you will have managed to put a cap to the losses you would suffer were the price to move against you. This is the reason options traders constantly rely on spreads to manage risk.

Using Options Orders

One of the simpler ways of managing risks is to make your investments in the different kinds of orders that are available to you. In addition to the four major options contracts we discussed in the first chapter, there are a few others that you could invest in to help reduce your risk and reliance associated with one particular order type.

One example of the additional orders is a market order, which is filled at the best possible price during the time it is executed. This is the typical way to trade options, but in a volatile market, there is no way to determine the best possible price. Your order may get filled at a lower or even higher price than you anticipated due to high volatility. However, market limit orders, you can choose the maximum and the minimum prices at which you want your orders filled. By doing this, you are able to keep yourself from buying or selling your orders at prices that are less favorable.

Some orders allow you to automate your exit from a position so that it locks in the profit you have secured, or it cuts off further losses from a trade that is not going well. You are only required to install a stop order, trailing stop order or a market stop order so that you retain control of the point at which you would wish to exit a position.

Diversification ensures that you are eating from all angles where profits are available. It helps you avoid missing potentially profitable positions and keeps you from holding on to positions that bring losses for too long, in the hope that the situation will turn around so that you close out of a bad position early enough. With options orders, you are able to limit the risks to which you are exposed to every trade you make.

Position Sizing to Manage Your Money

Before you manage the risks that come with investing, you must first properly manage the money you are investing in. There is not one without the other. Any investor has a limited amount of money to invest. Hence, it is important that he keeps a short leash in regards to where he is placing his money. Therefore, ensure that you do not lose sight of your budget so that you will not find yourself out of the ring.

The best money management strategy when trading is position sizing. This is a fairly simple concept, and it involves deciding on the maximum amount of capital you would want to invest before you enter into any given position. If you have taken up diversification, you must also ensure that you carefully calculate the amount you wish to invest in each venture, and take note of it in percentage, relative to your overall investment capital.

Position sizing facilitates diversification because it ensures that you are only using a small percentage of your trading capital in any single trade. Doing this helps to reduce your reliance on a single investment outcome and offsets losses made. You can be certain that even with years of experience, you still will be making trading mistakes, one time or the other. To ensure that the losses and the bad breaks don't turn you into a sad discouraged emotional trader, diversify your options trading investments. Venture into other investments also like stocks, ETFs, futures, real estate, and any other you fancy.

Diversification also ensures that in times of bad trades, you are not completely wiped out because you can use the returns from one trade to offset the losses of another trade, you will still have some money to buy your contracts when the bad trade turns around and becomes profitable.

Chapter 6: Credit Spread Strategy

When it comes to trading options, a trader has many options spread strategies from which he can choose. As we defined in the previous chapter, a spread refers to the purchase and sale of two or more options that have the same underlying asset in an attempt to take advantage of opportunities at both ends of a trade.

Spreads are classified in different ways, but the most basic of them is one that tries to figure out whether the strategy is a credit or debit spread. A credit spread, also called a net credit spread, is a spread strategy that has to do with the net receipts of premiums while a debit spread is one that involves net premium payments.

The Credit Spread

When creating a credit spread, the trader sells or writes a high-premium option and at the same time, buys an option with a low premium. The premium that the trader receives from writing the option is often more significant than the premium he pays to get the low-cost option. The difference is credited to the seller's trading account. When traders use the credit spread strategy, the maximum amount they receive, the one that is credited to their account when the position is entered, is called the net premium.

Looking at an example, let's say a trader takes up the credit spread strategy and writes a November call option whose strike price is $25 for $2, then simultaneously buys another November call option whose strike price is $30 for $1. Taking the usual multiplier, 100 shares per stock, then the net premium received will be $100, got from ($200 - $100). The trader will also enjoy more profits if the spread narrows.

When a trader is bearish, he is hopeful that the stock prices will go down, and he opts for long call options with a particular strike price before proceeding to sell a short all option within the same class, at a lower strike price. A bullish trader is often optimistic that the price of the underlying stock will go up and opts to buy call options at a particular strike price before proceeding to sell an equal number of call options at a higher strike price. The call options must be of the same class and have the same expiration.

The Debit Spread

We must mention a few details about the debit spread for your knowledge. A debit spread involves purchasing an option whose premium is high and selling one whose premium is low, simultaneously. The premium the trader pays for the long option of the spread is more than that of the written option.

The outcome of a debit spread is a debited premium, unlike the outcome of a credit spread. It is paid from the investor's account immediately; the position is opened. Because of this, traders use debit spreads to offset the costs that come with owning long options positions.

Let's see an example. Let's say a trader has purchased a March put option whose strike price for $15 is $3 and immediately purchases another March put option whose strike price of $10 is $1. The trader will have paid $2, or rather, $200, for the trade. Were the trade out-of-the-money, using the debit spread would have made for an excellent choice because it would have reduced the trader's maximum loss to $200 from $300.

Credit Spread Characteristics

Credit spreads have several unique characteristics with which you can differentiate them from other options trading strategies. They include:

- *Credit Spreads Are Useful Risk Management Tools*

We noted, in a previous chapter, that traders use spreads as tools to manage risk. In particular, credit spreads enable the traders to limit the risks to which they are exposed substantially by making them forego a limited profit potential. With the spread, traders can calculate the total amount of money they are risking even before they enter a particular position.

- *Credit Spreads Enhance Trading Versatility*

Traders are able to identify a combination of contracts to take either a bearish or bullish position by doing one of two things. First, they have the option of establishing a credit put spread, which is a bullish position whose short put has more premium. Second, traders can choose to create the credit call spread, a spread that takes a bearish position and has more premium on its short call.

Now, let's have an in-depth look at each of the strategies mentioned above:

The Credit Put Spread

Instead of outright selling your uncovered put options, traders take up the credit put spread. You see, selling an uncovered put option is a bullish move that is best taken when you expect the price of the underlying index or stock to go up. Traders sell the uncovered put option to generate income and then wait for the time limit to expire so that the option can be termed worthless. Although the risks involved when traders do this are somewhat limited, they can be substantial. The trader continues to lose money right until the value of the stock falls to zero.

Just like other spreads, the credit spread involves purchasing and selling options contracts simultaneously. Usually, the options are of the same class (whichever puts or calls) and riding on the similar underlying security. However, for vertical credit put spreads, the strike prices are different, although the expiration month is similar.

Also note that whenever you take up a bullish position using the credit put spread, the premium you receive for the option sold is higher than the premium you pay for the option. The result is that trading the option generates an income, although the amount will be less than what you would have got had you taken the uncovered call position.

Let's see an example. Suppose you buy 20 Company X March 65 puts each at $1 then sells 20 Company X March 70 puts each at $3, you will have a net credit of $2. In this case, the spread will be executed at $ 4,000 (($3 premium received - $1 premium paid) * (20 contracts each carrying 100 shares)).

If the market price of Company X shares closes above $67, you will make a profit. However, you will only maximize your profit (at least to get to $4,000) if the shares close at $70 and above. You will end up losing money if Company X's shares price goes below $67. For example, if the price fell to $65 or below, you stand to lose up to $2,000.

Kindly remember that taxes, fees, and commissions, though not included in this example, will affect the outcome of the trade, and ought to be factored in.

A trader would opt to take up this trade with the March 70 puts uncovered. Well, this could have resulted in a higher profit, $2,000, rather than the $1,500 profit received using the credit spread put. However, it is worth risking the $500 because the spread limits the risks involved significantly.

Had you sold the March 70 puts uncovered, essentially, your loss potential could have been a staggering $67,000 ($70,000 spent on buying the stock - $3,000 received on selling the puts), but that would only be if the company X stock value fell all the way to zero.

The credit spread scenario now appears better because under no circumstance can your maximum loss exceed $2,000.

Credit Call Spread

Usually, traders use credit call spreads instead of outright selling uncovered call options. Selling uncovered call options is a bearish trading strategy that traders can use when they expect the value of the security or the index underlying to go down. The goal of taking the credit call spread strategy is to generate income that could have been raised had the trader directly sold the uncovered call option and waited for the option to expire or become worthless.

Whenever you use the credit call spread to open a bearish position, the premium you pay for it will be lower than the premium you will receive once the option is sold. For this reason, the income you will generate using the credit call spread will be less than the income you would have raised had you taken an uncovered position.

The workings of the credit call spread are just like those of the credit put spread except that the loss and profit regions are on opposite sides of the breakeven point.

The Iron Condor

This is another type of credit spread for trading options, and it is the combination of the two strategies discussed above. The short iron credit option, for example, is a combination of the put credit spread and the call credit spread. For this reason, the iron condor position is neutral in regards to direction, and that it is most effective if the price is bound between the two spreads with time.

Here's a summary of the characteristics of the iron condor. It is directionally neutral, and the profits are only realized if the price maintains its position between the two spreads. The iron condor strategy gets better, or profits, with as time decays. The maximum profit a trader can derive from the iron condor is the credit received multiplied by the 100 shares of each option contract. The maximum loss is calculated by finding the difference between the width of the wider spread and the credit received, then multiplying the result by 100 ((Wider Spread Width – Credit Received) * 100).

To find the breakeven price using this strategy, find the upper limit by calculating the sum of the short call strike price and the credit received (Short Call Strike Price + Credit Received). The lower limit, you will get by finding the sum of the short put strike price less the credit received (Short Put Strike Price – Credit Received).

Advantages of Credit Spreads

- The margin requirement a trader needs is significantly lower than the one linked to uncovered options
- Spreads are useful tools for lowering risk substantially in the event the stock dramatically shifts against you
- The spreads limit the possible losses so that you do not lose more money than the margin requirement you have in your account when you enter your position. This is not the case with uncovered calls because, with them, you stand to lose even more than your initial marginal requirement.
- Spreads are adaptable because they have a wide range of expirations and strike prices, and most traders can find combinations of contracts that they can take up for their bullish or bearish positions, for both the credit and the debit spreads.
- Credit and debit spreads do not require as much monitoring as other trading strategies do. Once you have established your strategy, the spreads, you can

continue holding your position until expiration. However, they still may require some occasional review to certify that holding them up to when they expire is still beneficial. For example, if the underlying stock's price changes as fast or as far enough, the trader may still have the opportunity to close his spread position at a net profit, so long as the expiration date is yet.

Disadvantages of Credit Spreads

- The amount you send on the long option section of the spread reduces your profit potential.
- Since a spread requires the trader to choose two options, the cost of establishing both is high, even more than the commissions paid on a single uncovered position.

Chapter 7: Covered Calls

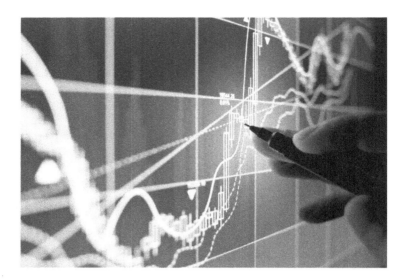

What Is A Covered Call?

A covered call is a financial market transaction that involves selling call options and simultaneously owning the equivalent amount of its underlying security. For example, if an investor already possesses a long position on an asset, then he sells call options of the underlying asset, raising higher profits than if he had only invested in one of them. The long position becomes the cover because the seller can deliver the shares in the event the call option buyer chooses to exercise it. Simultaneously buying a stock, then writing call options against that same stock is called a 'buy-write' transaction.

The covered call is a neutral strategy, and the investor takes it up when he expects only a small change, increase, or decrease, of the price of the underlying stock price within the life of the written call option. This approach is also suited for when an investor has a short-term neutral assessment of the asset he is holding, because of this, he clutches his asset for long but takes a short position by taking the option so that he can generate some income once he sells or writes the call option. He will receive a premium.

To put it in a simpler way, if an investor means to embrace the underlying stock for a long time but doesn't think such a substantial inclination in the price of the asset he is holding, in the near future, at least. The trader will seek to generate income by selling the option to receive a premium as he waits out to see how the market behaves.

As such, the covered call acts as a short-term hedge in regards to the long stock option and allows the investor to earn some income through the premium he gets. However, this is a trade-off because the investor forfeits the gains he would have received from the stock had the price moved above the option's strike price. If a buyer selects to exercise the option, after all, the trader who wrote the option is obliged to provide 100 shares for each contract he sold.

If an investor is very bullish or very bearish about the market, a covered call is not useful. Instead, if the investor is feeling very bullish, he would be better off not marks this option and should just hold the stock option. The reason is that option will cap profit the investor could have received if the stock price goes up, and this will decrease the total profit of the trade.

In the same way, if the investor is very bearish, he is better off just selling his stock because the premium he will receive for writing a call cannot do much to offset the loss he would suffer were the stock to plummet.

The maximum profit a trader can derive out of a covered call is equal to the strike price of the short call option in addition to the premium received for writing the call. The smaller the purchase price of the underlying stock. The greater the cost a trader can suffer in the acquisition price of the underlying stock, the lesser the premium collected.

If an investor wants to exercise an options contract (can be done at any time when dealing with US options, but on expiration if trading European options), trader sells his stock at the strike price, then if a buyer doesn't exercise the option, the trader (seller) gets to retain his stock.

As we have mentioned, a covered call, when sold, will typically be out-of-the-money, which permits profit to be made, both on the options contract and on the sale of the stock, but only if the stock price is maintained beneath the strike price of the option. On the other hand, a trader is certain that the stock price will decline, and still wants to keep his place, for the meantime, the trader may sell an in-the-money call option. The trader will collect an elevated premium for his call option, but the price of the stock will decrease lower the in-the-money strike price. Or else, the buyer of the option is entitled to collect the shares in contract traded so long as the share price is overhead the strike price of the option during expiration.

The Making of a Covered Call Trade

The first thing you must take note of is that when you purchase a stock, you should ensure that you purchase it in loads or bundles of 100-shares. When you vend the call contracts, sell it in 100-shares lots. For example, if you own 600 shares, you ought to sell them in 6 call contracts as opposed to the position you hold. You can likewise choose to sell fewer than 6 so that in the event the buyer exercises the call option, and you will not lose all your stock. If you sell 3 contracts and the buyer exercises the option, you will only lose 300 shares and still have 300 more shares.

When you write a call, you should wait for it to expire or to be exercised. If a contract expires, you get to make money off the premium the buyer pays. If the buyer does not exercise the option, you stand to keep the entire premium, and you can purchase back the option. However, there really is no good purpose to repurchase it.

The advantage of a covered call is that selling it helps offset the downside risks and adds up to the upside return. The risk, however, is that call sellers have to hold on to the underlying assets, lest they are holding naked calls.

Naked calls theoretically have a limitless loss probability if the underlying security goes up. So, if a seller wants to sell the contracts or shares, he must buy back option positions before they expire. Doing this increases the cost of transactions and lowers the net gain or the net losses from the trade activities.

Overall, covered calls are used to help gain income and to decrease the cost basis from shares or futures contracts.

Example of a Covered Call

Let's say an investor is in ownership of Company K shares and after analysis, the investor is optimistic about the long-term prospects of the company and its share price, but the investor feels that in short term, a stock is possible to trade flat, but maybe only within a few currency of its present value, say $20.

If the investor sells a call option on Company K shares whose strike price is $22, the trader will earn a premium from this sale but will cap the upper side on the stock to $22. In this case, one of three scenarios is likely to happen.

First, the shares might trade at a strike price below the $22, and if this happens, the option will be exercised useless, and the trader gets to retain the premium he received from the option. In this, the covered call approach will have helped the trader positively outperform the stock, and the trader will continue to own his stock and have an extra amount, the premium less the fees and commissions charged.

Secondly, Company K shares could fall, and the option will become worthless after expiry. The investor gets to keep the premium he received when he sold the options contract, and this helps to offset the decline he suffers when the stock price falls.

The third possible scenario is that Company K shares could rise above the $22 strike price. If the option is expired, the advantage of the stock will have been sealed at $22, but if the price goes higher, the sum of the strike price and the premium, it would have been better if the investor had held on to the stock alone. However, if the investor had intended to sell his shares at $22, he will have earned an extra amount, the premium he received.

Calculating the Rewards and Risks of a Covered Call

Covered calls are not without risks. The risk particularly comes from bearing a stock position whose price might decrease. The greatest cost a trader can suffer, however, is that which will be when the stock gets to zero. The maximum loss is calculated as follows:

Maximum Loss per Share = Premium Received + Stock Entry Price

E.g., Purchased a stock at $10 per share and on selling your call option, you receive a $0.02 option premium per share. The maximum loss you could suffer from your investment is $9.98 per share. The money you will have received as a premium reduces the maximum loss you would have suffered from owning your stock. However, selling your call option also limits the upside of your investment.

When using a covered call, your profit from the stock is limited to the strike price of the options contracts that you sold. The maximum profit you can reap from your trading is calculated as follows:

Maximum Profit = (Stock Entry Price − Strike Price) + Option Premium Awarded

Let's see an example. Suppose you bought a stock at $10 per share, and you sold it at $10.50 strike price, in addition to receiving a $0.05 premium. So long as the stock price remains at $10.50 at the time the option expires, you will maintain your stock position. However, if the stock price gets to $12, you will only receive whatever you gained up to $10.50. Your profit will remain $ ($10.50 - $10.0).

In the event you sell a call option, for you to maintain your shares, the value of the underlying stocks must fall beneath the call's strike price. If this happens, you will face a loss on your stock position, although the shares remain yours. However, the premium you will receive will help to offset your loss.

Generally, covered calls are considered a low-risk trading strategy, but it demands specific market conditions to work effectively. The best market condition in which to take it up is when the market is moving sideways, or when the market is moving up, slowly.

When a market is moving up or down quickly, the covered call trader will have problems. If the stock is moving up too quickly, the call option that was sold will be in-the-money, and the trader who wrote the option will have to give up his shares or to buy back the call options at a loss, as we have pointed out in the examples above. If the trader gives up his shares, but the stock goes on to increase in value, the trader will want to buy back his shares, but he will do so at a higher price.

On the other hand, if the stock is moving downward too quickly, the credit taken from the option will not be enough to cover the loss in value that the stock will experience over time.

You must understand, however, that no trading strategy and before you take up any of them, you must first take note of all potential risks.

Chapter 8: Strategies for Selling Covered Calls

Strategy for Picking and Selling a Covered Call

When you sell or write a covered call, you give away your right to buy a stock you own, at a particular price, and within a stated time. From the sale, you pocket the premium, and this amount acts as a cover for when the stock value increases above your strike price.

As you choose a stock from your portfolio, settle on one that has already performed well, but one that you wouldn't mind giving up if the call option was assigned. Avoid picking stocks that you feel very bullish about in the long-term, and that way, you will not be too discouraged when you have to give up stock and end up not receiving any net returns from your investment.

Once you have settled on a stock, it is time to pick the strike price with which you are comfortable selling the stock. Typically, your strike price should not be out-of-the-money, because the goal is to see the price of your stock rise further before you give it up. You must pick an expiration date also, the date by which your call option will be termed worthless. 30 to 45 days from now would be an excellent starting point but trust your judgment more. Select a date that would allow you to have a decent premium if you sold the option at your chosen strike price.

Do not struggle when deciding on an acceptable premium. Some traders fear that they are either selling themselves short or being greedy. One rule of thumb among investors is that an acceptable premium is one that is approximately 2% of the value of your stock. You must remember that options are sensitive to time decay. Therefore, the further you go in time, the more valuable your call option will be. However, going so far in time will make it harder to predict the market trends, and the investors will be apprehensive about taking up your options.

As you will realize in your consecutive trades, the time value is a good indicator of the viability of an option. If you notice that a premium is abnormally high, there must be an underlying sensitive reason behind it. Go on into the market and find out. Search for information in the news also, and find out what could be affective the stock price. Most times, when something looks too promising, it is.

The Three Possible Outcomes of Writing Your Covered Call Options

Your sale of covered call options could produce three different outcomes:

The Stock Price Could Go Down

If after the sale, at the time the option expires, the stock has gone down, your call option will expire worthless. The good news is that you get to keep the entire premium you received when you sold it. The bad news, however, is that the value of your stocks will be down. When the stock price is down, the risk lies in the stocks, not the options part. However, the profit you got when you kept the premium will help offset the value loss.

If the stock price falls before the options expire, do not worry. The fall will not lock you into your position. Although you will have lost in terms of the value of your stock, the value of the call option you sold will have fallen too. This is not bad at all because you now have the opportunity to buy back your option for less than you were paid for it. If you no longer fancy the option on your stock, just close your stock by buying back the low-priced option you sold and get rid of the stock.

The Stock Price Could Go Above the Strike Price

If the stock price goes above the strike price on the day of expiration, the call option will be assigned to you, and you will have to give up 100 shares from your stock. If the value of the stock now rises again after you have given up your shares, too bad for you because you will miss the gains from the price rise. You will have already committed yourself, on the basis of your conscious decision to part with the stock at the strike price. When this happens, dust yourself and move on, promising that you will make a better decision next time.

The Stock Price Remains the Same

In this scenario, the price of the stock could remain as is, or rise just a tiny bit. This is not a bad situation because the call option you sold will expire, and you get to keep all the money you received as premium. The underlying stock might also give you a few dollars as returns. Be happy that you get to keep your returns and your stock.

Here's a summary of the strategy for picking and selling call options as described above:

- Pick a low volatile stock
- Buy call options when in-the-money
- Sell your call option when out-of-the-money

Assignment to Sellers of Call Options

If a purchaser selects to exercise the option, your shares of stock might be collected from you, as we mentioned above. We use the word 'might' because it is not guaranteed that you would be asked to deliver your shares; it all depends on whether you are assigned.

The assignment process works through a random lottery system that the Options Clearing Corporation (OCC) runs. When an exercise notice gets to the OCC, the OCC assigns it to a member clearing firm, the brokerage. The brokerage then assigns exercise notices randomly to various short options in their books. You may or may not be assigned. It is possible that you will escape the assignment. However, if the call option is in-the-money, with more than a few cents, the likelihood of escaping this assignment is very low. In all this, whether the option is out-of-the-money or in-the-money, the call buyer retains the right to exercise or not to exercise his option at any time before the expiration, whether it makes sense or not.

Tips for Selling Covered Options

Think About the Volatility

It is best to take up the covered call strategy when dealing with stocks that exhibit medium implied volatility. For this, you will want to choose a stock that can move, but in a sort of predictable direction. If the implied volatility is low, don't expect to get much in terms of the premium. If the implied volatility is high, you will have the pleasure of getting higher premiums.

Unfortunately, when the volatility of the stock is high, the stock price could go either way, significantly. If the prices increase, your chances of having your stock called away increases, but if the stock price drops sharply, you stand to make a significant loss. Once the price rises too high and the buyer exercises his option so that your stock is called, you cease to be a stockholder, assuming you had traded in options for that represent all your shares.

As you see, neither of the extremes is good; it is best to work with medium volatility because it will make getting the premium for the call you write worthwhile. It also brings down the unpredictability that comes with high volatility. Therefore, be wise in choosing the premium amount that will make the strategy you have taken worthwhile.

If assigned, Do Not Panic

If what you dreaded comes to be and you are called to give up your stock, it may be surprising and upsetting to have to give up a long-held stock position. Luckily, in that situation, you have more choices than you know.

Suppose you have continually invested in Company G's shares, 100 shares each year, over the past 10 years, and each year, the price was higher than the price in the previous year. It then happens that you write one covered call that goes against your holdings.

If you are assigned, you get to choose the lot of shares you want to give up from the lots you have been accumulating over the years. It would serve you better to give up the most expensive of them, the ones you bought the latest, and to keep the less expensive ones you purchased earlier. By doing this, you will have avoided triggering a large tax bill that is charged on the capital gains of your stock. However, when this time comes, ensure that you seek the help and advice of your tax professional.

If you hold your stock close and are not willing to let any of it go, that is still okay. Instead, head on to the open market, buy stock on the margin and deliver it instead. When you do this, you will have better control of your long-term stock positions and of the tax consequences that will come up. However, keep in mind that if you choose to deliver the newly purchased shares, you will need to have anticipated your assignment so that you buy the new shares before the assignment notice.

It is also true that purchasing on-the-margin stock carries its own risks. Essentially, the margin is a line of credit for purchasing stock for which a trader makes a down payment and pays the broker an interest rate. Trading by this margin is risky because if suddenly the market moves against you, you will be required to add more money to the down payment you made, in what is called a margin call.

Think of Buy-Writes

Some people use covered calls to make some consistent income. They buy the stock then sell the call option in a bid to make some money, all in one transaction. This strategy is called the buy-write.

A buy-write offers many benefits. For one, it is convenient because the trader does not have to head back to the market after making the transaction. The strategy also reduces the trader's market risk by preventing legging. Legging into a trade is getting into a multi-leg options trading position by getting into more than one transaction. Since a lot can happen as the trader moves from one trade to the next, even when they are just a few minutes apart, legging can happen, and it complicates the situation while adding onto the risks to which a trader is exposed.

As such, allowing yourself to get into a multi-leg position can be quite tricky. Most of the time, traders have to pay two commissions and go through tough tax treatment, which depends on each individual's situation. However, before you take up a buy-write, consult a tax advisor.

Come Up with a Plan for When the Situation Turns Against You

If you are bullish about a stock, in the long-term, you would typically write a covered call. However, this call too, can go south, and you will need a plan to control the damage. Unlike what people believe, in this situation too, you will have a number of choices from which to choose.

Unlike what many investors assume, selling your call does not limit you to one position up until the call expires; you could always buy back your call and take away your obligation to give up your stock. We have mentioned this already.

The situation is different if you realize that the price of the stock has fallen since you sold the call. You might have the opportunity to purchase your call back, although this will be at a price lower than the initial sale price. Doing this will allow you to make a profit on your position.

If you want, you can also dump your long stock position, and this will prevent further losses, particularly if the stock continues to drop.

Make a Comparison Between If-Called and Static Returns

Covered calls are a smart way to earn an income out of your long stock positions beside the dividends that the company's payout to shareholders. The if-called and static returns enable you to figure out whether selling your call would be a smart move for your investment plan.

Static returns refer to the scenario where your covered call and the stock do not budge, giving you the right to keep the premium paid as part of your income. The if-called return assumes that you will be assigned and that you will have to give up your stock.

Before you take up the covered call strategy, ensure that you consider both scenarios described above. The numbers therein are important because they will ensure that you continually work towards reaching your investment goals. When you do this, you will be happy with your investment returns and whichever way the situation turns out.

Mistakes Investors Make When Selling Covered Calls

Factors like unpredictable markets often lead investors to make mistakes in their quest to build a profitable portfolio. Here are some of the mistake's traders make:

Selling Their Options Naked Rather Than Covered

In the case of covered calls, the premium marks the maximum profit a trader could receive. If the value of the underlying asset significantly increases, and the investor does not own stock of the underlying asset, the investor could suffer high losses. A call option without an underlying stock is called a naked call, and it is very risky because its upside potential is limited while its downside potential is unlimited.

As such, investors must purchase shares on the underlying stock before the option expires. Depending on the underlying stock's market cost, buying the stock could dig a large hole in your capital and end up in losses. Therefore, if an investor wants to take up the covered call strategy, he should mainly focus on selling covered calls on stocks he or she already owns or can afford to purchase.

Selling at Expiration or at the Wrong Strike Price

One of the critical trading mistakes options traders make is to sell the calls on the day they expire, or at the wrong strike price, having not fully understood the rewards and the risks that come with each move.

The strike price greatly influences your profitability. Therefore, when you choose your strike price, first consider your desired payoff, and the amount of risk you are willing to tolerate.

The strike price of an out-of-the-money call will be higher than the present value of the stock, while the strike price of an in-the-money option is less than the market value of the stock. When you sell an in-the-money option, you get to collect more premiums, and you increase your chances of being called away.

The expiration date is also very important. Lately, options expire after a week, a month, a quarter, and a year. A longer dater option gets a greater premium because its time of decay is far off. However, call sellers benefit more from shorter-term options.

Failing to Have A Loss-Management Plan

Most traders are not prepared for the reality that the trade could very well move against even their best predictions. Although no one goes into a trade hoping that it will go wrong, you should be ready for this possibility, and take measures to manage the risks that come with that.

Primarily, a plan to manage losses involves having an outlay of the money you are willing to risk in your trade even before you enter a position. You also should know how you will bail out of a trade if it goes the other way, so you may have a definite plan to help you cut your losses.

As you make your plans, it also makes sense to have a realistic picture of the profit you will be targeting. This, you will gauge by looking at the historical movement of your underlying asset, and you should leave enough room to wiggle should the market become unstable, and the stock prices start to fall or rise drastically.

Be careful that there isn't one loss-cutting strategy that will suit all trading scenarios; each trading style will need a new damage control strategy. Besides your style of trading, the size of your account and the position size will also matter.

The advantage is that when trading options, you get great flexibility. For instance, you may opt to buy back your option to relinquish your obligation to deliver your stock.

Only remember that when you notice that a trade is moving against you, the best strategy is not to add more money to it, stick to what you were doing and accept the loss. Keeping your emotions in check is critical in financial trading.

Failing to Factor in the Dividends

Dividends are an important consideration when it comes to evaluating option prices in your quest to choose the right stock. If you buy 100 shares, you will receive dividend payments if the company makes them out, so long as the ex-date comes before the day the contract expires. This is besides the premium you will receive when you sell your call option.

Undoubtedly, dividend payments will affect the call premium. The dividend payment causes the stock price to fall, and as such, the call premiums fall too, although the put premiums become higher. Therefore, if you are expecting dividend payments, it is better to exercise your call option early.

Expecting Returns Immediately

Options are not necessarily a short-term investment strategy; traders can also use them for long-haul investments. However, when they do this, they should not expect immediate returns. Options can be quite profitable, but they are by no means a 'get-rich-quick' strategy. Realizing the returns you want takes time. Realistically, traders should aim for 10 to 12 percent annual returns.

In addition, traders should have a plan that caters to the possibility of receiving lower returns than what they had expected. However, for the most part, they ought to have a consistent strategy, one that will produce consistent returns for the coming years.

Chapter 9: Advanced Strategies for Buying Calls

This chapter on advanced strategies for buying call options assumes that the trader already has a basic understanding of the fundamentals of options trading. As such, the strategies discussed herein are advanced. However, when it comes to financial trading, it all goes down to buying and selling call or put options at a particular strike price, with an expiration date attached. Therefore, the strategies are all about setting up different building blocks to guide you as you buy call options.

The advanced strategies are divided into four categories: bullish, bearish, neutral non-volatile, and volatile strategies. In this chapter, we will cover at least one from each categor

The Advanced Strategies

The Call Backspread

Call Backspread

The backspread is an options strategy that traders take up when they perceive that the market will be very volatile, though not 100% sure on the direction of the price. The stock's significant movement in the preferred direction earns them a big profit, but if it only moves a little, the trader earns a little profit. If the stock fails to move at all, the trader suffers a loss. Backspreads are also called reverse ratio spreads because they are designed to behave in the opposite direction of the ratio spreads.

When you are bullish on a particular stock, the backspread position you take is called the call ratio backspread, or simply, the call backspread. You enter this position when you buy a particular number of out-of-the-money call options (the kind whose strike price is more than stock value), and selling a smaller number of in-the-money call options (current stock price higher than the strike price). You have the liberty to choose the number of call options to sell or buy, but for now, let's only work with the case of a trader who buys 2 on-the-money call options then sells 1 in-the-money call option.

From buying the 2 call options and selling the 1 in-the-money call option, the trader has entered into what is called a credit position. This position allows the trader to earn a premium just by opening a call backspread. It happens when the trader buys the two call options, but since he is not willing to wait for the option to expire, he sells one option. However, even after the sale, the option owner still needs to buy back the option before it expires. These exchanges are what make taking this position quite risky.

If the stock price falls below the call option's strike price sold by the trader, then trader can allow the option to expire because, at this time, both strike prices are now meaningless. When this happens, the profit collected is the initial premium the trader made when he opened the position.

If the price of the stock rises high above the price of the strike price (in-the-money), but it is still below the strike price of the 2 calls, that the trader bought at the on-the-money price, the situation is no longer good. The 2 calls purchased on-the-money would become worthless, but the call the trader sold at the in-the-money strike price would still be worth something. It will need to be bought back before the contract expires.

Once the stock price has risen above the in-the-money strike price, the profits you can receive are limitless. The value of the in-the-money call rises, and even then, it must be bought back. The cost of purchasing the option, however, will be negated by the trader's possession of the 2 calls he bought at the in-the-money strike price. What's more, the two calls' value will be rising quickly, and the trader can sell them at a profit.

As a put, the backspread functions the same way, only in the opposite direction, in a bearish position.

Kindly remember that when it comes to the backspread position, you cannot allow your contracts to expire because the options you will have sold will need to be bought back to keep them from being exercised. As such, before you settle for the backspread, ensure that you have enough money to buy back the options in the event, the stock price fails to move.

The Synthetic Short Stock

The synthetic short stock is an options trading strategy that takes the form of buying or selling a stock, but with call or put options. It is taken up when the trader is bearish on a particular stock, and it involves buying a put option, then selling a call option with the same expiry date and at the same strike price.

In a typical situation where a trader only buys the basic put option, no profits would be realized until the stock price begins to fall under the strike price a bit. On the other hand, if the investor decides to invest in put options, he would have to pay the full premium, with the maximum possible loss being that premium.

In the case of the synthetic short stock, however, a trader can begin to enjoy some profits, once the stock price falls under the strike price, and the amount made after selling the corresponding call option makes up for the premium the trader spends buying the put option.

The advantages of the synthetic short stock strategy come with a big pay-off, unfortunately. The trader is now exposed to unlimited losses. For example, the more and more the value of the stock increases, the more the money the investor needs to buy back his call option before it expires. This makes taking this position very expensive, especially if the trader had made a faulty prediction concerning the likely direction of the stock.

The opposite of the synthetic short stock is the synthetic long stock. It behaves in a directly opposite behavior and is used by traders who feel bullish about their position to a stock.

That said, the synthetic stock strategies are thought to be excellent low-cost ways of dealing with basic options because their premiums are often offset once the trader sells the option under the opposite contract. However, this setup is seen to be almost similar to futures trading, and the thing with futures is that a wrong prediction could end up being too costly, just as we see with the synthetics.

The Long Butterfly Spread

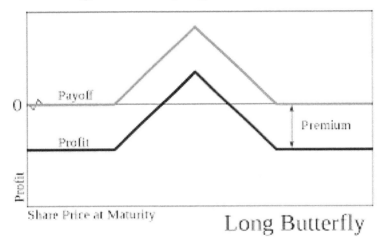

Long Butterfly

The Butterfly spread strategy is composed of 2 vertical spreads with a common strike price. The two spreads are the opening position where options are bought or sold, at 3 individual strike prices. These calls can be either calls or puts. The arrangement of the options makes the Butterfly spread a strategy that limits both profits and losses.

There is no difference between a Long Butterfly spread created with either calls or puts because, due to put-call parity, a Long Butterfly spread created out of put options behaves precisely like one created out of call options. Therefore, whichever you use, calls, or puts, you can create a Long Butterfly.

Take the example of a trader who purchases 1 in-the-money call option but sells 2 at-the-money call options, before purchasing another out-of-the-money call option. As you see, this strategy combines two opposing vertical spread options, which is how it got its name, the Butterfly Spread.

If you combine the profit profiles of the four call options mentioned above, you will realize that was the strike price to fall, the trader would only suffer limited losses. He would only lose the premium he paid trying to set up the entire butterfly arrangement. If the stock price were to climb very high, the losses would be limited too. However, if the stock price remained around the at-the-money strike price, the trader would receive some profit, but it too would be limited.

The Long Butterfly is thus a comfortably neutral strategy for when the market is experiencing low volatility because the trader will be making a correct bet, saying that the stock price would not be making much movement. Then he would receive the maximum profits, the limited ones we mentioned above.

Another advantage of the Butterfly strategy is that it is a low-risk approach. In case the stock climbs unexpectedly or crashes, the losses suffered will be limited.

The Short Butterfly strategy is just like the Long Butterfly strategy, but the roles are reversed. Its spreads are reversed, and it is taken up when the market is experiencing volatile shocks.

One keynote you ought to make regarding the Butterfly positions is that they involve three different strike prices, whether buying or selling options. To take it up, most brokers will ask you to pay 3 commissions to open the position, and you must pay 3 more commissions as you exit. Therefore, keep these commissions in mind when weighing the possibility of taking the Butterfly. See whether it will be a profitable strategy, given your circumstances. (Of course, the fees paid will vary from one broker to the next).

The Long Iron Condor

The Iron Condor strategies are an advanced strategy that, just like the Butterfly, uses two vertical spreads. The trader opens a call spread at a strike price higher than the current stock value of the underlying asset and opens a put spread too, at a strike price that is lower than the current stock value.

Of the Iron Condor strategies, the Long Iron Condor is the most popular, and it is also one of the most preferred advanced options buying strategies. Options trading instructors highly recommend it.

Using the Long Iron Condor strategy is similar to making a 'sure bet' although it leaves room for some modest profit and a few errors. The strategy is designed to be used on stocks that are not volatile, and those that maintain a neutral trading range. In addition, in case the stock price moves too much and the option reaches its expiration date, the losses resulting from this are very high, although limited.

The way to go about opening the Long Iron Condor position is by creating a bullish put spread and a bearish call spread. You create the call spread by selling 1 out-of-the-money call option and purchasing another call option whose out-of-the-money position is further along. You create the put by selling 1 out-of-the-money put option and then purchasing 1 put option that is further out-of-the-money. The spreads you will have created are credit spread, and once the position is opened, you can expect to reap some income from them.

Having this unique spreads together creates a target price range that falls between the inner out-of-the-money put strike price and the inner out-of-the-money call strike price. In the event the underlying stock price stays around this range by the time the expiry date comes, all four options will become worthless, and you get to keep the credit income you had at the start. If, however, the performance of the underlying stock becomes more volatile than you hoped and even gets out of the price range, you must close your in-the-money positions immediately. Unfortunately, doing this will reduce your profits and in the end, bring you a net loss.

In comparison to other neutral trading strategies, the Long Iron Condor stands out. If you compared it to similar strategies that deal with non-volatile stocks like the Strong Strangle and the Long Butterfly, you would note the differences. For example, if the price changes drastically, a trader using the Strong Strangle will suffer unlimited loss while a trader using the Long Iron Condor will only experience some limited maximum losses.

If the stock price remains at the same position without any movement, under the Long Butterfly, the trader will enjoy a maximum profit. However, the Long Iron Condor makes more room, with its more extensive price range, within which the trader can enjoy the maximum profit. This price range can be controlled too. If you make it narrower, you make room to receive more initial credit income, but this exposes you to the risk of having the stock price landing out of this range.

One significant disadvantage of the Long Iron Condor strategy is that it is made up of four individual options, and this could translate to higher commission costs, depending on the policies of your broker, in comparison to other strategies. What's more, the maximum loss potential that a trader stands to incur is often more than the initial credit income the trader placed when opening this position. These two factors are substantial, and they make the Long Iron Condor appear less profitable than people presume it to be. Therefore, before you take it up, it would serve you well to sit down and analyze all factors involved, weigh out the situation effectively, and see whether the strategy is appropriate for your trading goals. Do not forget to include the commission costs in your analysis.

The Short Iron Condor works in the opposite direction, and it is best suited for volatile stocks.

The Long Strangle

Strangle strategy options are strategies that thrive enable the trader's investments to thrive when the stock is volatile. The long strangle, for example, is the position a trader takes when anticipating high volatility in the underlying stock. The trader creates the Long Strangle position by purchasing 1 out-of-the-money call option, and 1 out-of-the-money put option. These options must share an expiration date.

Although the call option's stock price will be below the strike price, the call will not be worth anything, but once that stock price goes beyond the strike price, the call option will produce some profit. In the same way, the put option will be worthless so long as the stock price is above the option's strike price. However, once the strike price is higher than the stock price, the put option will begin to give some value.

When a trader brings together the two different profiles of the call and puts options, the result is the Long Strangle position. This strategy gives the trader the potential to make unlimited profits as the stock price climbs higher or falls lower. However, if the stock value stays within the confines of the two strike prices, both options will be rendered worthless, bringing a loss to the investment portfolio.

You ought to close your Long Strangle position before the expiry date of the options comes. You can do this by selling the option leg that has value and let the other option leg expire (expiry saves you some commission or fees charged when you transact). Therefore, if you realize that the stock has climbed, sell that call option and allow the put option to expire. If the stock price has fallen, expect the opposite. If the stock price remained stationary, you have to allow both options to expire, or if they have any time value left, you could sell them.

As we have mentioned, the Long Strangle is suitable for volatile stocks, those that you are sure will have dramatic climbs or falls in the future. This is a suitable strategy for when you are waiting for some big financial statement to be made, such as when a company is about to report on the performance of its stocks. If the performance has been good, the stock price will skyrocket, but if the performance was bad, the price would plummet. Other pieces of news that could cause volatility include the resolution of a lawsuit, the release of some research results, and a change of monetary or fiscal policy.

When it comes to strategy and execution, the Short Strangle is the Long Strangle is the exact opposite. The Short Strangle is best suited for stocks whose prices remain still and do not fluctuate. This makes it one of the neutral strategies that traders take up to reap profits out of very little if any, market activity.

The Call Ratio Spread

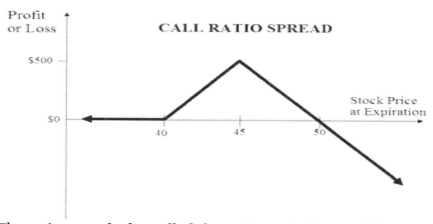

The ratio spread, also called the ratio vertical spread, is a strategy that is a variation of the vertical spread. It is a neutral spread that is built to be used in a neutral, non-volatile situation. With the word 'ratio' in its name, the strategy uses a 1-for-1 spread ration in which one option purchased is paired with another option sold. Traders set up this ratio spread by putting the options sold against options bought in a ratio. The ratio can have any numbers, but for the sake of understanding, let's work with a 2:1 ratio that represents 2 sold options put against 1 option bought.

As you can already tell, the Call Ratio Spread is a ratio spread created using call options. The trader buys 1 in-the-money call option and sells 2 at-the-money call options. The trader would be selling more options than he is buying, which essentially means that the seller is giving naked or uncovered options. A naked-options situation always brings with it many risks, and some brokers do not like to do business with traders dealing with uncovered options unless you demonstrate to them that you have adequate experience trading options.

The Call Ratio Spread strategy has some advantages, though. One of them is that the initial cost of opening this position is almost negligible, and the trader might even find himself earning some money. The second advantage is that the cost of the in-the-money call option is more than that of an at-the-money call option. Therefore, the cash you spend buying the 1 in-the-money call option will be offset by the premium you get when you sell 2 at-the-money calls.

Now that this strategy allows you to earn some income as you set things up, it has also earned the name Ratio Credit Spread.

At the time of expiry, in the event the value of the underlying stock has fallen below the in-the-money strike price, the three options become worthless, and the trader does not make any additional losses or profits. If the stock value has gone up high than the in-the-money strike price, the seller can sell the in-the-money call option he bought previously.

Your income increases as the stock value gets closer to the strike price of the call option at-the-money. If the stock value goes higher than the strike price of the call option at-the-money, you now will need to purchase back the 2 at-the-money call options that you had sold previously. This will cause you to suffer larger and larger losses as you try to buy back your two options, with only the premium from the 1 in-the-money option remaining to offset your losses.

A trader who has taken up the Ratio Credit Spread strategy is only able to realize a maximum profit when the stock value ends up at the position next to the strike price of the at-the-money call options. From there, the trader will sell the call option in-the-money for the maximum amount possible, while allowing the at-the-money calls to expire and become worthless. However, as the stock price rises, the losses increase too.

As such, the Call Ratio Spread strategy is suitable for neutral situations, where the stocks are non-volatile. If the stock value goes down, the trader experiences limited to no losses, but if the stock value has risen up, the trader suffers limited losses.

The Call Ratio Spread is similar to its counterpart, the Put Ratio Spread, only that the latter is constructed using put options rather than with call options. The Ratio Spread is also identical to the Butterfly and the Iron Condor that are also used when handling non-volatile stocks. The only difference is that the Ratio Spread allows for the recurrence of unlimited losses if the underlying stock is too volatile. However, the fact that the Ratio Spread only includes a few options limits the extents of the risks. In addition, there are fewer commissions because there are fewer positions to open and close.

Chapter 10: Technical Indicators

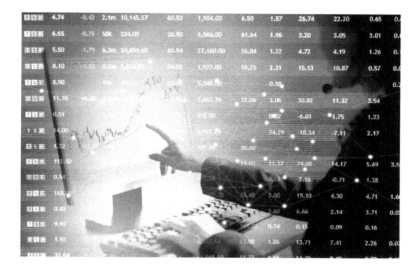

Depending on the type of security and the trading style a trader is handling, there many technical indicators in the market. However, this chapter discusses the most popular and most useful technical indicators for an options trader.

Generally, technical indicators are taken up in the short-term, and the choice of an indicator depends on the direction the price takes the range by which it moves, and the duration the price goes in a particular direction.

Another factor to remember is that the holding period of your options matters because options are subject to time decay. Options have time limits by which the positions must be executed, unlike other investments like stocks in which a trader can hold a position indefinitely. Since timing is critical, you will see that momentum indicators, the kind that is meant to show the options that are oversold or overbought, are popular among traders.

Technical Indicators Used in Options Trading

Bollinger Bands

Bollinger Bands is an indicator that shows the volatility of options. It is taken up to indicate the high and the low volatility levels on a price chart. This indicator cannot be used on its own; traders use it to complement oscillator-type, trend-following indicators, and this makes their trading activities more effective. For example, when there is little or no market activity, it is often difficult to predict the direction the price will take in the future, but with Bollinger Bands, traders can foretell the prevalent market phase.

Bollinger Bands are made up of a moving average and two lines that are extrapolated from the two standard deviations on whichever side of the central moving average. The two lines you extrapolate make up the band. If the band is narrow, the market is quiet, and if the band is wide, the market is loud. Therefore, the Bollinger Band can be used both in a trending and a ranging market.

When the market is trending, use the Bollinger Squeeze to mark your trade entry so that you can catch breakouts early enough. The Bollinger Squeeze is when the bands are close together, it appears like they are squeezing. The squeeze is a sign that a breakout is close by, although it will not tell you anything about the direction the price is likely to go.

The price movement is likely to continue in its downward trend if you see the candles breakout below the bottom band. The candles breaking out above the top band indicate an uptrend.

When the market is ranging, let the Bollinger Bounce guide you. During the bounce, the price bounces from one side of the band to the next but continuously goes back to the stirring average, in a sort of regression to the mean. Naturally, the value will get back to the average with time.

In a situation where the market is ranging, the bands become resistance and support levels, and if the value reaches the top of the band, the trader needs to place a stop-loss slightly above the band to keep it from breaking out. The price ought to revert to the average or the bottom band, and there, the trader can take profits.

In summary, the Bollinger Bounce in a ranging market indicates that the price will go back to the mean, and in a trending market, the Bollinger Squeeze indicates that the price is about to break out, although it does not indicate the direction the price is likely to take.

Relative Strength Index (RSI)

The RSI is an indication of the momentum, giving buy or sell signals to the trader. This indicator works under very simple logic: when the underlying asset is oversold, its price will be lower than what would be considered normal. An oversold asset is most likely to appreciate in the nearby future. If the underlying asset is overbought, the price will be higher than it usually should be, and it is expected to deflate in the near future. Therefore, with the RSI, you will differentiate the oversold and the overbought positions.

The setup of the RSI is relatively simple also. Usually, the indicator is plotted on a different scale, and a single line, with a scale ranging from 0 to 100, is used to identify the oversold and the overbought market conditions. If the readings are beyond 70, that is an oversold market, and if the evaluations are below 30, know that the market is oversold.

The idea behind using the RSI is to correctly identify the tops and bottoms so that the trader moves into the market just when a trend is reversing. The early entry allows the trader to take advantage of the entire market move before another cycle begins.

To confirm trend formations, you could also use the RSI. If the RSI is above the level of 50-marks, the market will be in an uptrend, and if the line is below the level of 50-marks, the market will be on a downtrend. A risk-averse trader should probably wait for trend confirmation before entering a position. However, he may not make as much as he would, had he moved in before the trend began.

You see, trading always involves a trade-off of two things. You stand to make lots of profit if you get into a trend early, but unfortunately, you stand to make mistakes much more often, and you could end up losing your trading capital. On the other hand, you might be able to wait to confirm the trend but only make conservative profits. However, when you wait, you increase your chances of being right most times. It all depends on your disposition to risk.

Ichimoku Kinko Hyo

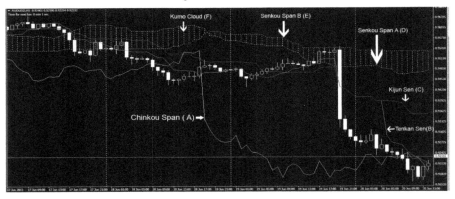

The Ichimoku Kinko Hyo, also called the Ichimoku Cloud, is a momentum indicator that shows future price momentum and indicates areas that are likely to provide support or resistance in the future. By its name and description, in addition to the number of lines that are plotted, it may appear like a complex indicator, but it really isn't.

Here's what each of the lines on the graph means:

- The green line called the lagging line or the Chikou Span is the closing price of the day plotted 26 periods behind.

- The red line called the turning line, or the Tenkan-Sen is one that is derived by getting the average of the highest highs and the lowest lows for the last 9 periods.

- The blue line, called the Kijun-Sen, the baseline, or the standard line, is a line determined by calculating the average of the lowest low and the highest high for the last 26 periods.

- There also is a red or green band called the Senkou Span. Its first line is computed by finding the median if the Kijun-Sen and the Tenkan-Sen, plotted 26 periods ahead. Its second line is calculated by averaging the lowest low and the highest high over the last 52 periods, but it is plotted 26 periods ahead.

The lines described above, it would seem, are difficult to translate when trading. However, that is not the case. The Senkou Span takes the role of offering dynamic resistance and support because if the prices go above the Senkou span, the top of the line will act as the first support point while the bottommost of the line will be the second support point. If the values fall under the Senkou span, its bottom line becomes the first resistance point while the top line becomes the second resistance point.

Traders use the Kijun-Sen to confirm trends. If the price breaks out at a point above the Kijun-Sen, the price will likely even go further up. In the same way, if the price drops below the line, it will unmistakably go lower.

The Tenkan-Sen is another line used to confirm trends. You will know that the market is trending when you see the line moving up and down. If it changes sideways, understand that the market is fluctuating. Take note that this red line indicates the price trend.

The Chikou Span, the colored-green one, is plotted 26 periods following the present period. It indicates trends of all sorts. Whenever this line crosses the price headed to the top from the bottom, know that the price will likely follow and go up. If the line crosses the price from up headed downwards, the price is likely to follow that direction too and will go from up to down.

As you see, this indicator shows quite a lot of information about a trade; you only have to recall what each line means. If you mixed up the colors, you could make a mistake and end up losing your investment, bringing down your portfolio.

Simple Moving Average (SMA)

This indicator is great for assessing the trend prevailing. There will be times when the direction a trend is taking will not be so obvious. The span a trend takes to complete also varies (there are medium-term and long-term trends). In cases like this, the SMA helps the trader to understand the market trends.

Traders can also combine the SMA with other indicators to get some clarity on some buy and sell signals.

The Moving Average Convergence Divergence (MACD)

This is a trend indicator, and like its counterpart, the Ichimoku Cloud, it has many parts to take note of. First, note that it is comprised of a slow line, a fast line, and a histogram. Understanding how they work can be confusing, so be attentive.

The inputs you need for this indicator are a slower moving average (MA-slow), a faster-moving average (MA-fast), a number that additionally defines the period of the third moving average, the MA-period.

The fast line of the MACD is a moving of the moving average of the difference among the fast-moving average and the slower-moving average (MA-fast – MA-slow). On the other hand, the MACD slow line is a moving average of the MACD fast line. The number of periods for which it moves is determined by the MA-period.

The final component, the histogram, is designed to indicate the difference between the fast and the slow lines of the MACD.

Let's look at an example to help you understand what I mean. Suppose to have a "12, 26, 9" MACD, which is a typical default setting, you will interpret it as follows: the first line will be the moving average among the 12-period and the 26-period moving averages. The slow line is the one in the 9-period moving average of the fast line. The histogram is the difference between the MACD lines.

Now that you understand that, let's now head on to explaining what the convergence and divergence are about. You will see that during plotting, the histogram and the moving averages are placed on separate charts and that the lines keep crossing over. As the difference between them continues to get smaller, the lines continue to get closer to each other. That is what we call convergence. If the difference is getting bigger and the lines are drawing further apart, they are diverging. Simple, right? When using the MACD indicator, take note of the distances and the tendencies of these lines.

Whenever a new trend is coming up in the market, the MACD lines converge, and when the trend reverses, they cross over and then begin to diverge. At the crossover point, the histogram disappears due to the dissimilarity among the fast and the slow lines will be zero.

One fact to have at the back of your mind is that the MACD indicator is made up of moving averages or other moving averages. As such, it tends to lag overdue the value a lot, making it a not-so-effective indicator for detecting trends early on. However, it is one of the best indicators for confirming trends.

Stochastic Indicator

This is the momentum indicator. It is aiding in helping determine the point at which a trend could end. The trader could use the end of a trend to pick an entry point so that he can get into the next trend at the very beginning. Just like the RSI indicator, it is used when the underlying stock or other asset has been oversold and overbought.

The stochastic indicator is made up of two lines, plotted on different charts. Once the lines are plotted above 80, it means that the market is oversold, there is possible to a downward trend. If the stochastic lines are plotted below 20, it means that the market is overbought, that there's about to be an uptrend.

As you try to get into trades early, be on the lookout because there are many fakeouts in the market. To prevent too much loss in the case, the market does not go in the predicted direction, install stop-losses.

Therefore, let the stochastic indicator only give you a clue of where the market is most likely to go; don't base the entire investment on it. Take on various risk management practices to keep your portfolio safe.

Money Flow Index (MFI)

Is the momentum indicator. It works by bringing together data regarding the price and volume of the underlying asset. Some investors call it the weighted-volume RSI.

The MFI measures how money is flowing in and out of an asset over a specified period, usually 14 days. The outcome it gives indicates the trading pressure in regards to the asset being traded. A reading beyond 80, just as with other indicators, is a sign that the asset is oversold whereas an analysis below 20 means that the security is overbought.

Since the MFI indicator deals with volume data, best suitable for stock-based options as against to index-based options, particularly the long-duration kind. Whenever the MFI moves in the direction reverse to that of the stock value, know that a trend change is impending.

Open Interest (OI)

The Open Interest is an indicator of the unsettled or open contracts in options trading. It does not indicate any specific information about where a trend is heading, but it does offer information about the strong point of the trend you are observing.

An increasing open interest is a sign that there is a new capital inflow, and this shows that the existing trend is sustainable. A declining open interest shows that the trend is weakening.

Options traders who seek to benefit from short-term trends and movements should take in the following scenarios:

- If the price is rising and the open interest is rising, the market or the security is strong.
- If the price is rising, but the open interest is falling, the market or the security is weakening
- If the price is falling, but the open interest is rising, the market or security is weakening
- If the price is falling and the open interest is falling, the market or security is strengthening.

Intraday Momentum Index (IMI)

This is an excellent indicator that high-frequency options traders use to wager on the price moves of the day. The indicator brings together the RSI and intraday candlesticks, creating a suitable range, like that of the RSI, for intraday trading; hence, it can accurately indicate what has been oversold and what has been overbought.

Using the IMI, an options trader will be able to take note of possible chances that could help him to initiate a bullish trade in a market that is trending upwards at an intraday correction. The trader is also able to initiate a bearish trade in a market whose trend is headed downwards at an intraday price bump.

Traders compute the IMI by finding the sum of up days and dividing it by the sum of up days plus the sum of down days (Sum of up / (Sum of up days + Sum of down days). The result is then multiplied by 100. The trader has the liberty to choose the number of days from which to look, but the most commonly used number is 14 days.

Just as when you use the RSI if the result goes beyond 70, the stock or other asset is considered overbought, if the digit is less than 30, the stock is oversold.

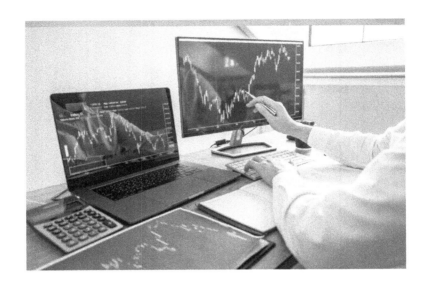

Chapter 11: Some Case Studies on Options Trading

Case studies allow traders to have a clearer understanding of the options strategies and the outcomes to expect so that they can avoid the errors or take up the same steps that the traders in the case study used. Here are a few case studies to provide you with a practical approach to options trading:

Case Study #1

This is a study of a metal works company that is concerned about the rising prices of one of its critical inputs, steel. The current market price of the steel is $400 per ton, but the manufacturer is afraid that the price could rise and get to more than $500 per ton.

To remedy the situation, the investor decided to buy a call option at $500 per ton. The call option strike price is equivalent to the forecast threshold that the investor is worried about.

Once he purchases the call option, the investor pays a premium to the writer of the option so that if the market price does not go above the $500 per ton, the option will expire out-of-the-money. If this happens, the investor will not experience too much loss when the option expires because he will still be able to buy his steel below the $500 threshold. The only loss he will incur is the premium he paid to the writer of the option.

In the event the market price exceeds $500 per ton, the option will expire in-the-money, and the option holder will make a profit from it. For example, if the price goes as high as $550 per pound of steel, the investor will exercise his option and will purchase a ton of steel at $500, from the option writer. He makes a profit of his savings, less the premium he paid. In case the premium was $10, the profit will be $40. This is found by ($550 -$500) - $10. Hence, the investor will be protected against the steel price going above $500 per ton.

In this example, the call option serves as a hedge against the changes in the steel market. The call option's interactions remain the same despite the changes in the market. In the investor's case above, it is clear that the out-of-money option puts a limit to the downside to the premium paid on the option, $10. All market prices will experience a downside up to, and including, premium and the strike price. However, once the market price exceeds the sum of the premium and the strike price, the investor will enjoy a profit. Luckily, the profit or the upside is unlimited.

In this example, the option purchased will have been a successful hedge against an anticipated rise in the price of steel. The call option limits the downside to the price of the premium but maintains an open door to the profits through the unlimited upside.

Case Study #2

Here's a case study borrowed from the Terry Tips blog.

Costco had begun trading in 2015 at $141.87, and at that time, Terry Tips' portfolio, one that uses COST as the underlying asset, was valued at $6223. Had this money been devoted, it would have produced 43.8 shares or roughly 44 shares of the stock.

Early in that year, the price rose steadily but fell from a $153 high to a $135 low within the first week of September. By the end of that month, the stock was now trading at $3 higher than it had traded when the year began.

If you were to compare the value of the 44 COST shares and the current value of the Terry Tips portfolio had it traded options in that same period, the situation could have been as follows:

When the stock fell a little in January, the value of the portfolio could the value of the portfolio followed and fell by an even more considerable amount. However, as the value of the stock recovered, the portfolio outdid it again and outperformed on the upside also.

Over the nine months between January and September, investing in stocks could only have produced returns of $1.20 per share, which means that for the 44 shares, the investor would have received $52.80. The stock obtained $2.70 per share above the 9-months that the 44 shares would have increased their worth by $118.80 compared to their value at the beginning of the year. This increase translates to a $171.60 net gain, adding the $52.80 dividends paid out. The net gain represents a 1.2% gain in the value of the stocks in 9 months.

Above the equal period, the definite COST options portfolio had risen in value to $12,900 from $6,223, a net gain of $6,667, which represents a 107% increased value.

Looking at the trading strategy used, Terry Tips owned seven calls, all of which expired in April, and two others that would extend until July. They had also sold 8 calls that expired on January 15, of which 3 had a strike price just under the stock value, while the remaining 5 were somewhat out-of-the-money. The company also have 1 long uncovered call against, that they could have sold a short-term call; nevertheless, they thought it better to maintain a higher net delta. With that portfolio, and with different options positions, Terry Tips owned about 218 shares of stock, which does not compare to directly owning 44 shares.

By the end of the nine months, on September 25, all the long calls had been pushed to January to April of the next year, 2016, and the company still held a few put positions. In May, when the COST shares were selling at $144, the company had sold a bullish credit put spread. (It had bought October-15 135 puts but sold October-15 140 puts). Terry Tips figured that if the price were above $140 at the time when the puts expire on October 16, the puts would have been rendered worthless, and the company would have 51% on the quantity it had risked when it sold its spread in May.

Halfway through 2015, Terry Tips decided to switch tactics and change how it traded its portfolio. By now, they were now short some weekly options for numerous dissimilar series. Therefore, individual week, when some calls would expire, Terry Tips would repurchase them on a Friday, typically, and then sell the new ones, which would have a four-week time limit.

The company was careful to pick out only the strikes that would balance out its risk profile by carefully weighing its portfolio. This also gave them the opportunity to tweak its investment profile each week, and to make small changes, rather than waiting to make some grand alterations at the end of the month when the options expired. The company credits its superior performance while managing the profile to its style of trading, saying that it would not have been possible had the company not taken up the weekly options.

At the end of every week, on Friday, the company would create a risk-profile graph so that it would act as the guide in helping them choose the strike prices to use when it buys back the expiring weekly options to change them with new short calls whose expiry was further out.

The value gained from trading options does not compare to one gained trading stocks. With a starting value of $6,223, the company realized a 107% portfolio gain, even higher than the income the investors started with. A person who chose to safely invest in stocks by buying COST shares would only have gained $172, 1.2% of his portfolio. The options portfolio outperformed the gains from the stocks so many times over.

The Terry Tips example clearly illustrates, beyond all doubt, that when options strategies are correctly executed, they can out-perform the direct shares purchase. Indeed, it is much easier to buy stock, and it involves less risk, but although trading options is demanding and involves much more risks, it is sure worth investing it because, with attention and time, it performs many times better than shares.

Case Study #3

Let's see how this second case compares to the COST investment example (both made by Terry Tips).

Terry Tips decided to invest in Starbucks because its stock had been doing so well, particularly in the first 9 months of the year 2015. At the beginning of the year, the stock started at $81.44 then rose steadily to $98 before the two for one stock split in early April. By the end of the ninth month, September, the stock was trading at $57.99, which got to $115.98 as the pre-split price. Starbucks paid three $.16 dividend then paid another $0.48 to the total adding up to a total of $35.02, which translates to a 43% gain in the 9 months.

Terry Tips started the year by investing $6032 and invested in Starbucks options. Had they purchased the shares themselves, at $81.44 per share, the company would only have afforded to purchase 74 shares. In only 9 months, the portfolio would have procured $11,768 or 195% in value.

Unfortunately, Terry Tips' portfolio did not gain much because they had also invested an equal amount with the Keurig Green Mountain (GMCR), another coffer company. Over the same period, the GMCR portfolio lost $8905 because the stock value fell from $130 to $50s. However, the company did drop GMCR stock in August, and the company added FB to its portfolio, now dealing with FB and Starbucks stock, but in separate portfolios.

The portfolio established at the beginning of the year reached $10,604, and by the end of the nine months, it had gone up to $12,708. The value increase was $2182, which is 20.5%. This was a small, though not bad, value gain over the 9 months, considering that the market had fallen by 6.7%. However, this does not compare to the 195% the company would have enjoyed had it stuck to the Starbucks investment alone.

The three case studies described above are enough proof that if options strategies are correctly executed, they can outright outperform the direct bought of shares, by numerous times over. Absolutely, it's safe, uncomplicated, and less demanding to choose to invest in the stock, but if you are willing to put in the work, by giving your portfolio the time, the attention, and the research it demands. You will end up earning profits of 195% instead of a mere 43%, or 107%, rather than 1.2% with the same investment, using the same stock.

If you wish to take up options trading but don't have the time or the knowledge you would require to run a self-directed options trading account, opt for the auto-trade services that most brokers offer. The trades will be made automatically for you, and although you might have to pay some commission, it doesn't compare to getting the 1.2% returns you would get investing in stocks under the buy-and-hold setup.

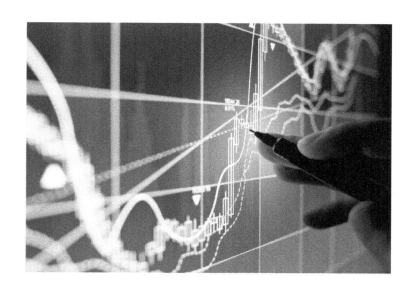

Chapter 12: Strategies to Apply Easily to Options Trading

There are many options trading strategies available, and each comes with the promise of increasing returns, protecting what you got by minimizing risks, or both. With only a clear understanding of how the strategies work, potential traders can learn how to take advantage of the opportunities that come up.

Below is a discussion of some of the strategies investors can take up:

Options Trading Strategies

The Long Call

The long call is the choice options trading strategy is popular among aggressive investors who feel very bullish about an index or a stock. When a trader is feeling bullish, he expects that the stock price will go beyond the strike price at the time of expiration.

The advantage of taking up this strategy is that the upside, the profits side, is uncapped so that when the stock price goes up, the trader can make profits as far as the stock price can go. Theoretically, the upside is infinite, and if the stock continually rises before expiration, the call continues to climb also. This one advantage makes long calls one of the most popular to bet on the stock price.

Let's look at a sample. If a particular underlying stock, Y, is exchange at $15 per share and its call, at the strike price of $15 that expires in four months is trading at $2, your contract (typically of 100 shares) will cost you $200. If the shares go up by $2, the share price will be $17. As such, for every change in value above $15, the options contract will increase in value by $200. If the value drops under the $15 strike price, the options contract will be worthless.

The downside of the long call is the complete loss of your investment. If the stock closes under the strike price, the call will become useless, and the trader will lose the premium that he paid when purchasing the option.

Seeing that the risk can be quite significant, opt to take up the long call strategy only when you expect that the price of the stock will rise significantly within the stipulated time limit. If the rise only rises a little bit above the strike price, the option will still be in-the-money, but it is less likely to return the premiums you have paid. You will only experience loss.

The Long Put Strategy

The long put strategy is quite different from the long call. The first thing you need to note about their differences is that buying a call is the opposite of buying a put. When you are bearish about a stock, you buy the put option, but when you are bullish, you purchase the call option. The put option allows the buyer the right to sell stock to the put seller at a predetermined price, and this limits his risks. As such, the long put is a bearish strategy, and traders invest in it to take advantage of the falling market.

Suppose stock Y is trading at $10 per share, and its accompanying options have a $10 strike price, is retailing at $1, and expiring in four months. For every dollar decline in price, the $10 put will increase in value. Above $11, the put will expire, become worthless, and the trader will have lost his $100 premium.

Your long put's upside is similar to that of holding a long call: the upside is not capped, and the value of the option premium can increase many times over. However, the upside is not theoretically unlimited because the stock can never go below zero. As you see, the long put presents an exciting way to take on the decline of the stock, and they tend to be safer than shorting a stock.

The advantage of the long put is that its downside is capped at the $100 premium you paid, and this only happens when the stock closes at a price above the strike price. If this happens, your put option immediately expires, and you remain with nothing.

Therefore, use the long put strategy when you expect that the value of the stock will drop to heights significantly lesser than the strike price before the time limit is up. Be careful, though, because if your prediction is not as accurate and the price falls just slightly lower than the strike price, although it will be in-the-money, you could end up losing your premium altogether.

The Short Call

In a case where a trader anticipates that the stock price will rise in the future, the trader opts for the long call strategy. However, when the trader predicts that the value of the underlying stock will fall, the trader will take up the short call strategy. The short call strategy is also called the Short Naked Call strategy because the investor does not hold any underlying stock when he is shorting.

The investor begins to sell call options because he or she is bearish about a particular index or stock, and he expects the prices to fall later. The short call is one position that offers minimal chances of making profits, and the situation could quickly turn around so that the investor begins to suffer losses, in the event the underlying price begins to increase instead of decreasing.

Although the short call strategy is easily implemented, it can get quite risky, mainly because it exposes the seller of the call option to unlimited risks.

The Short Put Strategy

Just as you would expect, the short put strategy is the exact opposite of the long put strategy. However, in this case, the trader sells his put because he anticipates that the stock price will rise before the set time limit expires. In exchange for the put option, the trader gets a cash premium, and this is the best possible outcome a short put can have. If the stock closes at a price lower than the strike price, the options trader must now buy it at the strike price.

An example might make it easier to see how the short put strategy is used. Let's say a specific stock, stock K has its shares selling at $10 each, its options are trading at $1, and that the option expires in the next four months. Taking into account the fact that an options contract typically holds 100 shares, the contract will attract a premium of $100.

In the event the option breaks even at $9, under the short put strategy, the short put will cost the trader $100 per dollar decline in value. If the value goes above the strike price, say, $11, the seller will earn a clean $100 premium.

The upside of the short put does not go above the premium the seller received, in this case, the $100. As such, the maximum returns the seller can enjoy under the short put is the amount that the buyer presents upfront.

The downside, on the other hand, is the total value of the underlying stock, a lesser amount of the premium the seller has collected. However, this would only happen if the value of the stock got to zero. In the example above, the trader would be asked to buy stock worth $1000 ($10 * 100 shares). However, the premium the trader would receive would offset the $100 premium the seller received, causing the total loss to be $900 ($1000 - $100).

The short put strategy is best taken up when the seller expects the stock to rise in value, high beyond the strike price, by the time it expires. The stock only needs to be above or just around the strike price for the option to lose its value. If that happened, the seller would keep the entire premium received. That said, your broker will still be concerned to see whether your account holds enough equity to buy the stock if the opportunity to do so comes up. If the put closes while still in-the-money, the money will be left in your trading account.

The Long Straddle Strategy

The long straddle strategy is also called the 'straddle' or the 'buy straddle' strategy. It is one of the neutral options trading strategies, and it involves simultaneously buying a call and put option of the same underlying stock. Since the positions are long in for both the put and the call, the strike price and the expiration date of the options are the same. This strategy can achieve large profits, whichever direction the price shifts to because the trader has covered both sides. However, just like the other positions, the move the price makes must be strong, for the trader to enjoy any significant progress.

The investor buys the long straddle when he thinks that the underlying stock or index will have some significant volatility in the near future. Any risk that the investor experiences is limited to the initial premium paid.

The Short Straddle Strategy

The short straddle strategy is the exact opposite of the long straddle strategy. An investor takes up the short straddle strategy when he or she perceives that there will not be much movement in the market in the coming days. For this reason, the investor sells a put and a call option of the same stock or index. The pair, the put, and call often share the strike price and the maturity date, just like those of the long straddle.

The result is that selling the two options generates a net income for the seller. If the underlying stock or index does not make much movement in either direction, the investor keeps the premium, and neither of the two options is exercised.

Unfortunately, this strategy exposes the investor to unlimited risk while the reward is limited to the premium the investor will receive for the options sold. If the stock happens to move significantly, either upwards or downwards, the investor stands to lose a significant amount. Since this is a risky strategy, investors should exercise caution before adopting it by studying the market hard to ensure that their predictions are right. The strategy should only be adopted once the trader is sure that the expected volatility in the market will be limited.

The Married Put Strategy

The married put strategy is similar to the long put strategy, only that it has a twist. For this one, the trader already owns stock but goes ahead to buy a put of that same underlying stock. This strategy is done to hedge the existing stock in a case where the trader expects that the stock price will go up but still wants to have some form of insurance, just in case the stock falls. If the stock price were to fall, the long put would offset the loss.

Theoretically, the married put's upside is uncapped, for as long as the stock continues to rise. Taking this strategy puts the trader at a hedge position, having paid the premium as insurance to allow the stock to rise, while still limiting how far it goes to the downside.
 The married put's downside, therefore, is the value of the premium paid, and as the value of the stock goes down, the value of the put itself increases, covering the fall in price. For this reason, the options trader only loses what it costs to buy the option rather than the more significant value of the stocks he owns.

The best time to take up the married put option is when the trader expects that the price of his stock will rise significantly before the options' expiry date, but also understands that there is a slim chance that the price could fall dramatically. With the married stock, you get the satisfaction of holding the stock that comes with enjoying its upside when it rises, but still be covered in case of a substantial loss, when the stock falls.

Traders buy the married put when they expect news and events in the future that could drive the cost of their stock upwards or downwards but still desires to be covered.

The Covered Call Strategy

When it comes to dealing with calls, one of the best strategies is to go ahead and buy a naked call option. You could also structure a buy-write or a basic covered call.

The covered call is quite widespread among traders since it helps to generate income while reducing the risks associated with the long stock. However, to do this, you must be willing to trade your shares as the predetermined price at the strike price of the short call. Therefore, to use this strategy, you must first get into the market, purchase the underlying stock as a normal stock investor would, and then write a call option on those same shares.

E.g., a call option on a stock that carries 100 shares in each call option. To cover the call, you must sell 1 call option against the 100 shares of stock that you have purchased. If the stock you have purchased skyrockets in price, your short call will be covered by the long stock position you have taken. This is the reason it is called a covered call.

Traders take up the covered call strategy when they hold a short-term position in the stock, and a neutral opinion on the direction the price of the stock is headed. The investor could be looking to sell the call, get the premium and gain some income, or they could be making an effort to protect their stock against a possible decline of the value of the underlying stock.

The Protective Collar Strategy

The protective collar strategy is the one in which traders purchase out-of-the-money put options and at the same time, write an out-of-the-money call option of the same underlying asset, and with a similar expiration date. It is a mix of a long put and a covered call.

The combination creates a neutral setup that protects the trader in case the stock falls, but on the other hand, it gives the investor the responsibility of selling his long stock at the short call strike price. This is not too bad for the investor because he will have experienced the benefits of holding the underlying shares.

Investors use the protective collar when in a long position, and the stock they are holding has had some substantive gains. The stock and options combination allows the investor to enjoy downside protection through the long put so that he or she locks in the profit, while at the same time, getting the pleasure of selling his shares at a high price.

Suppose an investor is long on some Company Y shares, 100 shares at $50, and the value of the shares rises to $100, the investor will create a protective collar by selling one call at $105, and simultaneously buying another at $95. As such, the trader will be protected below the $95, but this is a trade-off with the obligation to sell his shares at $105.

There is an infinite number of strategies that investors can take up to trade options. However, what will be of help to you, in the long run, is to approach the market with a lot of caution, to be systematic and to be probability-minded. Whichever strategy you take up, ensure that you have done your homework first by gaining a sound knowledge of the market and being conscious of the goal you intend to achieve. You must choose the most suited strategy for the market condition you are in.

While the risks involved might appear to be quite significant, the options trading strategies with a risk limit will control the risk to which the trader is exposed. As such, even the risk-averse traders can invest in options to increase their overall returns, protect their current stocks, and reap other benefits that options have to offer. However, as we have pointed out earlier, it helps to understand all the upside and the downside of each investment strategy before you take it up so that you are fully aware of what you stand to lose if the market does not go your way, and what you stand to gain if it does.

Description

The resources people find on the internet in the form of articles and research papers are excellent and informative, but the problem with that kind of knowledge is its lack of arrangement. Most of these resources will give you distorted information because however, you concentrate, you will find something that will distract you. As you are reading about options, you will find an attached article on cooking styles, and as you read on, you will find a funny cat video or an ad. Once you are on that trail, there is no going back. It is no wonder the greatest minds of our time insist on books, not videos or articles. They say that distorted knowledge leads to a distorted mind. It is a joy to bring you an ordered, well-written book on options and options trading.

Options Trading Strategies: Advanced Guide with All the Latest Winning Strategies, Practical Tips, and Suggestions That Will Make the Difference in Your Trading. Start Generating Income Now is designed to equip you with the latest and most practical knowledge on tips, techniques, and strategies that will get you more informed and equipped to trade efficiently.

You see, almost everyone wants to have multiple streams of income. We read about it in motivational books. We also have motivational speakers pounding information into our heads about how important it is to begin projects that will help us to raise both passive and active income-generating projects and looking at various industries; we can agree that the financial market is one of the most lucrative.

Instead of marching forth and doing something, our journey towards self-improvement ends with us nodding our heads and scribbling some illegible words on our notepads. Well, this ends today because I am here to remind us of one incredibly lucrative venture: options trading. Through this reading, I take you back to the basics of options and options trading strategies, starting from the basics and building up to advanced knowledge.

In this book, you will find:

- Basic training on options and options trading
- Information on various commissions, fees, and the effects of slippage
- The most informative discussion on about brokers and trading platforms, along with advice on how to find the best ones
- An identification of risks involved in trading and techniques you can use to limit your risk exposure
- Training on how you can develop your own trading strategy
- The most explicit instructions on how to use technical indicators to analyze your trade positions
- The most insightful discussion of several basic options trading strategies
- A comprehensive review of several advanced options trading strategies
- The most in-depth assessment of some case studies that demonstrate the effectiveness of options as a trading tool in comparison to other techniques

Buy it Now and let you Customer get addicted ti this Amazing Book !

Conclusion

Thank you for making it through to the end of *Options Trading Strategies: Advanced Guide with All the Latest Winning Strategies, Practical Tips and Suggestions That Will Make the Difference in Your Trading. Start Generating Income Now,* let's hope it was informative and able to provide you with all of the tools you need to achieve your goals, whatever they may be.

With all the myths debunked and all the misinformation corrected, I am confident that you feel more optimistic and convinced that options' trading is the way to go. It is surprising to see that with rich resources like this, not many people take up this lucrative trading business. However, it is said that success is the path less traveled, and I am glad you are on it.

Writing this book was a revelation for me, too. I realized that there exist many hidden pockets of knowledge I had not known about. It is incredible how, in the course of pass knowledge to you, I ended up learning a lesson or two myself.

It is my sincere hope that through this book, you have learned and increased your knowledge of options and how they are traded. You have also learned about the types of options, the risks involved in trading, and the techniques you can utilize to manage that risk. You also know how to use technical signals and indicators to interpret trends in the financial market. You also now understand basic and advanced trading strategies.

The next step is to take the bull by its horns. Do not waste your knowledge. If you are new to options trading, go on and make plans to start trading soon. If you have been trading, take up the tips and techniques, and implement them in your trading to make it more efficient. If you can, pass this knowledge also to other traders and would-be traders. Go ahead and begin the movement that will sensitize people on the wonderful benefits of options trading.

Options Trading Crash Course

Intensive Guide to Options Trading, With All the Winning Strategies, Tips and Tricks, That Will Allow You to Invest and Make Money Income by Options Trading All Step by Step

Trading Club America

Introduction

Thank you so much for purchasing the book *Options trading crash course Intensive Guide to Options Trading, with all the winning strategies, tips, and tricks, that will allow you to invest and make money Income by Options Trading all Step by Step.* In this book, we will show you how to make money from options trading. Many people don't realize it, but options trading is one of the most revenue-generating ways of trading money.

To this day, many people believe in generic stock investing. Although it is excellent, it is still required for you to invest a ton of money to make some money. Whereas in options trading, you will make money without spending a lot, that being said, we will teach you how to invest using options trading and how to make money from it. This will be a beginner's guide on options trading so that you can learn how to make money the right way. We will talk about what options training is and how to trade using short-term strategies and long-term strategies.

 If you feel like the information is getting repetitive, please understand that this is a very technical book and requires you to understand it thoroughly before you start investing your money. Overall, this book will be a crash course for options trading. You will learn many things when it comes to options trading, and it will help you to be successful, if you enjoy this book, then we will highly recommend that you recommended your friends and families who would like to invest their money.

and truthful when it comes to the recounting of facts. As such, any use, correct or incorrect, of the provided information will render the Publisher free of responsibility as to the actions taken outside of their direct purview. Regardless, there are zero scenarios where the original author or the Publisher can be deemed liable in any fashion for any damages or hardships that may result from any of the information discussed herein.

Additionally, the information in the following pages is intended only for informational purposes and should thus be thought of as universal. As befitting its nature, it is presented without assurance regarding its prolonged validity or interim quality. Trademarks that are mentioned are done without written consent and can in no way be considered an endorsement from the trademark holder.

Chapter 1: Options Trading 101

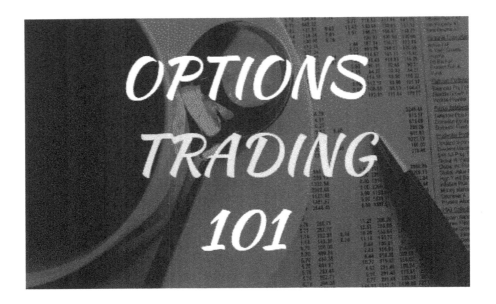

So, you're interested in getting your feet wet in the ocean of options trading, are you? Well, option waters are deep, and when storms are brewing the waves of loss vs. risks can bury beginners if they don't know how to swim through all the variables. It's a volatile ocean of options, where the difference between mere survival and success is dependent upon a speculators' preliminary knowledge, patience, and their primal gut instincts. There are many threats within this broad ocean of options trading, but the greatest danger of all is an over-zealous beginner with little to no skills. With no basic knowledge of options trading, beginners have nothing to keep them afloat until they master the sport. So, you've come to the right place to get your first instruction on options trading. Even though at first, you may be a little fish in a big pond, we'll teach you how to hold your own with the trading sharks. As soon as you learn the principles and strategies of options trading, you'll know how to maneuver your way through the maze of possibilities and experience the challenges and rewards of investing in the options market.

Introducing options, I assume the first few paragraphs didn't send you packing, so let's give you a definition for options trading, and then we'll break it down so you can better understand its parts. A more formal definition of an option is as follows: "A contract that gives the buyer the right, but not the obligation, to buy or sell an underlying asset at a specific price on or before a certain date. An option, just like a stock or bond, is security. It is also a binding contract with strictly defined terms and properties (1)." If you're like many beginner speculators, you don't know much more now than you did before reading the definition. This illustration may help to clarify the basics of an option. Imagine you found the perfect home for you and your family. It's just the right size with all the amenities you wanted, and today's selling price is only $400,000. You've been looking for a long time and know that's a reasonable price for a home in this location. There's just one small problem. You won't have enough cash to purchase the home for another three months.

Your decision is, do you wait and hope the home doesn't sell or the interest rates don't go up, or could there be another option? Of course, there could be another option; what you have to do is investigate the possibilities. Now let's take it to the next step. You want to strike a deal with the homeowner and see if together, you can negotiate a way for you to secure the home at a price you can afford. The owner agrees to put a contract on the home—to secure it for three months at which time you have the right to purchase the home for the agreed-upon price of $400,000. For the privilege of making this option available to you, the homeowner asks for $5,000 to be paid upon the writing of the contract. Remember, this is the right to buy the home on or before that three-month period of time. However, you are not obligated to purchase. You could choose to walk away and let the contract expire, but you would lose your entire $5,000 investment. Now we get into the fun things that often happen with options trading. Back to the purchase of the home. Let's say you make a wonderful discovery about the home; it was the former home of a famous artist, and the living room mural is worth a million dollars. The market value of the home is now $1,400,000. With this discovery, the owner could have sold the home for much more money, but he is obligated to honor the contract he has with you. You are under no obligation to purchase the home, but should you decide to exercise your right to buy, you stand to make a profit of $995,000 (discounting the cost of the option and the price of the home). If the situation was reversed and the homeowner discovered there was black mold and that the home was termite invested, making it worth much less than his asking price of $400,000, he still came out ahead to have taken the option.

Obviously, you won't exercise your option to purchase at $400,000, but the owner at least gets to keep your $5,000 fee, which will help to go toward the repairs. Bear in mind, when you decide to let the expiration date of the contract pass, in this case, the three months, and not exercise your option, you lose 100 percent of your investment—or the total cost of the option privilege. The more practical definition for an option is this: "A legally binding agreement or contract between two people to buy and sell stock at a fixed price over a given period of time (2)." As we get further into this book, you'll learn how options can be extremely risky, yet quite profitable. Because of the high risk that accompanies options trading, they are not for the faint at heart. If you fail to do your homework, you will put yourself at a definite disadvantage when trading options. When you are options trading, you really do not own the stock, you purchase a right or have an obligation. This is what marks options with a different pen, so to speak. The single and only product for sale in the options trading market is one's risk, and the level of risk you buy or sell depends on whether you are accepting or transferring.

For example, if you wish to avoid a risk, you can purchase an option. Or, if there is a risk you want to assume for a substantial fee, then you can be compensated through the options market for accepting the risk for another person (2). If you are entirely confused, that's okay; you'll pick it up as we move forward. Although more and more investors are taking advantage of the options market, you will still see some disclaimers like this one: "Options involve risks and are not suitable for everyone. Options trading can be speculative in nature and carry a substantial risk of loss. Only invest with risk capital (1)." We'll cover many of the benefits of options trading in another chapter, but one of the most desirable elements of options is their versatility. While options trading, you can be as speculative or conservative as you would like. Options give you the opportunity to protect a position from a decline or bet the market is trending upward. You'll often hear options called derivatives because they derive, or get, their value from something else. What they derive their value from is known as an underlying asset. For example, in our illustration of the person who wanted to buy the $400,000 home, it was the home that was the underlying asset.

In Chapter 1, we're going to go over a lot of specific terminologies used in the world of options trading. In fact, it's the language that turns a lot of would-be traders away from options.

In the next chapter, we'll begin introducing you to a whole new options trading language. Along with the words and their definitions, we'll include illustrations to give you "visual learners" better understanding. Before it's over you'll be bi-lingual; your second language will allow you to speak fluent options trading.

You have already been introduced to several unique words of the options trading world, but now it is time to jump in. Most of what you'll be introduced to in this chapter will be definitions with examples that further illustrate their meaning. If all you do is memorize definitions, you're not going to understand options trading. Instead of knowing a rote definition, it's critical that you internalize the meaning of these terms so you can apply them when it comes time for you to invest. People who sell options are known as writers, and those who buy options are called holders. There are two types of options:

1. **Calls**: This type of option gives the holder a right to purchase an asset at a specified price within an agreed-upon period of time. Holders (buyers) of calls want the stock price to increase before their option expires.

2. **Puts**: This type of option gives the holder a right to sell an asset at a specified price within an agreed-upon period of time. Holders (buyers) of puts look for the stock price to fall before their option expires. There are four types of participants in the options market, and the different types depend on the position those participants take.

Examine the illustration above and you will see that there are call options and put options. Let me show you an example of each to clarify their meaning and distinctions. An everyday call option that most people have been exposed to a thousand times are coupons. Let's say you have a coupon for pizza. It looks something like this: You were offered this coupon, and as its holder, you have the right to buy one large pizza with up to three toppings at the fixed price of $10. To use this coupon, you must redeem it on or before the expiration date of October 1, 2016. Just like a call holder, you are under no obligation to use the coupon. You could choose to toss it in the garbage, and there are no consequences to you.

All the elements you see in this coupon can be found in a call option: Call Options Consist of A RIGHT to BUY at a FIXED rate Over a given PERIOD OF TIME

Note: The store offering the coupon has an obligation to sell you the pizza at the price offered on their coupon, irrespective of whether the amount of supplies increases. Papa's Pizza is the writer, you are the holder, the pizza is the underlying asset, and the expiration date is October. The reason this is known as a "call" option is that it gives you the right to "call" the stock or underlying asset (pizza) away from another person. Now let's look at an example of put options. A typical example of put options given to beginners is an insurance policy. Insurance policies are a good illustration of risks—those who want to protect their risks and those who are willing to assume the risk for a fee. What's one of the first things the owner of a new car does when he drives his vehicle off the dealership's lot? Right! Call your insurance agent and make sure your new car is covered. Not that you plan on having an accident—God forbid! However, should the unthinkable happen, you need to make sure your investment is not going to be lost. At the same time, your insurance company hopes you don't wreck your new car as well. You agree on a new premium price depending on the worth of your vehicle and your driving record, and your agent writes a new policy for you. If you should total your new car, you can always "put" it back to the insurance company who agreed to assume the risk for a fee, and in an ideal situation, you'll get the cash value of your car, minus depreciation. If the policy expires and there has been no accident, the policy is worthless unless you renew.

Put options allow the holder to "put" stock back, or sell, to someone else in exchange for cash.

Put Options Consist of A RIGHT to SELL at a FIXED rate Over a given PERIOD OF TIME Note: If you are the seller of an option, this is called writing the option, just like your insurance company writes policies.

Although these are some of the major concepts, you will need an options dictionary of terms to help learn how to make those terms work to make you money.

Options Trading Terminology

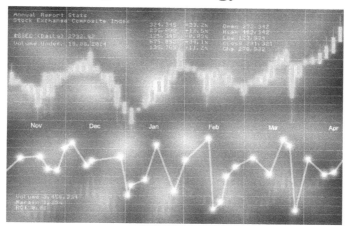

There is a language web that traps beginners in the options trading market, but don't be discouraged. Once you delve into options trading, the terms begin to link one concept to another until the beginner starts to internalize the meaning behind the options trading terminology. Two of the more common terms used by many traders and brokers are "long" and "short." Let's dig a bit deeper and see how these two terms relate to options trading. A contract in options trading equals 100 shares, so when you hold a contract, you have 100 shares. When you buy 100 shares of stock, you are said to be "long" the position. The term "long" means you own the stock. It is the same for options; if you buy a call option, you are "long" the call option. You own the option. So, if owning it means "long" does selling it mean "short?" It should be so easy. Looking at an example of short is much easier than presenting a definition. Imagine you have 100 shares of Microsoft, and you accidentally sold 200 shares. Wouldn't the computer, or the Wizard of Oz, or somebody stop this from happening? No! The computer has no way of knowing just how many shares you own. And, the Wizard is busy with other emergencies, so you end up selling more shares than you own. I said accidentally, but it's rarely by accident.

So, a "short" position is when you sell shares you don't own. You are now short 100 shares of Microsoft. To profit from stock on the downturn, traders will often intentionally sell short. Why? Let's assume Microsoft is trading for $100 a share, but you heard about some problems they were having rolling out a new product, and it is your opinion that the stock is going to drop. If you're correct, you could earn a tidy profit if you sell short. Okay, you sell short 100 shares of Microsoft at $100 a share, but now the shares have decreased in value, and they are assessed at $50 per share. You are obligated to pay back the number of shares, not the dollar amount the shares were worth when you decided to sell short. When you sold short 100 shares of Microsoft at $100 per share, you put $10,000 in your account. Now you ask your broker to find 100 shares of Microsoft that you can borrow. You have a savvy broker who borrows 100 shares of Microsoft stock at only $50 per share. Congratulations! You only had to take $5,000 out of your account to pay back the 100 shares that you initially sold for $100 a share. This left you a profit of $5,000 (minus the broker fees). Wait, you say! What if you were incorrect in your assumption that Microsoft stock would decline? What if the stock price was higher? That's the risk you take. If the stock is higher when your obligation is due, then you suffer a loss since the shares will cost you more than you initially received. I'm sure you've at some time or another asked a financial expert how to play the market, and they said those famous words— "Buy low—sell high." It's in the reverse order when you sell short—you want to sell high, buy low. To make the options market work, the long call may buy while the short call must sell. Selling short creates an obligation to complete the contract and pay back the shares owed. It's the long position that has all the rights. Back to Papa's Pizza, you are the holder of the coupon; you have the right to use it, so you are the holder of long position.

The pizza owner has an obligation to sell you the pizza at a fixed rate on or before the expiration date, so he is short position. If you are long a put option … You are in control—you call the shots, you have the rights, you have the option to decide, you have the right to sell your stock for the fixed price at any time while your policy is in effect. When it comes to the insurance example, you have the right to "put" the car back to the insurance company, so you are long the policy. The insurance company was paid a fee to assume the risk, and they are obligated to give you cash if your car is damaged. They are short because they have the obligation. If you are short position, you have an obligation to fulfill the contract within the given time period

Note: The short position is regulated by the Options Clearing

Corporation (OCC). They make sure everyone meets their obligations.

The OCC acts as the middleman in every transaction. You sell and buy through the OCC. They guarantee performance on every contract.

Strike Price: This is the price at which you "struck" a deal to buy the option. For the pizza, the strike price was $10. Sometimes the strike price is also called the exercise price. It is known as the exercise price because, in order to use your option, your broker must submit exercise instructions, but it's only a phone call away.

In-the-Money: When the share price is higher than the strike price, this is known as being in-the-money. Put options are in-the-money when the share price is below the strike price. Think of being in-the-money as being in a potentially profitable position.

Intrinsic Value: The intrinsic value of the option is the amount by which that option is in-the-money.

Premium: The entire price or cost of the option.

Equity Options: Equity options or options on stock, will always expire by the third Friday of the expiration month.

There are two styles of options, each being a bit different in their time of expiration.

1. **European Style Equity Options**: These options can

ONLY be exercised on the third Friday of the month of expiration.

2. **American Style Equity Options**: These options can be exercised ANY TIME THROUGH the third Friday of the expiration month (1) (2).

As one of the most successful financial products, equity options offer you control to protect your portfolio. They also help you generate additional investment income, while still providing flexibility and diversification. Even though some investors still cling to yesterday's beliefs that options are way too risky, especially for the beginner trader, others who have made incredible profits will tell you differently. Having a better understanding of the options market, they understand that you can be as conservative or speculative as you like; options are merely a tool that gives you that choice.

Are options risky? Sure, but so is any investment in the stock market. If you are looking for safe, put your money in the bank and watch it grow about as fast as winter grass. Anybody that promises you instant profits from options trading isn't giving you the whole story. However, where there are risks, there is also great opportunity to make significant returns on your investment. The beautiful thing about options is that they allow you to speculate without investing near the money as you would to buy the stock outright. We have only covered some of the terminologies of options trading in this chapter, but it's enough to get you started. As we go through the other chapters, there'll be more terms and concepts that arise. We'll explain to them as they occur in the writing.

Chapter 2: How to Start Options Trading

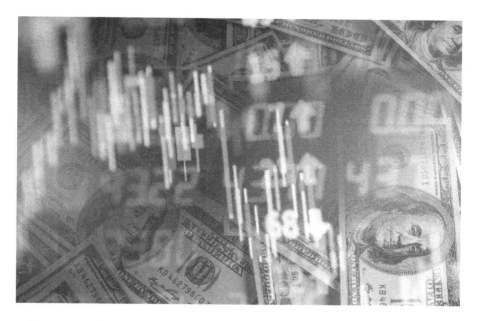

After you have a clear idea of everything that goes into determining the pricing of specific options, you will be ready to stop learning theory and start putting it into practice. Before you get started, however, it is important to determine your personalized trading plan. Create a plan the fact of the matter is that there is simply no way you can expect to be successful in the long term when it comes to day trading if you don't have a plan that has been personalized based on your very own strengths and weaknesses. While skipping this section, and finding a generalized trading plan online, maybe the fastest way to start trading as soon as possible, it is far from the most efficient.

Determine Your Current Level of Skill

In order to ensure that you create a plan with a realistic chance for success, the first thing that you are going to want to do is determine what your current competencies are when it comes to trading in general and the underlying asset you are hoping to focus on specifically.

The more experience you have, the more elaborate and ambitious your plan can be but it is important to determine your level of experience honestly as overestimating your experience is only going to make it more difficult for you to start turning a profit in the first place. During this step, you are also going to want to catalog your general strengths and weaknesses as they relate to trading in general and options trading specifically. It is especially important to be honest with yourself when it comes to your strengths and weaknesses, especially when it comes to your ability to properly maintain your composure when your emotions are running high. Remember, this isn't a test that you can either pass or fail, it is simply an examination of the ways you can be the most effective trader possible. As such, if you fudge the results then the only person who is going to be losing out is you. With enough forethought, you can maximize your strengths and minimize your weaknesses, leading to overall greater success in both the short and the long term.

Decide How Much Risk Is Right for You

When it comes to determining how much risk is the right amount, the final solution is going to be different for each trader. This is because there is no singular amount of risk that is perfect for everyone, the risk is more individualized than that. To get started figuring out the perfect amount of risk for you, the first thing that you will want to do is to determine how much capital you are going to allot solely to trading, as well as what that amount means to you. If you have saved a few thousand dollars in a month or so to give something new a try, then your overall risk is going to be low. If you saved that same amount over nearly a year of dedicated saving then that same amount might represent a much higher risk. Regardless, it is important to never put more into a single trade than you can ever afford to lose. A good rule of thumb is that each individual trade should encompass no more than 5 percent of your total options trading fund to ensure that a small mistake doesn't end up costing you dearly. What's more, when it comes to deciding to take chances on potential trades you are only going to want to pull the trigger when you have a reasonable suspicion that the trade in question is going to end with you making three times as much in profit as what you originally put in prior to paying any related fees. To determine this amount all you need to do is take the potential payout and divide it by the buy-in amount, if the result is greater than three then you can move ahead with the trade with a clean conscience. This advice is what is known as the risk/reward ratio and it is key to trading in options successfully. Besides the financial realities of your situation, you are also going to need to consider how much time you ultimately plan on spending concentrating on options trading to the exclusion of all else along with the amount of profit you hope to see in the process.

If, after determining the amount of time you hope to spend trading your financial estimates aren't as high as you might like, you can then either change the amount of time you are planning to spend or the amount of risk you are willing to put up with, there are only these three variables to work with. Be wary when it comes to raising your risk too high as major amounts of risk are as likely to lead to major losses as they are too major windfalls.

Prepare Yourself

Ideally, you will be spending the early hours of the day reading up on the likely state of the market for the moment when it opens so that you can take advantage of your planning as much as possible. As such, when it comes to creating your plan it is important to understand how much time you realistically have to commit to maximizing your trade advantage and what other parts of your life are going to interfere with this preparation.

There is certainly money to be made by trading options at less regular hours, but the only way that you will be prepared to do so is if you know about the discrepancy ahead of time and work to minimize its impact as much as possible. In addition to the daily preparations that will be required of you, you will also need to be aware of various important due dates, both for your underlying asset of choice as a whole, as well as any holdings you might have specifically. Earnings reports of all types are sure to have a noticeable effect on the market and if you are caught unaware you have no choice but to take a loss that, in many cases, can be quite serious. You will also need to be aware of when any dividend payments are coming due for any options that are related to stocks that you might own. Owning an option does not entitle you to a dividend so you must know when to exercise your options if you hope to maximize your profits at all times.

Understand when you will want to get while the getting is good: When it comes to creating a successful strategy, it is important that you take the time to determine exactly when you are going to want to exit every trade that you make, no matter what. Choosing this point means considering your acceptable level of risk and will ultimately serve to limit your losses, though also doing the same to your profits. Specifically, this means that when scenarios arise such as when a stock drops out of the money from a previously profitable position, you will always want to be realistic about the situation and understand that the best thing is to do is sell rather than wait for it come back around, risking even greater losses in the interim. This logic is flawed, and what's worse, will lead to future negative habits if you are lucky enough for it to work out in your favor the first time as it will always result in a loss in the long run. Instead, you will want to determine what the best strategy is for you and your holdings based on numerous personal factors including other trades you are currently pursuing, what you believe to be an acceptable level of risk and how closely you plan to micromanage each individual trade. Essentially, what this means is that the specific details behind the exit strategy that you choose don't matter, what does matter is that you plan out what it is going to be, before you make your first move, and then stick with it no matter what, even if every emotional cell in your being is telling you to change horses midstream and do something that is almost certainly stupid.

To keep your losses to a minimum, you are going to want to use what is known as stop losses. Stop losses are a way to automatically buy or sell options based on a predetermined set of specifications. As such, they are not terribly useful when it comes to trading in options that are likely to move a great deal in both directions over a short period of time but can be extremely useful in other, more stable, situations. It doesn't matter if you are the holder or the writer, stop losses are a must for everyone involved in the interaction. You will also find that secondary stop orders are also useful when it comes to securing a predetermined amount of profit while still ensuring that you can take advantage of any ongoing positive trends as well. This is done thanks to what is known as a price target which is the amount you feel is realistic to expect to make from the trade in question. You then simply set your first stop loss at this point and then set a second stop loss much higher. This way when the first level of profit is reached you can sell off half of your holdings while still retaining the rest in case the positive trend continues in a big way.

Find the Right Place to Start

Once you know when you are going to get out of any trade that you place, the next thing that you will need to consider is the right time to capitalize on the trend of a specific option. The best way to go about doing this is to consider the amount of risk that you deem acceptable before considering what type of purchase you want to make when you come across an option that meets your criteria for purchase based on your earnings goals and your risk assessment. As a new options trader, what you are going to likely be the most interested in is making a single option purchase per trade. While this might not seem like a lot, it is important to keep in mind that each option is going to be worth 100 shares which means that it only takes a little bit of movement from the underlying asset to cause significant gains or losses for any trades that you make. This means that you are going to want to be discerning when it comes to choosing the right entry point, one that is relaxed enough to ensure that you aren't waiting days between trades and strict enough that every option you come across doesn't automatically qualify. Goals It is important to ultimately consider what goals you have for trading and how likely each trade is to help move you one step closer to achieving them. A good way to do so is to determine if each of your goals related to options trading is not only realistic but SMART. The first SMART goal that you set should be one that is at the same time straightforward enough to more or less ensure your success while at the same time being relevant enough to your day to day life that actually succeeding will be a moment that you can easily recall in the future when success on a future goal is not nearly so assured. This way you will start forming the right type of neural pathways as soon as possible, which will then form into patterns that will eventually become habits. With this in mind, you want to start off with a goal that is, at least tangentially connected to the negative pattern that you are the most anxious to start to change. You don't need to have an exact goal in mind at this point, just the start of an idea that you can build into something larger later on. Consider the following to ensure that you are on the right track. SMART goals are:

Specific: The best goals are the ones that you will always be able to clearly determine where you stand in relation to the goal. The goal should then have a clearly defined fail state as well as state that will clearly let you know when you have crossed the finish line. Specific goals are also going to be much easier to chart out over time as their specificity will lend to clear sub-goals that can be linked to their success or failure. When you choose a specific goal, you are going to want to guarantee that you have a clear idea of the following details to ensure that you have chosen a goal that is truly specific enough for your needs. You must know who you will need to work with in order to make the goal a reality, what you will need to do in order to get started on completing the goal, where you will need to go in order to see the goal through to completion, why you wanted to get started completing the goal in the first place, when you can realistically expect the goal to be completed, how you will go about completing the goal in various steps.

Measurable: A good goal is one where progress towards success can easily be measured, giving you a feeling of accomplishment and a serotonin boost every time you take another step in the right direction. With your first few goals, it is extremely important to keep them measurable in order to nurture the growth of the proper neural pathways.

To determine the metric of success you should be using, start by determining the easiest criteria by which you can measure success. This metric can either be one that is based on achieving certain predetermined outcomes or one that is based on cold, hard facts, the important thing is that there are clearly defined points that can be used to ensure you are always on the right track. Early goals tend to work better when a success metric is a number that can be easily defined as it helps to be able to constantly see a stream of new progress unfolding. Once you know how you will be able to tell if you have achieved a specific goal, it is important to keep a visual record of your progress that you can look back on in times of hardship to snap your mind out of trying to make excuses. The visual proof of effort already exerted can be a powerful motivator when it comes to silencing excuses and making goals seem more attainable which in turn keeps motivation high throughout the ordeal. This is especially true once you have reached the halfway point as everything after that is downhill when compared with the effort you have already put in. Keeping detailed notes of your progress can be as simple as charting your progress on a graph or as complicated as keeping a detailed journal of your experiences. Try various methods of keeping track of your progress and see which works best for you.

Having this record will help to keep the entirety of the goal in the appropriate perspective as well as helping to mitigate any concerns and excuses you might have about not making any headway to your ultimate goal.

Attainable: SMART Goals are always attainable. Ideal scenarios are nice, but including goals that have only a slim probability of materializing is doing little more than wasting your time. This is not saying that complicated or difficult goals should be avoided, rather it is about really knowing your limits and when they can be expanded. Setting long-term goals is good for the self-image of the business and it can help every member of the team grow in an attempt to reach them.

Relevant to your current situation: It is important that the goal you choose is relevant to your current situation as well as being simply something that is attainable with only a reasonable amount of effort. Relevance is key to turning the SMART goal system from a one-time thing into a pattern and eventually a life-long habit that you can rely on to help you meet the challenges of life no matter what they may be. Remember, you want these early goals to be as meaningful as possible so that you think back on them regularly and fortify the neural pathways as quickly as possible so they become your brain's default way of acting.

If you take it slow you will find that completing part of the task related to achieving your current goal will become a habit just like anything else which will then make it easier to work on even more complicated tasks in turn. As with everything else described above, when working on cementing SMART goals in your life you will want to remember that practice makes perfect.

Timely: Studies show that you are statistically more likely to continue to works towards the completion of a complicated or difficult task if it has a deadline associated with it. What this means is that you will want to determine what your ultimate goal will be, determine a timeline for completion, and then do the same for each of the sub-goals you set as well. When it comes to setting a due date for your goals, you will want to consider periods of time that are long enough to allow you to really experience a few setbacks along the way, without being so lax that you never actually get around to accomplishing anything. What you are shooting for is something that will force you to stop dreaming about financial freedom and start working towards it, not something so strict that you have no realistic chance of success. Track your progress instead of being in a rush to look into how effective your plan is or setting daily trading goals that are, frankly, completely unrealistic, especially so early on, you will want to make a point of sticking to the plan that you created and keeping detailed notes on every single trade that you make, what the results are and what all of the relevant details turned out to be. To determine the metrics that are most relevant to your overall success, you are going to want to first ask yourself what type of trader you are. If you are someone who is always hunting for big risks and bigger rewards, then you will be much better served by finding out how successful you have been overall in a given time period (starting with one month of data) as opposed to the number of successful or unsuccessful trades. On the other hand, if your overall number of trades is very low because you only make extremely safe moves, then you will want to ensure that each trade you make is as profitable as possible.

Chart Your Success

After you have waited long enough that you have some data that can be genuinely useful to you, the next thing you are going to want to do is chart out how effective your initial trading plan has been so far. Charting out this type of data will make it easier for you to see if all of the rules you are basing your trading decisions on hold up to a critical analysis. This will help you to determine if the plan that you are working with is going to be reliable moving forward to help to assure yourself that it is going to continue to line up with the goals you have for profit generation. This is also a way to create the baseline for future historical volatility analysis. Once you have charted out the data that you have so far, the next thing you are going to want to do is to create a summary that reflects the details in the data that you have generated so far. You will want this summary to include all of the details of every single trade that you made in your first month of trading. Seeing all of this data, clear of any daily biases will make it much easier for you to ultimately see the forest, not the trees.

This broader focus will, in turn, make it easier to determine not just how profitable your venture has been thus far but also to illuminate patterns ultimately related to either failure or success that may be hiding in the apparently random data. The more you study your results, the more likely it is that you will be able to turn apparently random instances of good luck into a repeatable pattern of success. Results that matter most: If you have been following along as suggested, then by now you will certainly have all the data you could ever need when it comes to determining the efficacy of your system. Luckily, you aren't going to need to use all of it regularly, and can instead rely on a few important indicators that will tell you what you really need to know. Net profit: To determine the total net profit that you have brought in by trading options thus far, all you need to do is add up all of the profitable trades that you have made thus far and compare that number to the total number of trades where you lost money and determine which number is higher. This is the most basic and broad determination of whether or not your plan is successful if the number you end up with is negative, it is time to go back to square one and find a more profitable plan, anything else is akin to burning money.

Profit Factor

Once your total net profit is facing the right way, the next thing you are going to need to consider how much you are likely to make on your plan per dollar spent assuming everything else remains equal. To find this number, you take your total profit number and divide it by the total amount of any losses you had. This number needs to be above 1 to indicate an effective plan, and anything higher is hugely profitable.

Percent Profitable

You can think of the percent your project is valuable as how likely you are to win at any given trade. To determine what the number is, you take the name of trades that ended in success and divide it by the total number of trades that you attempted. There is no target number in this scenario, as the right amount depends on whether you prefer significant gains and higher risks, in which case you should aim for few trades with higher margins; or you will want a high number if you prefer lots of small, safe trades.

Trade average net profit: The trade average net profit is the amount you are likely to make on each trade you complete, given your history of trading. To find this number, all you need to do is divide the total amount of profit you made by the total number of trades, regardless of whether or not they were ultimately successful. This number should be positive, and ideally, the higher, the better. If the number ends up being negative, then you need to stop trading until you come up with a plan that is somewhat more effective. When finding this number, it is important to leave out any trades that you may have made that were extreme outliers compared to all of your other trades as they can skew this number to the point of irrelevance.

Chapter 3: Short Term Strategy

As you know, there are many people following short-term option trading strategies to make a quick buck. Keep in mind that, for you to be successful short-term trading, you have to be very meticulous with the stocks you are dabbling with. The truth is that the stock can be very high and can be very low within minutes, which is why you mustn't necessarily act on a specific company or a particular stock, based on the information provided to you via news or newspapers. With that being said, there are many ways to see success with options trading with short-term strategies. That being said, we will now discuss the main strategies that will help you to see tremendous results with your options trading.

20-Day System

This is one of the techniques we use to make some short-term gains. If you look at the stock that has recently gone up, chances are it will go down drastically within 20 days. 99% of the time, this is the case, which is why we like to wait 20 days before we make any investment on a stock. If you wait 20 days, you will hit the lowest price point of that particular stock. When it is at its lowest, it is ideal that you invest your money into that stock. Chances are the stock will go up again, many top traders have been using this technique with fantastic success. The trick is to wait 20 days at least before you make a trade. Depending on the company, the stock prices will drop down within 20 days of it going up drastically. And on the 20th day, this is when you invest your money into that stock and see it grow. You can see capital gains within ten days of the spending that money.

A great example would be marijuana stocks that took place recently. Many people were investing like crazy on these stocks. However, it hit an all-time low within 20 to 30 days, and then it levels back up. Our main goal is to wait for the shares to level back up, as it will give you a better understanding of where the stock is headed and what you should do about it. Ideally, you never want to invest in stock as soon as it goes up. There will be millions of people investing in the capital when that happens. Take your time with the stock and watch it grow.

Don't Sell Until the Stock Price Hits Back up to Its All-Time High

After understanding the basics of the 20-day strategy, you need to know that you should not sell your stock unless and until it has gone back up to its highest stock price in those 20 days. Most of the time, when the stock hits its all-time low, it will rise again up to its all-time high if not higher, which is why it is advised that you wait for the stock to grow back up to its highest point or above. Meaning that you should not sell your stock unless and until it is leveled back up to its highest price point. A great rule of thumb would be to wait another 20 days after you've invested your money. Once you do that, except for the stock to climb back up, once it climbs back up to a price where it was at the highest or even higher than that, then you can most definitely pull out that money and enjoy it. We understand that you are always very emotional with the money you're investing. One of the most excellent advice I can give you is not to be emotionally attached to your stock. Meaning that even if you make less or more money, it is always better to be safe than sorry. For instance, if you decide to sell your stock once it hits the highest peak, you ever have seen, and the next day it goes even higher don't be sad as you still made profits. When it comes to making the short-term strategy work, you mustn't ponder on the lost money. Chances are if you kept waiting on it then you might have even lost some money, which is why it is essential not to get emotionally attached to your stock and to also not be scared. You need to find that right balance when you are selling your stock.

Look at the Trend

They must start looking at the pattern when you are trying to achieve short-term capital. Always look at the trends that are taking place and invest your money accordingly. If you have a feeling that a particular stock will go up in a short period, then make sure that you invest in that stock. If you look at the transcript history, then it shouldn't be hard for you to see which stocks will go up soon and which won't. This will allow you to make fantastic capital gains with your options trading. However, when following trends, you must keep an eye on your stock. As trends go, they will go up quickly, and they will go down even quicker. This is why it is ideal they keep checking up on your stock as much as possible and pull the trigger when you think it's right. As always do not get emotionally attached to your stocks and if you feel like it is slowly dropping down then perhaps sell the stock.

Control Risk

Controlling risk is one of the most important things when it comes to option trading. Short-term trading involves a lot of chances, so you must minimize the risk by maximizing all your returns. You can use things like sell stops or buy stocks as protection from a market reversal. It would be to sell a particular stock once it reaches a specific price. Once the prices reach, it will be ordered to sell at the market price. Buy stock is the complete opposite and is used in a short position when the stock has risen to a specific amount, at which point it becomes a buy order. Both of these options have been designed to limit your downside off you losing money. A general rule of thumb and short-term trading is that you want to set yourself stop or buy something within 7.5% to 12.5% that's where you purchased the stock or initiated the short. The premise behind this theory is for you to not lose money or lose little money. So, the gains you make will be a lot more frequent.

Target Stocks Which Will Make Big Moves Very Soon

Similar to looking at Trends, this is one of the long terms / short-term strategy options. The strategy can be both used in a long-term and short time. However, it's right to a short-term options trade, and you'll need to focus on stocks that may have a history of making significant moves in a short period. This is the kind of information you can get by reviewing stock charts, and by looking up their account. To put it, let's talk with history reading that suggests dramatic price swings are going to make money in the short term. There are also many technical indicators that you can refer to to get your short-term trading strategy decisions. For instance, what type of stocks goes up and down in a 20-day plan. If you see a lot of prices going up and down, then the chances are that it will reoccur once again. Make sure that you act on it when the stock is at its lowest, so you make sure that you can sell it at the highest. However, it is more important to see stocks that have a history of going up and down more frequently. Most of the time, the past is an excellent indicator of where the stock is going to be in the future and how they're going to react. Although not accurate as always, they will still give you a great insight into where the stock is heading so you can make a decision. Make sure that you do some digging on the company you're going to invest in, look at the upcoming products they're going to sell or what is it that they're going to do which is going to be a revolutionary. These are essential things to look at if you're looking to make short-term money out of it, as it will help you to see where to put your money and when. If the product launch goes hugely successful, the chances are you will be benefiting from it as much as the third person.

Determine Your Exit Plan in Advance

Cashing out and short-term gains from your stock are amazing. Unfortunately, if you'd be able to create a concrete exit plan in advance, you will find yourself in a worse position than you started. If you remember, we talked about buying and call options recently. It is essential to have a grand exit plan before you start trading your money. You need to ask yourself these questions how long should you keep the money in the stock? Or do you want to close out a loser immediately? Or do you want to wait to see if the stock starts making more money? These are the questions you need to ask before you invest the money and go with it. It is essential to have a grand exit plan strategy, as it will not only help you to save more money, but it will give you a clear idea of what you're doing before you invest your hard-earned money. Answers to these questions may vary depending on person to person. However, you must play it smartly if your goal is to see a lot of capital gains. Before you make any investment in a stock, make sure you sit down and think about what you're going to be doing with the money that has been invested and when and how are you going to exit out of it. Like you said before, you do not want to get greedy with the money that you're investing. Make sure that you take your sweet time with the money that you've spent, and use it the right way. Make sure they don't get greedy with the profits as they can go down very quickly, and also be very smart with investments that you're making or you can lose a lot of money. Nonetheless, if you follow the advice provided to you in this book, then you will have no problem seeing capital gains in the long-term and short-term. Make sure that you very smart with the Investments that you make, and you always do your research before you make any investments.

With that being said, we conclude this chapter. This chapter should give you a great idea on how to invest money in the short-term. Make sure that you understand what the sections are trying to convey to you, as you must know how to invest money in the short-term before you do spend the money. More specifically, I want you to understand that you will have to use your brain when it comes to investing money. We can give you great advice on how to spend money, and however, sometimes you will have to use your gut feeling on when you should exit and when you should enter a stock and how.

Nonetheless, make sure that you look at the stock history, and which stock is trending based on that, you should invest. Whatever it is that you do, make sure that you understand that your money will be at risk, so use the money wisely and that if done correctly tell for sure you will see capital gains. If you are stupid with your money, then you will most definitely lose all your money, regardless after reading this chapter you will be in a much better position to seeing capital gains from your short-term investments.

Chapter 4: Long Term Strategy

Fundamental Analysis

While it should come as no surprise that you are going to need to gather as much data as possible in order to make the best trades, regardless of what market you are working in; it is important to keep in mind that if you don't use it in the right way then it is all for naught. There are two ways to get the most out of any of the data that you gather, the first is via technical analysis, and the second is via fundamental analysis. As a general rule, you will likely find it helpful to start with fundamental analysis before moving on to technical analysis as the need arises. To understand the difference between the two you may find it helpful to think about technical analysis as analyzing charts while fundamental analysis looks at specific factors based on the underlying asset for the market that you are working in.

The core tenant of fundamental analysis is that there are related details out there that can tell the whole story when it comes to the market in question while technical analysis believes that the only details that are required are those that relate to the price at the moment. As such, fundamental analysis is typically considered easier to master as it all relates to concepts less expressly related to understanding market movement exclusively. Meanwhile, technical analysis is typically faster because key fundamental analysis data often is only made publicly available on a strict, and limited, schedule, sometimes only a few times a year meaning the availability for updating specific data is rather limited.

Fundamental Analysis Rules

The best time to use fundamental analysis is when you are looking to gain a broad idea of the state of the market as it stands and how that relates to the state of things in the near future when it comes time to actually trading successfully. Regardless of what market you are considering, the end goals are the same, find the most effective trade for the time period that you are targeting.

Establish a Baseline

In order to begin analyzing the fundamentals, the first thing that you will need to do is to create a baseline regarding the company's overall performance. In order to generate the most useful results possible, the first thing that you are going to need to do is to gather data both regarding the company in question as well as the related industry as a whole. When gathering macro data, it is important to keep in mind that no market is going to operate in a vacuum which means the reasons behind specific market movement can be much more far-reaching than they first appear. Fundamental analysis works because of the stock market's propensity for patterns which means if you trace a specific market movement back to the source you will have a better idea of what to keep an eye on in the future. Furthermore, all industries go through several different phases where their penny stocks are going to be worth more or less overall based on general popularity. If the industry is producing many popular penny stocks, then overall volatility will be down while at the same time liquidity will be at an overall high.

Consider Worldwide Issues

Once you have a general grasp on the current phase you are dealing with, the next thing you will want to consider is anything that is going on in the wider world that will after the type of businesses you tend to favor in your penny stocks. Not being prepared for major paradigm shifts, especially in penny stocks where new companies come and go so quickly, means that you can easily miss out on massive profits and should be avoided at all costs. To ensure you are not blindsided by news you could have seen coming, it is important to look beyond the obvious issues that are consuming the 24-hour news cycle and dig deeper into the comings and goings of the nations that are going to most directly affect your particular subsection of penny stocks.

One important worldwide phenomenon that you will want to pay specific attention to is anything in the realm of technology as major paradigm shifts like the adoption of the smartphone, or the current move towards electric cars can create serious paradigm shifts.

Put It All Together

Once you have a clear idea of what the market should look like as well as what may be on the horizon, the next step is to put it all together to compare what has been and what might to what the current state of the market is. Not only will this give you a realistic idea of what other investors are going to do if certain events occur the way they have in the past, you will also be able to use these details in order to identify underlying assets that are currently on the cusp of generating the type of movement that you need if you want to utilize them via binary option trades. The best time to get on board with a new underlying asset is when it is nearing the end of the post-bust period or the end of a post-boom period depending on if you are going to place a call or a put. In these scenarios, you are going to have the greatest access to the freedom of the market and thus, have access to the greatest overall allowable risk that you are going to find in any market. Remember, the amount of risk that you can successfully handle without an increase in the likelihood of failure is going to start decreasing as soon as the boom or bust phase begins in earnest so it is important to get in as quickly as possible if you hope to truly maximize your profits.

Understand the Relative Strength of Any Given Trade

When an underlying asset is experiencing a boom phase, the strength of its related fundamentals is going to be what determines the way that other investors are going to act when it comes to binary options trading. Keeping this in mind it then stands to reason that the earlier a given underlying asset is in a particular boom phase, the stronger the market surrounding it is going to be. Remember, when it comes to fundamental analysis what an underlying asset looks like at the moment isn't nearly as important as what it is likely to look like in the future and the best way to determine those details is by keeping an eye on the past.

Quantitative Fundamental Analysis

The sheer volume of data and a large amount of varying numbers found in the average company's financial statements can easily be intimidating and bewildering for conscientious investors who are digging into them for the first time. Once you get the hang of them, however, you will quickly find that they are a goldmine of information when it comes to determining how likely a company is to continue producing reliable dividends in the future. At their most basic, a company's financial statements disclose the information relating to its financial performance over a set period of time. Unlike with qualitative concepts, financial statements provide cold, hard facts about a company that is rarely open for interpretation.

Balance Sheet

A balance sheet shows a detailed record of all of a company's equity, liabilities and assets for a given period of time. A balance sheet shows a balance to the financial structure of a company by dividing the company's equity by the combination of shareholders and liabilities in order to determine its current assets. In this case, assets represent the resources that the company is actively in control of at a specific point in time. It can include things like buildings, machinery, inventory, cash and more. It will also show the total value of any financing that has been used to generate those assets. Financing can come from either equity or liabilities.

Liabilities include debt that must be paid back eventually while equity, in this case, measures the total amount of money that its owners have put into the business. This can include profits from previous years, which are known collectively as retained earnings.

Income Statement

While the balance sheet can be thought of as a snapshot of the fundamental economic aspects of the company, an income statement takes a closer look at the performance of the company exclusively for a given timeframe. There is no limit to the length of time an income statement considers, which means you could see them generated month to month, or even day to day; however, the most common type used by public companies are either annual or quarterly. Income statements provide information on profit, expenses, and revenues that resulted from the business that took place over a specific period of time.

Cash Flow Statement

The cash flow statement frequently shows all of the cash outflow and inflow for the company over a given period of time. The cash flow statement often focuses on operating cash flow which is the cash that will be generated by day to day business operations.

It will also include any cash that is available from investing which is often used as a means of investing in assets along with any cash that might have been generated by long-term asset sales or the sale of a secondary business that the company previously owned. Cash due to financing is another name for money that is paid off or received based on issuing or borrowing funds. The cash flow statements are quite important as it is often more difficult for businesses to manipulate it when compared to many other types of financial documents. While accountants can manipulate earnings with ease, it is much more difficult to fake having access to cash in the bank where there is none that really exists. This is why many savvy investors consider the cash flow statement the most reliable way to measure a specific company's performance.

Finding the Details

While tracking down all the disparate financial statements on the companies you are considering purchasing stock in can be cumbersome, the Securities and Exchange Commission (SEC) requires all publicly traded companies to submit regular filings outlining all of their financial activities including a variety of different financial statements. This also includes information such as managerial discussions, reports from auditors, deep dives into the operations and prospects of upcoming years and more. These types of details can all be found in the 10-K filing that each company is required to file every year, along with the 10-Q filing that they must send out once per quarter. Both types of documents can be found online, both at the corporate website for the company as well as on the SEC website. As the version that hits the corporate site doesn't need to be complete, it is best to visit SEC.gov and get to know the Electronic Data Gathering, Analysis, and Retrieval system (EDGAR) which automates the process of indexing, validating, collecting, forward and accepting submissions. As this system was designed in the mid-90s, however, it is important to dedicate some time to learning the process as it is more cumbersome than 20 years of user interface advancements have to lead you to expect.

Qualitative Factors

Qualitative factors are generally less tangible and include things like its name recognition, the patents it holds and the quality of its board members.

Qualitative factors to consider include:

Business Model

The first thing that you are going to want to do when you catch wind of a company that might be worth following up on is to check out its business model which is more or less a generalization of how it makes its money. You can typically find these sorts of details on the company website or in its 10-K filing.

Competitive Advantage

It is also important to consider the various competitive advantages that the company you have your eye on might have over its competition. Companies that are going to be successful in the long-term are always going to have an advantage over their competition in one of two ways. They can either have better operational effectiveness or improved strategic positioning. Operational effectiveness is the name given to doing the same things as the competition but in a more efficient and effective way.

Strategic positioning occurs when a company gains an edge by doing things that nobody else is doing.

Changes to the Company

In order to properly narrow down your search, you will typically find the most reliable results when it comes to companies that have recently seen major changes to their corporate structure as it is these types of changes that are likely to ultimately precede events that are more likely to see the company jump to the next level. The specifics of what happened in this instance are nearly as important as the fact that statistically speaking, 95 percent of companies that experience this type of growth started with a significant change to the status quo.

Technical Analysis

When working with technical analysis you are always going to want to remember that it functions because of the belief that the way the price of a given trade has moved in the past is going to be an equally reliable metric for determining what it is likely to do again in the future. Regardless of which market you choose to focus on, you'll find that there is always more technical data available than you will ever be able to realistically parse without quite a significant amount of help. Luckily, you won't be sifting through the data all on your own, and you will have numerous technical tools including things such as charts, trends, and indicators to help you push your success rates to new heights. While some of the methods you will be asked to apply might seem arcane at first, the fact of the matter is that all you are essentially doing is looking to determine future trends along with their relative strengths. This, in turn, is crucial to your long-term success and will make each of your trades more reliable practically every single time.

Understand Core Assumptions

Technical analysis is all about measuring the relative value of a particular trade or underlying asset by using available tools to find otherwise invisible patterns that, ideally, few other people have currently noticed. When it comes to using technical analysis properly you are going to always need to assume three things are true. First and foremost, the market ultimately discounts everything; second, trends will always be an adequate predictor of price and third, history is bound to repeat itself when given enough time to do so. Technical analysis believes that the current price of the underlying asset in question is the only metric that matters when it comes to looking into the current state of things outside of the market, specifically because everything else is already automatically factored in when the current price is set as it is. As such, to accurately use this type of analysis all you need to know is the current price of the potential trade in question as well as the greater economic climate as a whole. Those who practice technical analysis are then able to interpret what the price is suggesting about market sentiment in order to make predictions about where the price of a given cryptocurrency is going to go in the future. This is possible due to the fact that pricing movements aren't random. Instead, they follow trends that appear in both the short and the long-term.

Determining these trends in advance is key to using technical analysis successfully because all trends are likely to repeat themselves over time, thus the use of historical charts in order to determine likely trends in the future. When it comes to technical analysis, the 'what' is always going to be more important than the 'why'. That is, the fact that the price moved in a specific way is far more important to a technical analyst then why it made that particular movement. Supply and demand should always be consulted, but beyond that, there are likely too many variables to make it worthwhile to consider all of them as opposed to their results. Price charts Technical analysis is all about the price chart which is a chart with an x and y-axis. The price is measured along the vertical axis and the time is measured via the horizontal axis. There are numerous different types of price charts that different types of traders prefer, these include the point and figure chart, the Renko chart, the Kagi chart, the Heikin-Ashi chart, the bar chart, the candlestick chart, the line chart, and the tick chart. However, the ones you will need to concern yourself with at first are going to be included in any forex trading platform software and are the bar chart, the candlestick chart, the line chart, and the point and click chart which is why they are outlined in greater detail below.

Line Chart

Of all the various types of charts, the line chart is the simplest because it only presents price information in the form of closing prices in a fixed time span. The lines that give it its name are created when the various closing price points are then connected with a line. When looking at a line chart it is important to keep in mind that they will not be able to provide an accurate visual representation of the range that individual points reached which means you won't be able to see either opening prices or those that were high or low prior to close.

Regardless, the closing point is important to always consider which is why this chart is so commonly referred to by technical traders of all skill levels.

Bar Chart

A bar chart takes the information that can be found in a line chart and expands upon it in a number of interesting ways. For starters, the chart is made using a number of vertical lines that provide information on various data points. The top and bottom of the line can then be thought of as the high and low of the trading timeframe respectively while the closing price is also indicated with a dash on the right side of the bar. Furthermore, the point where the currency price opened is indicated via a dash and will show up on the left side of the bar in question.

Candlestick Chart

A candlestick chart is similar to a bar chart, though the information it provides is much more detailed overall. Like a bar chart it includes a line to indicate the range for the day, however, when you are looking at a candlestick chart you will notice a wide bar near the vertical line which indicates the degree of the difference the price saw throughout the day. If the price that the stock is trading at increases overall for the day, then the candlestick will often be clear while if the price has decreased then the candlestick is going to be read.

Point and Figure Chart

While seen less frequently than some of the other types of charts, a point and figure chart has been around for nearly a century and can still be useful in certain situations today. This chart can accurately reflect the way the price is going to move, though it won't indicate timing or volume. It can be thought of as a pure indicator of price with the excessive noise surrounding the market muted, ensuring nothing is skewed. A point and figure chart is noticeable because it is made up of Xs and Os rather than lines and points. The Xs will indicate points where positive trends occurred while the Os will indicate periods of downward movement. You will also notice numbers and letters listed along the bottom of the chart which corresponds to months as well as dates. This type of chart will also make it clear how much the price is going to have to move in order for an X to become an O or an O to become an X. Trend or range: When it comes to using technical analysis successfully, you will want to determine early on if you are more interested in trading based on the trends you find or on the range. While they are both properties related to price, these two concepts are very different in practice which means you will want to choose one to emphasize over the other. If you decide to trade according to trend, then you are more interested in going with the flow and choosing stocks to trade while everyone else is having the same idea.

Chart Patterns to Be Aware of Flags and Pennants

Both flags and pennants show retracement, which is deviations that will be visible in the short term in relation to the primary trend. Retracement results in no breakout occurring from either the resistance or support levels but this won't matter as the security will also not be following the dominant trend. The lack of breakout means this trend will be relatively short term.

The resistance and support lines of the pennant occur within a larger trend and converge so precisely that they practically form a point. A flag is essentially the same except that the resistance and support lines from the flag will be essentially parallel instead. If you are looking for them, both flags and pennants are more likely to be found in the mid-section of the primary phase of the trend. They can last up to two weeks before being absorbed back into the primary trend line. They are typically associated with falling volume which means that if you notice a flag or a pennant and the volume is not falling then you are more likely actually seeing a reversal which is an actually changing trend instead of a simple retracement.

Head Above Shoulders Formation

If you are looking for indicators of how long any one particular trend is likely to continue, then looking for a grouping of three peaks in a price chart, known as the head above shoulders formation, can indicate a bearish pattern moving forward. The peaks to the left and to the right of the primary peak, also known as the shoulders, should be somewhat smaller than the head peak and also connect at a specific price.

This price is known as the neckline and when it reaches the right shoulder the price will likely then plunge noticeably. The inverse head and shoulders (or head and shoulders bottom) is a sign that the price of the security in question is about to rise in the face of an existing downward trend. It typically forms at the lowest overall price of the trend. Based on the analysis of the peak-and-trough pattern from the Dow Theory, an upward trend is then seen as indicative of a series of successive rising troughs and peaks. Meanwhile, a downward trend is indicative of a series of lower peaks and deeper troughs. If this is the case, then the head and shoulders pattern represents a weakening of an existing trend as the troughs and peaks deteriorate. The head and shoulders top forms at the peaks of an upwards trend and signals that a reversal is often forthcoming through a process of four steps. The first of these starts with the creation of the far-left shoulder which can be formed when the cryptocurrency reaches a new high before dropping to a new low. This is then followed by the formation of the head which occurs when the security reaches an even higher high before retracing back to the low found in the left shoulder. Finally, the right shoulder is formed from a high that is lower than the high found in the head, countered by a retracement back to the low of the left shoulder. The pattern is then completed when the price drops back below the neckline. The inverse head-and-shoulders pattern is the exact opposite of the head-and-shoulders top, as it signals that the security is set to make an upward move. Often coming at the end of a downtrend, the inverse head and shoulders are considered to be a reversal pattern, as the security typically heads higher after the completion of the pattern. In both instances, the price dipping below the neckline signals the true reversal of the trend in question which means the security will now be moving in the opposite direction. This breakout point is often the ideal point to go either short or long depending. It is important to keep in mind, however, that the security is unlikely to continue smoothly in the direction the pattern suggests. As such, you will want to keep an eye out for what is called a throwback move.

Gann

While not universally trusted, Gann indicators have been used by traders for decades and remain a useful way of determining the direction a specific currency is likely to move next. Gann angles are used to determine certain elements of the chart include price, time and pattern which makes it easier to determine the future, past and even present of the market as well as how that information will determine the future of the price.

While you could be forgiven for thinking they are similar to trend lines, Gann angles are actually a different beast entirely. They are, in fact, a series of diagonal lines that move at a fixed rate and can likely be generated by your trading program. When they are compared to a trend line you will notice the Gann angle makes it possible for users to determine a true price at a specific point in the future assuming the current trend continues at its current strength. Due to the fact that all times exist on the same line, the Gann angle can then also be used to predict resistance, support, and direction strength as well as the timing on bottoms and tops as well. Gann angles are typically used to determine likely points of support and resistance and it is easy to get started with as it only requires the trade to determine the proper scale for the chart before drawing in the relevant Gann angles from the primary bottoms to the tops. Essentially, this means that they make it less complicated for the trader to properly frame the market and thus makes it easier for them to predict the way the market is likely to move in the future based on the way it is currently moving in the predetermined framework.

Angles that indicate a positive trend determine support and

angles that show a downward trend outline resistance. This means that by understanding the accurate angle of a chart, the trader can more easily determine the best time to buy or sell far more simply than what could otherwise be the case. When utilizing Gann angles, it is crucial that you keep in mind all the different things that can potentially cause the market to change between specific angles.

Cup and Handle Formation

The cup and handle formation most commonly appears if the given security reaches a peak price before dropping off significantly for a prolonged amount of time. Sooner than later, however, the security will rebound, which is the perfect time to buy. This is an indicator of a trend that is rapidly rising which means you are going to want to take advantage of it as soon as possible before you miss out. The handle will form on the cup when those who purchased the security at the previous high-water mark and couldn't wait any longer begin to sell which makes new investors interested who then begin to buy as well. This type of formation does not typically form quickly, and indeed, has been known to take a year or more to become visible. Ideally, you will then be able to take advantage of this trend as soon as the handle starts to form. If you see the cup and handle forming, you will still want to consider any other day to day patterns that may be interfering with the overall trend as they are going to go a long way when it comes to determining the actual effectiveness of buying in at a specific point.

Trend Lines

Trend lines represent the typical direction that a given underlying asset is likely to move in and, thus, can be very beneficial for traders to highlight prior to trading.

This is easier said than done, however, due to the high degree of volatility that assets of all types experience on a regular basis. As such, you will find it much more useful to consider only the highs and lows that the underlying asset experiences as this will make it far easier to determine a workable pattern. Once you have determined the highs and the lows for the underlying asset it then becomes much easier to determine if the highs are increasing while the lows are decreasing or vice versa. You will also want to remain alert to the possibility of sidewise trends, where the price doesn't move much of anywhere, as this is a sign that you should avoid trading for the time being. When watching the trend lines, you will likely notice that the price movement of a given underlying asset tends to bounce off the same high and low points time after time. These are what are known as resistance and support levels and identifying them makes it easier for you to determine the supply and demand of the coin in question. The support level is the level that the price is unlikely to drop below because there are always going to be traders who are willing to buy at that point, driving demand back up.

Once the price reaches the point where traders feel the price is unlikely to go any higher, they start to sell, and a level of resistance is created.

Moving Averages

The most commonly used confirmation tool is one that is referred to as the moving average convergence divergence or MACD for short. This tool measures the amount of difference that there is between two averages that have been smoothed to minimize ancillary noise. The difference between the two results is then further smoothed by the process before then being matched against the moving average that it relates to as well. If the resulting smoothed average is still greater than the existing moving average, then you can be sure that the positive trend you were chasing actually exists. Meanwhile, if the smoothed average ends up below the existing moving average than any negative trends will be confirmed instead. The moving average convergence divergence indicator is a type of oscillating indicator that primarily moves between zero and the centerline. If the MACD value is high then you can assume the related underlying asset is nearly overbought and if the value is low, then the stock is nearly oversold. The MACD chart is typically based on a combination of several EMAs. These averages can be based on any timeframe, though the most common is the 12-26-9 chart. This chart is typically broken into multiple parts, the first of which is the 26-day and 12-day chart. Mixing up the EMAs will allow you to more accurately gauge the level of momentum that the trend you are tracking is experiencing. If the 12-day EMA ends up above the 26-day EMA, then you can assume the underlying stock in on an uptrend and the reverse indicates a downtrend. If the 12-day EMA increases more quickly than the 26-day EMA then the uptrend is going to be even more well-pronounced.

However, if the 12-day EMA moves closer to the 26-day EMA then you can safely assume that it is starting to slow, and the momentum is waning, which means it is going to take the trend with it. The MACD uses the EMA by considering the difference between them once they are plotted out. If the 26-day and the 12-day are the same, then the MACD equals out to 0. If the 12-day ends up at a higher point than the 26-day then you can assume the MACD is positive, if not, it will be negative. The greater the difference between the two, the greater the difference between the MAACD line and zero. From there, you will then want to take into account the 9-day EMA as well. The 9-day EMA is different in that it determines the trend of the AMCD line as opposed to that of the stock price. As such, if the 9-day EMA smooths out the movement of the MACD line the results are going to be far more manageable. If the result then generates a trend that indicates a negative amount of divergence, then you can be quite certain that the positive trend that is currently taking place is ultimately going to hit a level of resistance that it simply won't be able to overcome.

Chapter 5: Put Them All Together

This chapter is going to be one of the most brutally honest sections, and this chapter we're going to talk about combining all the methods to see substantial gains with options trading. For some of you that might not know, options trading Stock Investing and forex trading are very similar. Which is why it is essential to understand the basics first, since you have understood the basics by now, we will talk about how to find success with options trading using the techniques provided to you in this book. And also go through a Q&A, which will allow you to get a better understanding of options trading and how it can benefit you or befall you.

Finding Success in Options

Since you understand the basics of options trading, you are ready to learn the strategies that traders use to attain success on the market. As we tried to drive home in the previous chapter, success in stock trading is all about how you approach the game. Understanding what you are attempting to accomplish with your trades as well as appreciating that less is more when it comes to trading. Before we jump into the strategies that will aid you in turning a buck in stock trading, let's spend a moment reiterating some of the essential concepts that have led us to this point. There are many vital points that you need to understand before you even start talking about strategies.

Successful Trading Strategies

When all is said in done, you are the one responsible for turning your venture into stock trading into a successful endeavor. That is one of the great things about Options. You do not have a boss screaming down your neck, telling you to do something that you do not agree with. You can come up with your trading plan based on your research and your knowledge. That being said, success can come more quickly for some than for others, and a lot of the time this has to do with approaching this endeavor with the right strategy. In this chapter, we will provide you with three strategies designed to help you make this foray into Options as profitable as possible (with as little loss as possible).

Strategy 1. Buy Low and Sell High

This is a strategy that we have discussed before, and it's not as straightforward as it seems. If you began stock trading today with $25,000 in your pocket and access to a trading platform, all ready and raring to go, how would you know what is low and what is high? It's your first day. Naturally, for you to understand what would represent an excellent small investment and conversely what is high, you need to have some knowledge of the exchange rate history of that stock. Maybe the exchange rate for Japanese yen seems low but compared to last year or a few months ago, it's a little high. Now it would not be a good time to buy. Maybe the pound seems low right now, but yesterday the British government announced that the first round of the Brexit negotiations with the EU failed and therefore the pound may have room to go lower than it is when you logged onto your trading platform. Maybe you should wait and see what the pound is later today or tomorrow and buy then. The point here is that buying low and selling high requires understanding the patterns associated with that stock and what might cause it to go up or down. And that's merely the buying side of things. Once you have bought low, you need to figure out when you are going to sell. This is where a good trading plan will come into play. A good idea will prevent you from selling too soon, or even not selling soon enough.

Strategy 2. Focus on Not Losing Money Rather Than on Making Money

This may not be an easy strategy to understand initially, in part because not losing money and making money seem like two sides of the same coin. They are, but they are not identical. One of the personality types that is associated with difficulty in finding success in trading is the impulsive type. This type of person wants to make money, and they want to make it quick. They have a vague strategy about how they plan on doing that, but the most important thing to them is that they have a high account balance to make as many trades as they need to turn a profit. This is the wrong approach. Currencies are not the same as stocks. The value of a stock may change very little even over a week, so I strategy that involves a lot of trades to make money is usually not the best. You want to have a crystal-clear idea of when you are going to but, yes, because you want to make money, but mostly because you don't want to lose. Every market that involves exchanges, like the stock market, has some inherent risk, and stock trading is risky, too, because you may be tempted to give up the advantage you have to try and make money quickly.

Strategy 3. Develop a Sense of Sentiment Analysis

Alright, the third strategy was going to be about Fibonacci

retracement, which is a type of technical analysis of the market, but as this is the basics of stock trading, we are going to go into a different strategy that is not any easier than a Fibonacci retracement, just different. Sentiment analysis is a term that is used in many different specialties, not just finance, and it is not easy to describe. It is essentially a type of analysis that is not based on a chart showing exchange rates over time (technical analysis) or on an understanding of a factor that might today be affecting the value of the stock (fundamental analysis). Sentiment analysis attempts to gauge the tone of the market, the direction the market is heading in, by parsing all of the available information. A key to understanding sentiment analysis is likening it to public opinion. The economy may be booming, people have more money in their pocket, so the stock of this hypothetical country should increase in value, but maybe it doesn't. Maybe there is something that is causing the market to be bearish and which therefore might cause the stock to drop. As you perhaps can tell, as this analysis is not based on any concrete information, it can be thought of as intuitive, and no one has intuition on day 1. Let's be honest about that. Intuition comes from experience. But the purpose of this strategy is to introduce to you the idea that not the stock trading market, like any market is not going to behave like a machine because it's not a machine. Exchanges are places where human beings come together, and humans are unpredictable, often in a frustrating way. Perhaps one day, stock trading may be handled by machines (that wouldn't be fun), but that day is far off, and so you will have to develop your sense of where the market seems to be going and use this as a strategy to achieve success in this endeavor.

Frequently Asked Questions

- **Question 1. What Is the Stock Trading Market or Options?**

  The stock trading market, also called Options or FX, is a marketplace where various actors are engaged in buying and selling the stock. Stock trading has been around since the 19th century, at least, but it did not become big business until the 20th century when various economic accords made it profitable for banks to buy stock on a speculative pattern. Before the mid-19th century, exchange rates were strictly regulated by central banks, so it would not have been profitable for many institutions to speculate on the stock. As these regulations were relaxed, i.e., as most central banks ceased pegging their currencies to other currencies, it allowed the industry to develop where banks and other bodies could purchase stock to make a profit. Retail trading, or an individual purchasing stock to make a profit for themselves and not for a large bank or investment bank, did not become popular until the late

'90s when an electronic network was created that allowed brokers to buy and sell stock directly with the holders of capital, like the large banks.

- **Question 2. What Is an Options Broker? Will I Be an Options Broker?**

A stock trading broker-dealer is the contact that is actually engaged in the stock trade with the bank or other financial institution. As we mentioned in the first two chapters, stock trading was long a reserve of banks as they bought stock from other banks and helped to influence the value of stock in a world where a central bank no longer set stock value. The long and short of it is that you will necessarily be a trader engaged in stock trades with these broker-dealers. This book is designed to help traders gain a better understanding of the stock trading market so that they can enter it with confidence.

- **Question 3. What Role Will I Play in the Stock Trading Market?**

Your role in the stock trading market will be as a retail trader engaging in trades through a broker. You will most likely be using your capital to buy and sell the stock while the broker makes a profit by a minimal cut in the exchange or by the commission.

- **Question 4. Do I have to be a member of a professional organization to be involved in stock**

trading?

Brokers and other firms engaged in the stock trading market are required to become members of the National Futures Association (NFA) as well as other organizations that oversee securities and commodities exchange. Some retail traders will also become members of this organization, especially if they are working with a funded trading program.

- **Question 5. Do I need a certain minimum amount of capital to be involved in stock trading?**

There is no minimum account balance required to be involved in Options. Some brokers may need you to have a minimum, but this is often very low. Though you can trade with as little or as much capital as you want, it is essential to remember that the money to be made on an individual transaction is often very small, so if you are trading more significant numbers you are more likely to see a noticeable payout, both in the short term and the long term. Some people consider $10,000 or $20,000 to be the right amount for a retail trader to start with, but some traders begin with less than that.

- **Question 6. As a trader, do I have to work with a bank or can I operate independently from them?**

As a retail trader, you will be working with a broker. The

broker will be the ones making trades on your behalf, often through an electronic platform that directly connects you with another entity that is also attempting to make a trade.

- **Question 7. What level of access will I have on the stock trading as an independent trader?**

As a retail trader, you will not have access to the information on the interbank market that comes from the banks and which the brokers will have access to. You will have access to the information posted on the brokerage platform that you are using, most of which are closely tied to the exchange rates on the interbank market.

- **Question 8. Are there any risks associated with stock trading?**

Much like the stock market, there is always a risk that you will lose money while engaged in stock trading. You are essentially taking your account balance and making a (hopefully) informed decision on what to buy or sell and when. Though the goal is that, with a thorough trading plan, you will make money based on your exchanges, there is no guarantee that you will. Losses that you may experience may be dictated by your behavior, leaving aside the purchases that you make. For example, maybe you hold on to stock too long when you should have sold it days ago. Perhaps you should have waited until the price was a little lower to buy. Just like the stock market, participating with Options comes with risks.

- **Question 9. What is the interbank market? Will I have access to the interbank market as a trader?**

The interbank market is the marketplace that large banks use to make trades. Banks have vast reserves of capital and assets that allow them to easily make deals in the millions and billions of US dollar range every day. That is why they have they have an interbank market. The last thing they need is someone with \$10,000 walking into their market like they own the place. Joking aside, banks are dealing with high volumes and frequent activity. It makes more sense for you to interact with them through a broker, and this is basically how the system works. You will not have access to the interbank market as a retail trader.

- **Question 10. Is it true that I will not have to work with a dealing desk if I choose to trade with individual dealers over others?**

To answer this question, let us try to understand what a dealing desk is. This refers to the site where a stock trading contract, an agreement to exchange say X amount of US dollars for X amount of stocks, occurs. The broker that you use will have a dealing desk that they use to trade stock. The idea is that if you do not have to go through a dealing office, you may get better pricing. The reason for that is that, in a dealing desk scenario, you are basically on the other side of a trade from the broker so there is a perception that the broker has an interest in maybe charging you more than a non-dealing desk broker would. This may or may not be correct, but the idea that you do not have to deal with a dealing desk at all is a myth. As you are not a bank and are not able to purchase stock as an independent financial entity, your purchase will involve dealing with someone's dealing desk, even if you are not directly dealing with a broker that has a dealing office.

- **Question 11. So basically, if I am stock trading using a stock trading platform, I am primarily dealing with a broker?**

Unless you are a professional trader working for a financial institution or a broker with a license to trade on ECN, then you are a retail trader dealing with a broker.

Question 12. Why is it that stock prices are necessarily the same no matter which platform or dealer I use?

Many factors influence stock values, including actions that central banks may take to attempt to stabilize the stock. The large banks involved in the interbank market are vast influencers of stock values so individual brokers, though they may quote slightly different prices, do not have much wiggle room when it comes to prices as they are mostly either getting their stock from a bank or they are setting the costs of their reserves based on the rates set by the bank. For this reason, one could argue that choosing one broker or another should probably be based on how they make their money, by taking a cut or by the commission, and not by individual prices as the variation here is not much.

- **Question 13. Is options trading replacing the stock trading market?**

So, this is a question people often ask. Stock is all over the news as of late because many of the early investors have quickly seen their relatively small initial investments transformed into millions almost overnight. Although stock, in particular, does not appear to be going anywhere anytime soon and indeed seems likely only to grow in the coming decade, it is difficult to say whether it will ever compete with stock trading. Although much of stock trading is operated independently of government involvement as exchange rates are no longer commonly fixed (at least not for the major currencies), the stock is still tied closely to nations and governments can always intervene to make sure that their share does not lose value. Stocks, on the other hand, is no different from a group of private individuals coming together and agreeing to utilize a stock amongst themselves. Though it may grow in value as the stock has, there is nothing in place to maintain that value. What is worth $10,000 today might be worth 10 cents tomorrow, and that is unlikely to happen to a significant stock on the stock trading as a government can use various means to prevent their share from falling. The potential payout from investing with capital today is possibly more significant than they are with Options, but that is because the risk is more significant. The stock industry runs the risk of becoming a bubble that may one day burst, while this is not true of stock trading. As long as there are governments in operation, it is unlikely that stock trading will ever become unprofitable, even if it means that the profit margins are relatively small.

- **Question 14. How much money can I expect to make on Options?**

This is not an easy question to answer as it is impacted by numerous variables, not least of which is how much capital you have to invest in the first place. In reality, though, account balance or money is merely one of the variables that influence how successful you will be on stock trading, and it may not even be the most important one. Many retail traders with large amounts of capital to invest fail, losing much of their money, while traders investing less often succeed. Success in this business is as much a function of how you use your money as it is impacted by how much money you have. You have to approach stock trading with a mind towards developing a strategy that you will use and stick to that strategy. It is easy to fall into the trap of spending all of your account balance on a few trades early on. You need to make sure that you understand the long-term nature of this business and that you may only make a few dollars here and there on trades.

As you can tell nothing is cut clear, which is why it is essential to understand the basics of options trading at go by your gut. One of the best advice I can give you is to go by your gut but do not get emotionally attached to your trade. This is very important to understand as if you get emotionally attached to your trade, and you will have disappointments later on. Keeping that in mind, you need to make sure you fully understand all the techniques before you act on it as it can lead to disappointments if you don't do it correctly. When it comes to any trading, nothing is guaranteed one day you could be making a lot of money, and the next day it will dropdown. But if you look at the charts correctly, you will be in a much better position to being successful over and over again. At the end of the day, it is just a mind game and knowing the right market. So, make sure you treat it as such and have fun with it.

Chapter 6: How to Avoid Risk

Between the many variables of options trading, it's difficult for beginners to focus on the direction of the move, the timing, the price of the underlying stock or index, the stock's volatility, its dividends, and perhaps even changing interest rates. Just familiarizing themselves with options trading terminology can be a daunting task, but couple that with the beginner's lack of knowledge and confidence, and you have the perfect storm. With most other activities, mistakes can be easily rectified. If you forget to consider all elements to a decision, usually it won't result in significant financial losses. However, make a mistake in options trading, and you could lose your hat, boots, and the horse you rode in on. The thrills and excitement of doing something new like options trading can turn into your worst nightmare if you start your trading career, making small mistakes that cost you big money.

Recognizing the traps that beginners fall into can be a game-changer. Knowing how to avoid the common mistakes most beginners make will put your head and shoulders above the rest of the newbies. So, take a look at the following mistakes many novice traders make. In fact, keep a list of these mistakes close to your computer if you're doing online options trading, just to act as a reminder when you're tempted to consider a real novice move.

- **Mistake #1:** Beginners Treat Options Trading Like Equity Investment

  This mistake especially applies to those who have some experience trading equity stocks. They tend to treat options trading in the same way they do equity securities, failing to recognize these are completely different financial instruments. Because there are some familiar patterns between the two, those with some experience buying stock, fail to take advantage of all the variables in options trading. Experienced investors have been taught that adage—buy low, sell high.

  They have difficulties wrapping their heads around the fact that with options there are times when you have to reverse the process by buying low, selling high. For you with a little experience, you may need to reboot with a "start over" when it comes to playing by a whole new set of options trading rules. If you are a beginner in options trading, open your mind to a more volatile, flexible, and potentially profitable market.

- **Mistake #2**: Beginners Start with OTM Call Options

  Buying out-of-the-money (OTM) call options seem to the beginner to be a great place to start. It follows that familiar pattern of buy low—sell high, right? To set the record straight, buying OTM calls outright is one of the most challenging ways to consistently turn a profit with options trading. Relying so heavily on OTM's may cause beginners to suffer losses early on, convincing them that options are what they've often heard—too risky. Buying calls are fine, but only buying calls create additional issues for the beginner who is already having trouble focusing on all the new knowledge spinning around in their heads. Remember, with OTMs; you have to be right about both the timing and the direction of the move. If you're right about one and wrong about the other, your trade may result in a total loss of the option premium you paid. Do yourself and your pocketbook a favor. Learn other strategies so that you can improve your ability to earn some solid returns as you build your knowledge and your portfolio.

- **Mistake #3**: Beginners Tend to Use One Strategy in All Market Conditions

Options trading is not a "one-strategy-fits-all" endeavor. It's impossible to take advantage of all the flexibility options trading offers if you only use one favorite trading strategy regardless of the market condition.

Even if you are still making small profits, think of how much higher your profits could be if you were able to implement many more of the techniques of options trading. In Chapter 6, we're going to be examining spreads. As a beginner, you'll want to learn as much as possible about buying spreads offers. Increasing your understanding of spreads will enable you to know when and how to use them in options trading. One of the great benefits of trading spreads instead of buying options is that it neutralizes the effect of time decay. Again, with the foreign language, right? No worries, we'll discuss spreads further in Chapter 6. If nothing else, remember this: even though spreads may limit the maximum potential gains, it also limits the maximum potential losses. So, beginners, be patient. Don't try to make all your money in one trade. For beginners, it should be all about baby steps.

- **Mistake #4**: Beginners Fail to Have an Exit Plan

  When you're in the middle of a contract, emotions run high, especially with beginners. That's one of the most challenging things to control, your emotions. Whether you are excited about what could be substantial profits or depressed about a dismal loss, letting your emotions get the better of you is nonproductive. One of the ways to avoid letting your emotions dictate your actions is to have an exit plan in place in advance of the contract. You cannot be led by the whims of the market. By having an advance plan, you can control your actions in all markets. It's important to set both upside and downside exit points, along with the timeframes you plan to follow. Once the plan is set, be determined to stick to your plan. It's only natural that you don't want to leave money on the table, so when things are good, you're tempted to ride it out a little longer.

  However, you'll make profits more consistently when you follow your plan—not to mention the fact that following your plan makes it much easier to sleep at night. When you follow your plan, you won't be sitting on pins and needles wondering if you've made the right decision. When you pre-set your timeframes, it takes much of the guesswork and worries out of trading. You have a system that works, so let it. The cost of pushing the envelope is too high a price to pay for a few more dollars. When you decide ahead of time what gains you will be satisfied with, then be happy when you reach them. You've accomplished what you set out to do. Likewise, when you decide what you will be able to tolerate as a loss, then cut your losses and move on to the next transaction.

- **Mistake #5**: Beginners Play Make-up

When beginners sustain some heavy losses, the temptation is there to want to make it up by doubling down. When you're beginning to trade, and you find an option that's going your way, it's so tempting to ride that horse 'til it drops. A word of warning—don't do it! Set some absolutes. Absolutes are necessary when you first begin options trading. Telling yourself you'll "never"... or, it's "always" good to... will keep you on track. Later on, as you gain more knowledge and experience, you can be a bit more flexible. However, for now, have "absolute" resolve. Remember that owning options aren't like holding stock, so doubling down to play "makeup" when you're experiencing loss just doesn't make sense most of the time. Options are derivatives; their prices don't move like stock nor do they have the same properties as the underlying stock. You've got time decay to consider, and that can throw a wrench into the works. It's better to take a small loss than suffering a blow-up when things get dicey.

- **Mistake #6:** Beginners Often Don't Factor in Options Liquidity

A liquid market is one where you have plenty of buyers and sellers who are ready and willing to trade. If an option is said to be liquid, it can be quickly bought or sold without creating much of a price movement. In other words, can you look at your option and quickly figure its probability? Is it likely that the next trade will happen at approximately the same price as the last? Options trading is, by nature, not as liquid as the stock market. There are so many variables to consider in options that it causes illiquidity. If you have the opportunity to buy a more liquid stock, but you are starting at a 10 percent loss point, you may want to rethink your position. Here's a good rule of thumb for beginners—or any options trader, for that matter. Time to introduce a new term: open interest. Open interest is the number of outstanding options contracts at the same strike price and expiration date that have been bought or sold to open a position. Opening transactions increase open interest, and closing transactions do just the opposite— they decrease it. When options trading, you want to make sure the open interest is equal to 40 times or more the number of contracts traded.

For example, to trade a 10-lot, your liquidity should be 10 x 40, or an open interest of at least 400 contracts. Open interest is always calculated at the end of every business day. Following this rule-of-thumb to trade liquid will save you the worry of trying to move forward with illiquid stocks, even when the strike price seems much more reasonable. There are plenty of liquid opportunities out there. Keep looking for liquid.

- **Mistake #7**: Beginners Don't Understand Buy Backs

  If the market is right, be open to buying back short options early. Sometimes traders justify their hesitancy to buy back short options by reasoning that they'll have to pay more commissions, or they're betting that the contract will expire and be worthless, or even that they want to squeeze every penny out of their trade. Waiting too long to buy back a short option can turn on you. Here's a way to determine when to buy back short options.

  When you can keep 80 percent of what you initially gained from selling the option--buy it back right away.

- **Mistake #8**: Beginners Forget to Factor in Dividends and Earnings When Planning Options Strategies

If you decide to hold short options near or in-the-money close to the ex-dividend date, you risk early assignment, which means you will not collect dividends. Your risk of assignment is especially high if the dividend is expected to be large. Remember, as an options holder, you only have a right to buy—there is no ownership of stock. To take advantage of dividends, you must buy the stock before the ex-dividend date. As options traders, you also need to factor in whether you're trading during a stock's earning season.

If you are, your option is likely to be higher priced. Let me illustrate my point by using a real-world example. Remember how we previously discussed insurance being an option. You pay the insurance company a fee for assuming the risk, right? Okay, pretend you own a beachfront home on the Florida coastline. You've decided you need to look for a new provider for your homeowner's insurance. It would be safe to say that your premiums will be higher if you purchase homeowner's insurance during hurricane season, right? This will be the case if you are trading options as well. Not to say you can't purchase during the earning season, just keep in mind your premiums will likely be higher, and the option will be more volatile. For beginners, it might be easier to predict profits if you wait for earning season to pass so you won't be dealing with the possibility of inflated prices for the underlying stock.

- **Mistake #9**: Beginners Are Ignorant About Early Assignment

Beginners rarely think about assignments and can be thrown for a loop when it happens to them. Let me explain what is meant by assignment. The definition of an assignment is as follows.

An assignment is the transfer of an individual's rights or property to another person or business (10). Assignments can happen when the written option is exercised by the options holder. If a call option is assigned, the options writer is forced to sell the obligated quantity of the underlying security at the strike price. It would be more profitable to sell the options. If a put option is assigned, the options writer will have to buy the obligated quantity of the underlying security at the strike price. For this reason, most options are exercised before the time of expiration. The deeper in-the-money the short option is, the more likely it will be exercised. Exercising a call means that the trader will have to spend cash now, versus later when the options could bring them greater profits. An example of a real-world assignment is when a mortgage company sells off a mortgage to a third party, like another lender. The borrowers aren't informed until after the transaction, even when it might mean a change in terms and conditions of the contract. In discussing these common mistakes that beginner options traders make, we have also introduced you to some new terms and trading strategies.

Chapter 7: Advanced Options Trading

Now it is time to move on to some of the steps that you can take to maximize your profits with the help of options. Options are a great way to earn an advantage because they allow you a way to reduce your exposure and the amount of risk that you take on while increasing the number of profits that you could potentially make. Some of the tips that you can use to help maximize your earnings while options trading includes:

You Can Profit No Matter the Market Situation

One of the first things that you will notice when you are working on the options market is that you can benefit from any location in the market when you work with options. Most of the strategies that work with this investment vehicle are carried out by combining the different option positions, and sometimes they will even use the underlying area of the stock. You can use either different trading strategies, or work with a few together, to profit no matter what market situation is going on. When you enter into the market with options, you always stand to make a considerable amount of profits, while still keeping your risk to a minimum.

Ordinary stock trading isn't as reliable, and it comes with a lot more risk. The most crucial aspects of options trading are to know when you should enter a trade and how you should exit it. Knowing how and when to exit will ensure that you keep any losses to a minimum and that you can increase your profits as much as possible. You will find that options strategies are considered one of the most versatile when it comes to the financial market. They are going to provide investors and traders alike with a lot of profit-making opportunities, and there is a limited amount of risk and exposure present. This is one of the main reasons that a lot of investors like to take some time and invest in options instead of the other asset choices. Since you can profit no matter what the market situation is doing, this gives you a lot of freedom when working with options. But it also means that you may have to learn a lot more strategies than usual. You should learn at least a few plans for a rising market, for a stagnant market, and a downturn market. This will ensure that you are ready to go no matter which way the market is heading. While the ability to make a profit in any exchange is a great thing and can open up many new opportunities to make money compared to just investing in the stock market, it does make things a bit trickier to work with. You have to understand where the market is going, you have to know which strategies work for the different market directions, and you have to be ready to switch back and forth depending on how the market is doing.

Take Advantage of the Volatility of Options to Make a Profit

Options have some similarities to stocks, but they are a bit different. And one place you will notice these differences is with the time limit. Shares can be held for as short of a period, or as long of a period, as you want, but options have an expiration date. This means that the time you get to make the trade is going to be limited. And as a trader, missing this window is going to be a costly mistake, one that you need to avoid if at all possible. If this chance is lost, then it may be a very long time before you see it again. This is why it is never a good idea to work with a long-term strategy when you are trying to trade with options. Strategies, such as working with the average down, are seen as bad choices for options trading because you don't get the right time frame to see them happen. Also, make sure that you are careful about margin requirements. Depending on what these are, they could have a significant impact on the requirements for the number of funds you can invest. There are also times when multiple factors may affect a favorable price. For instance, the cost of the asset you choose may go up, which is usually seen as a good thing. But it is possible that any of the accruing benefits could be eroded due to other factors, such as volatility, time decay, and dividend payment. These constraints mean that you need to learn how to follow some of the different strategies for profit-taking.

Always Set a Profit-Taking Stop Loss

The following advice that you should follow is to set up a profit-taking stop loss. You can set up a stop loss at about five percent. This means that you want it to reach a target price of $100 if the trailing target is going to be $95. If the upward trend does continue and the price gets to $120, then the trailing goal, assuming the 5 percent from before, is going to become $114. And it would keep going up from there, with the amount of profit that you wish to make in the process. Now, let's say that the price is going to start to fall. When this happens, you will need to exit and then collect the profits at this level, or the trailing target that you set. This ensures that you get to enjoy some protection as the price increases, and then you will exit the trade as soon as the price starts to turn around. The thing that you need to remember here is that the stop loss levels should never be too high or too low. If they are too small, you will be kicked out of the market too soon in most cases. But if they are too large, they will make it impossible to enjoy profit-taking.

Sell Covered Call Options Against Long Positions

Selling options Is an income-generating process that is pretty lucrative. Depending on the amount of risk that you take and what kinds of trades you decide to do, you could easily take home more than two percent in returns each month. However, this is not the only method you can use to make it rich on the market. You can also go with something that is known as naked puts and sells these. This is similar in the way of trading stocks or shares that you don't own. When you go through the process of selling naked put options, you will be able to free up some of your time to do more. Stock trading allows you to have an opportunity to trade stocks of shares that you don't already own, and then you can earn a profit. This will free up your capital, allowing you to invest it or trade with it indefinitely. To make this method work, it is best if you work with stocks that you already understand well or those that you wouldn't mind owning. This way, you know when there are any significant changes to the capital, and you can make some changes to the way you invest before the market turns and harms your profits. There is still a level of hedging that is associated with this options trading method, so you must always be on the lookout for that.

Pick the Right Strategy

There are a lot of different strategies that you can choose to work with, and we will discuss a few of them in the following chapters. And often the one that you pick will lead you to find the right options to sell. Some of the options trading strategies are going to work in a downturn, some are going to work the best in an upturn, and some do well when the market is more stagnant. When you pick out a strategy, you will then be able to choose the options that fit in with that strategy the best. With that said, there are a few guidelines that you can learn to follow when it is time to purchase an option for trading. Following these guidelines will make it easier for you to identify the options that you should choose to make a good profit.

Determine whether the market is bullish or bearish. Also, make sure that you determine whether you are strongly bullish, or just mildly bullish. This can make a difference in how the market is doing and which assets you would like to work with. Think about how volatile the market is right now and how it could affect your strategy with options trading. Also, you can think about the status of the market at the time. Is the market currently calm, or is there a lot of volatility that shows up? If it is not very high, then you should be able to buy the call options based on the underlying stock, and these are usually seen as relatively inexpensive. Consider the strike price and the expiration date of any options you want to trade-in. If you only have a few shares at this time, then this may make it the best time to purchase more of the stock or asset. Your overall goal of working with the options trading market is to make as much profit as possible. No one goes into the market, or any investment, with the idea that they want to lose money. But if you follow some of the tips above, you will be able to maximize your profits and see some great results.

As an options trader, there are many different types of assets that you can work with, and even different markets that you can enter. Getting started provides you with a lot of choices to help you earn a profit, no matter which direction the market is heading. When you are ready to get started with options trading, make sure to use the following tips to make things easier and to help you become more successful with all of your trades.

Always Be Flexible When Trading Options

When you are working with stocks and some of the other securities out there, you will need to do it on the idea of buying low and selling high. But when you are working with options, this approach often doesn't meet all of your needs. With options, you can profit even if the market is going down. Options work well no matter what the market conditions are, either there is a lot of volatility, stagnation, downturns, and upturns. As someone new to the idea of trading, you need to think about all of the different options before you. Always be ready to look at all the various opportunities that are out there, and be prepared to seize them, even in places you may not have considered before. Flexibility is great with this kind of trading because it allows you to see more opportunities and new trading strategies in the process. Options can be a different game compared to what you may be used to with other forms of trading. If you have been working in the stock market in the past, then you may be unsure about the differences. Make sure that you learn how to trade in options and the differences between stocks and options before you get started with this at all. This ensures that you are ready to take on more opportunities and still earn as many profits as possible.

Use Options to Hedge and Minimize Your Risk

Hedging is a great technique that you can use as an options trader to help to reduce your exposure and reduce some of your chances. So, let's say that you hold onto a stock from a blue-chip company. You are worried about how the stock may end up going down in value in the following weeks. To avoid this disaster, something that could cost you a lot of money, you would instead choose to do a put option. This allows you to sell the shares at market price, even if the number of your stocks end up dipping. This is an excellent method to use to save your investments and protect your money. The issue of hedging is such a compelling one that many traders will try out options to keep their investments safe. Remember that there isn't any guarantee and it is possible that you could lose out on this for a bit. But the history of options and functional analysis can show that this can help increase your chances of being successful with options.

Working with Break-Even Points

Another thing to consider when it comes to options trading is the break-even points. As a trader, you must understand these break-even points, so you know the best time to get out of a trade, and you don't exit too early and take a loss without even realizing it. The break-even points often going to be a specific point, whether it's high or a low, that the stock needs to reach before you can start to earn a profit. These break-even points need to also take into account the amount you paid to get into the trade, as well as any fees or costs that you got from your broker to get started. Figuring out your break-even points can help you to avoid some of the shocks later on, and any surprises that come out then. Many times, traders forget to work with the fees and commissions that they have to pay their broker when it comes to the trades. They will only figure out the break-even part based on how much they originally invested. Then, when they take the money out at the break-even point, and they have to pay the commissions and fees, they end up losing money in the process. Figuring these numbers out ahead of time an take out all of the surprises. Figure out how much it will cost to get into the trade. Then figure out any extra fees and commissions that you will owe to the brokers when you are all done. From there, you can determine what the break-even point is to get started. You can then move on from here and figure out the point where you can begin to earn a profit and make your plans on whether this is a good trade or not, based on those calculations.

Always Do Your Research

Before you enter into any trade with options, make sure that you do sufficient amounts of research. Charts are going to be crucial when you work on your technical analysis. But this isn't always enough on its own. When you begin, take some time to figure out what kinds of stocks and underlying assets interest you the most, and then do some further research into those particular assets. Take your time to learn about the markets that you want to enter. Watch the charts and find out how they work. Learn the history of those assets, and about the companies that own them. Talk to a broker or someone else who works in the market and get their advice.

The more research you can do ahead of time with these options, the easier it will be. You will gain a full understanding of the assets, and be better prepared to make the right decisions when it is time to do your trades. You will find that there are a ton of different sources that you can use to help you do your research and utilizing as many of them as possible can make a big difference in how well you are going to do with your trades in the long run. Before even entering into the market, make sure that you spend at least a few weeks researching the options and their underlying assets that you are most interested in. The more knowledge that you can add to your arsenal, and the better you understand these underlying assets, the better you will be able to do with your trades. With that said, you will need to take some time to find the best resources. You will need to find charts so that you can learn the history of the underlying assets. Find several assets that you would like to work with, and bring out as many historical charts as possible. Then move on to other tables about the industry as a whole, and even the whole market, to see where these underlying assets come from. This helps you to get a good idea of whether it is performing under average, at average, or over average based on how other companies are doing. You shouldn't stop right there, though. You must make sure that you work with additional resources as well. You need to have information from different online sources (make sure that they are reputable and stay up to date), newspapers, and more. You need to know what is going on in the market and the industry, and how that is going to affect any of the different assets that you want to trade-in. You never know when a change in the market can make a significant change in how your options, and their underlying asset, are going to behave.

Going with the Flow

As much as possible, you should go with the flow and do a trend with the trend. With options trading, you will often find that the trend is going to be your friend. This can be true in any kind of investment that you choose to go with, and even seasoned traders know that jumping on the trend, especially early on, is an easy way to make some good money in the market. Any time that you are looking at underlying security and trying to assess its worth, never try to make guesses or estimates. Especially when you are a beginner, these estimates are going to be wrong, and your investing actions are going to be like gambling. But if you trust the trend (which means you have to watch the market and the charts), you will be right most of the time, and you will earn a profit on your trading endeavors.

Your Exit Point, or Your Escape Plan

All successful traders have one thing in common, they have a strategy in place, and they choose to stick with it. They refuse to let their emotions take charge of their trading goals. Feelings are unreasonable and erratic, while a trading plan is thought-out and logical. As part of your trading plan, you must have a clearly defined exit strategy, one that you stick with no matter what. To keep this simple, that exit point is the place where you will close out the trade and walk away if the business starts to head south and you start to lose money. If you follow this, you can protect your investment, and it ensures that you don't stay in the market for too long. But if you let the emotions take control, you can end up losing a lot of money because you remain in the trade too long. Before you ever enter into a business, make sure that you list out your exit points. Know precisely what criteria need to come into play for you to stay in business, and which ones you need to follow to leave the company. If you can stick with this, you can limit your losses and ensure that you can make the most profit possible.

Chapter 8: Tips for Success

While sticking to your plan, even when your emotions are telling you to ignore it, is the mark of a successful trader, this in no way means that you must blindly follow your plan 100 percent of the time. You will, without a doubt, find yourself in a situation from time to time where your plan is going to be rendered completely useless by something outside of your control. You need to be aware enough of your plan's weaknesses, as well as changing market conditions, to know when following your predetermined course of action is going to lead to failure instead of success. Knowing when the situation is changing, versus when your emotions are trying to hold sway is something that will come with practice, but even being aware of the disparity is a huge step in the right direction.

- **Avoid trades that are out of the money**: While there are a few strategies out there that make it a point of picking up options that are currently out of the money, you can rest assured that they are most certainly the exception, not the rule. Remember, the options market is not like the traditional stock market, which means that even if you are trading options based on underlying stocks buying low and selling high is not a viable strategy. If a call has dropped out of the money, there is generally less than a 10 percent chance that it will return to acceptable levels before it expires which means that if you purchase these types of options what you are doing is little better than gambling, and you can find ways to gamble with odds in your favor of much higher than 10 percent. Avoid hanging on too tightly to your starter strategy. That doesn't mean that it is the last strategy that you are ever going to need, however, far from it. Your core trading strategy is one that should always be constantly evolving as the circumstances surrounding your trading habits change and evolve as well.

What's more, outside of your primary strategy you are going to want to eventually create additional plans that are more specifically tailored to various market states or specific strategies that are only useful in a narrow band of situations. Remember, the more prepared you are prior to starting a day's worth of trading, the greater your overall profit level is likely to be, it is as simple as that.

- **Utilize the spread**: If you are not entirely risk-averse when it comes to taking advantage of volatile trades, the best thing to do is utilize a spread as a way of both safeguarding your existing investments and, at the same time, making a profit. To utilize a long spread, you are going to want to generate a call and a put, both with the same underlying asset, expiration details, and share amounts but with two very different strike prices. The call will need to have a higher strike price and will mark the upper limit of your profits and the put will have a lower strike price that will mark the lower limit of your losses.

When creating a spread, it is important that you purchase both halves at the same time as doing it in fits and spurts can add extraneous variables to the formula that are difficult to adjust for properly.

- **Never proceed without knowing the mood of the market**: While using a personalized trading plan is always the right choice, having one doesn't change the fact that it is extremely important to consider the mood of the market before moving forward with the day's trades. First and foremost, it is important to keep in mind that the collective will of all of the traders who are currently participating in the market is just as much as a force as anything that is more concrete, including market news. In fact, even if companies release good news to various outlets and the news is not quite as good as everyone was anticipating it to be then related prices can still decrease. To get a good idea of what the current mood of the market is like, you are going to want to know the average daily numbers that are common for your market and be on the lookout for them to start dropping sharply. While a day or two of major fluctuation can be completely normal, anything longer than that is a sure sign that something is up. Additionally, you will always want to be aware of what the major players in your market are up to.

- **Never get started without a clear plan for entry and exit**: While finding your first set of entry/exit points can be difficult without experience to guide you, it is extremely important that you have them locked down prior to starting trading, even if the stakes are relatively low. Unless you are extremely lucky, starting without a clear idea of the playing field is going to do little but lose your money. If you aren't sure about what limits you should set, start with a generalized pair of points and work to fine-tune it from there.

More important than setting entry and exit points, however, is using them, even when there is still the appearance of money on the table. One of the biggest hurdles that new options traders need to get over is the idea that you need to wring every last cent out of each and every successful trade. The fact of the matter is that, as long as you have a profitable trading plan, then there will always be more profitable trades in the future which means that instead of worrying about a small extra profit you should be more concerned with protecting the profit that the trade has already netted you. While you may occasionally make some extra profit ignoring this advice, odds are you will lose far more than you gain as profits peak unexpectedly and begin dropping again before you can effectively pull the trigger. If you are still having a hard time with this concept, consider this: options trading is a marathon, not a sprint, slow and steady will always win the race.

- **Never double down**: When they are caught up in the heat of the moment, many new options traders will find themselves in a scenario where the best way to recoup a serious loss is to double down on the underlying stock in question at its newest, significantly lowered, price in an effort to make a profit under the assumption that things are going to turn around and then continue to do so to the point that everything is completely profitable once again. While it can be difficult to let an underlying stock that was once extremely profitable go, doubling down is rarely if ever going to be the correct decision. If you find yourself in a spot where you don't know if the trade you are about to make is actually going to be a good choice, all you need to do is ask yourself if you would make the same one if you were going into the situation blind, the answer should tell you all you need to know. If you find yourself in a moment where doubling down seems like the right choice, you are going to need to have the strength to talk yourself back down off of that investing ledge and to cut your losses as thoroughly as possible given the current situation. The sooner you cut your losses and move on from the trade that ended poorly, the sooner you can start putting energy and investments into a trade that still has the potential to make you a profit.

- **Never take anything personally**: It is human nature to build stories around, and therefore form relationships with, all manner of inanimate objects including individual stocks or currency pairs. This is why it is perfectly natural to feel a closer connection to particular trades, and possibly even consider throwing out your plan when one of them takes an unexpected dive. Thinking about and acting on are two very different things, however, which is why being aware of these tendencies are so important to avoid them at all costs.

This scenario happens just as frequently with trades moving in positive directions as it does negative, but the results are always going to be the same. Specifically, it can be extremely tempting to hang on to a given trade much longer than you might otherwise decide to simply because it is on a hot streak that shows no sign of stopping. In these instances, the better choice of action is to instead sell off half of your shares and then set a new target based on the updated information to ensure you are in a position to have your cake and eat it too.

- **Not taking your choice of broker seriously**: With so many things to consider, it is easy to understand why many new option traders simply settle on the first broker that they find and go about their business from there. The fact of the matter is, however, that the broker you choose is going to be a huge part of your overall trading experience which means that the importance of choosing the right one should not be discounted if you are hoping for the best experience possible. This means that the first thing that you are going to want to do is to dig past the friendly exterior of their website and get to the meat and potatoes of what it is they truly offer. Remember, creating an eye-catching website is easy, filling it will legitimate information when you have ill intent is much more difficult. First things first, this means looking into their history of customer service as a way of not only ensuring that they treat their customers in the right way, but also of checking to see that quality of service is where it needs to be as well.

Remember, when you make a trade; every second counts. This means that if you need to contact your broker for help with a trade you need to know that you are going to be speaking with a person who can solve your problem as quickly as possible. The best way to ensure the customer service is up to snuff is to give them a call and see how long it takes for them to get back to you. If you wait more than a single business day, take your business elsewhere as if they are this disinterested in a new client, consider what the service is going to be like when they already have you right where they want you. With that out the way, the next thing you will need to consider is the fees that the broker is going to charge in exchange for their services.

There is very little regulation when it comes to these fees which means it is definitely going to pay to shop around. In addition to fees, it is important to consider any account minimums that are required as well as any fees having to do with withdrawing funds from the account.

- **Find a Mentor**: When you are looking to go from causal trader to someone who trades successfully on the regular, there is only so much you can learn by yourself before you need a truly objective eye to ensure you are proceeding appropriately. This person can either be someone you know in real life, or it can take the form of one or more people online.

The point is you need to find another person or two who you can bounce ideas off of and whose experience you can benefit from. Options trading doesn't need to be a solitary activity; take advantage of any community you can find.

- **Knowledge is the key**: Without some type of information which you can use to assess your trades, you are basically playing at the roulette table. Even poker players show up to the table with a game plan. They can adapt to the circumstances and learn to read other players. That way, they can tell the contenders from the pretenders. Options trading is no different. If you are unable to use the information that is out there to your advantage, then what you will end up with is a series of guesses which may or may not play out.

Based purely on the law of averages you have a 50/50 chance of making money. That may not seem like bad odds, but a string of poor decisions will leave you in the poor house in no time. So, it is crucial that you become familiar with the various analytics and tools out there which you can use to your advantage. Bear in mind that everyone is going to be looking at the same information. However, it is up to you to figure out what can, or might, happen before everyone else does. This implies really learning and studying the numbers so that you can detect patterns and see where trends are headed, or where trends may reverse. The perfect antidote to that is vision and foresight. Practice building scenarios. Try to imagine what could happen is trends continue. Or, what would happen if trends reversed? What needs to happen in order for those trends to continue or reverse? When you ask yourself such tough questions, your knowledge and understanding begin to expand. Your mind will suddenly be able to process greater amounts of information while you generate your own contingency plans based on the multiple what-ifs. That may seem like a great deal of information to handle, but at the end of the day, any time spent in improving your trading acumen is certainly worth the effort.

Chapter 9: Put It All Together

Overtrading

Overtrading occurs when a trader or a broker buys or sells stocks in excessive quantity. This is not a good way to conduct a trade. Below are some of the disadvantages of overtrading. Capital loss Most traders overtrade with the expectation of earning an extra coin, but the majority of these trades end up with multiple losses. While overtrading, the trader opens multiple positions. In each, they invest a certain amount of money. In the end, the trader has high expectations that some if not all of the investments, will bear fruits. The biggest problem is that most of the time, the trades invest blindly. They fail to put into consideration the various principles governing trade. They may have overlooked the type of trade the choice. This could have been coupled up by failing to consider the various option strategies. As a result, they end up making wrong trade choices which results in a loss. It at all the trader took some time to evaluate these trades, and they could have avoided the loss. However, it may seem difficult to evaluate each trade since they are many. If the trader engaged in at least two trades, it could be manageable. Being unable to handle a loss What happens when the trader engages in multiple trades and makes a loss in all or most? You can imagine the likely situation that such a person will find themselves in, in case such a thing happens.

Overtrading is not any different from gambling. It mainly depends on luck but fails to consider how things work. When you gamble, you can either encounter a loss or a profit. However, the probability of encountering a loss is more than that of getting a profit. You may find that the person invested in all the money that they had and end up losing all of it due to a single bad decision they make. This will be difficult for them to accept. They may take long before they come into terms with the loss that they have incurred. Some even get to extreme points of committing suicide since they feel like there is nothing to live for. In some cases, individuals have been diagnosed with depression and other mental health issues. All these are not good situations to be in. you would rather avoid overtrading. Over-leveraged accounts Overtrading can lead to over-leveraged accounts. One of the benefits of day trading is that it provides room for conducting multiple trades. You may find that the trader can trade as many times as they would like without a limit. If they are careful enough to analyze the probable outcome, they are likely to encounter a profit. This will involve making the right decisions on the type of trade that they engage in. they will also need to use the right trading strategies to get to a profit out of a trade. On the other hand, they will need to have an effective trading plan. However, a trader will overlook all of these while engaging in multiple trades. As a result, the trader may encounter a loss that they may not be able to recover from.

When this happens, the brokerage account that they use to trade may become over-leveraged. Loss of capital is better than an over-leveraged account. In an over-leveraged account, the trader may have to pay back that entire capital, he or she owed the broker. In some cases, it may involve high-interest rates so as to compensate what they owed the broker. Misuse of funds Overtrading can lead to misuse of funds. You find that an individual has accumulated a lot of funds from previous trades. The capital may be part of the savings or earning from the various investments the individual might be having. After some thinking, the individual decides to multiply the capital. There is nothing wrong in making that decision, the only challenge comes in when you decide on the method to use. There are plenty of ways in which an investor can earn an extra income.

Overtrading can be a possible option but it is not the best option that one can have. Unless you are very sure that you can manage, do not risk investing in multiple trades. You find that the individual decides that out of all the options that they have, overtrading is the best. This person engages in multiple trades without proper planning and ends up making a loss. When this happens, the person loses the money that he/she has worked hard for, instead of increasing it as they would have expected. If you care about your earnings, you wouldn't gamble on luck. You would carry out a proper evaluation on how best you can invest. To avoid the challenges that come with overtrading, have a trading plan. A plan will help you in selecting the best options to invest in. you will get to know the advantages and disadvantages of engaging in some trades. It also helps you in proper timing in that you get to invest at the right time. Proper timing helps in maximizing the profits as you minimize the losses. It also allows you to make proper investment decisions that allow you to generate an income. In the previous chapters, I have talked about developing a trading plan, you can use the information while making one. Keeping a journal is also important. It allows you to write down your progress in option trading. You can write down some of the factors that contributed to a loss in a certain trade. In the future, you can refer to the records to avoid making such a mistake.

A journal can be useful in avoiding overtrading since it shows the dangers of making a bad decision. A risk management plan can also help in reducing the possibility of incurring a loss due to many risks. The important factor involves making the right decisions while trading.

How to Succeed in Trading Options

Have a trading plan to succeed in anything in life, and you first need to have a plan. A plan allows you to focus on an end goal, and you do all you can to ensure that you keep your end of the bargain. In the previous chapter, I have discussed the various factors that once need to consider while coming up with a suitable plan. We have also identified that one of the major mistakes people make while trading option is failing to have a trading plan. A plan consists of many things that make trade matter. Having a good plan will guarantee that you become successful at trading option and that you keep maintaining that position. It acts as a proper guide in knowing when to execute a trade and when to avoid making a trade. This helps a lot when it comes to timing, the trader can exercise their trade at a time that can generate an extra income. Have proper knowledge of the option strategies There are many ways to kill a rat. When it comes to trading options, there are many ways to trade. These ways are what we refer to as option strategy. Lack of information regarding option strategies has caused many people to make huge losses while trading options.

Limited knowledge of the option strategies has also led to low returns. In an investment, this is not a good thing to occur, considering that the aim of trading options is to earn high returns. Anyone hoping to make it in option trading has to give his/ her best in getting all the needed information. As the industry expands, new discoveries are being made. More and more option strategies are coming up and one has to keep up with the trend. If you take your time to invest in something, it is equally important to know how you will sustain that investment by letting it grow. Often, we work really hard to get the money that we wish to invest. The problem is that we do not put in that energy when it comes to sustaining the investment. Take some time and learn more about the strategies. Having a vision What makes you get out of bed with bursting energy to tackle each day? Do you have something that you find worth living for? If someone asked you why you think you deserve being in this world, what would be your reason? Do you find yourself worthy? Take some time and deeply reflect on these questions. They are not only relevant to success in options trading, but to overall success in life.

Often, we are advised that we are what we think we are. This is true since our way of thinking shows us what type of people we are. Success in option trading is entirely dependent on the individual. If you would like to earn a fortune out of option trading, you will need to have a vision. Have something that motivates you to push on even when you feel like giving up. I will not say that trading options is a walk in the park because it is not. The risks involved may end up in a loss. When such a thing happens, you will need to stay strong and focused on your vision. This will help you embrace setbacks with a lot of enthusiasm that you will manage to bounce back. Have a renewed mindset You will be surprised how limiting your brain can be. There are those negative things that you tell yourself that limit you from getting to positions you ought to be in. When it comes to trading options, our mind can limit us from achieving what we would like. For you to break free from that limitation, you will need a renewed mindset. We have had people being discouraged to engage in options trading because it is a scam. Most of the people who say this have either been frustrated by the trade they made or they also had the rumors from another source. This allegation has caused a lot of people not to engage in trade. I think one should come to a conclusion after trying something out. That way, you get to say things that you are well aware of. The other issue is that most people fail because of the lack of needed information. There is a very low possibility of failing if you are aware of the trading strategies and have proper timing while executing a trade. Work on reforming your mindset and see your success rates increase. Know how to handle success We are all looking forward to becoming rich but we never consider how we will sustain the wealth once we acquire it. If you wish to be a successful trader, this is one thing that you will have to consider. Failure to which, you will remain stagnant at one point and never make a progress.

Once you get profits from trading options, you get to misuse them and nothing productive comes out of it. If you hope to make a difference and keep boosting those profits to a larger profit, there are some things that you will have to do differently. For instance, you can open up a savings account with any bank and transfer a portion of the profits earned. If you are confident enough in your trading skills, you can reinvest the money in trading to keep increasing the earnings. Alternatively, you can invest in another investment to allow the money to grow. All these strategies will ensure that you sustain the money earned from option trading. You can also set a budget in which you spend the money required. This limits you from making unnecessary purchases. Have self-control You are probably wondering how self-control can help you succeed in trading options. Well, self-control has everything to do with our overall success in life. At times we need to do some things with a limitation so that we do not overdo the. Trading can be really addictive. One can trade today and make a loss and still give another shot the following day and still end up with a loss. You could come across someone who keeps trying and trying and in all times he or she keeps getting a loss. Such an approach can make you lose everything that you have worked so hard to get.

At times one has to know that option trading is not like gambling. You cannot entirely depend on luck without having a proper plan and a strategy. This shows that everything that you do will be in vain and it may not amount to anything major. In such cases, one needs to have discipline. Once you make two losses in a row, you need to stop trading and figure out where you are going wrong. This will prevent the likelihood of incurring a loss in the next trade. Have a risk management plan Each option has its own downsides and upsides. There are also risks involved in each option. How you tackle an option is for you to decide. The only way to earn a profit while trading is to minimize the risks that are involved so as to reduce the chances of getting a loss. One of the best ways of minimizing the possible risks is having knowledge of all the option strategies that you can use in a trade. This is the main way you can reduce such risks. The option strategies are made for this reason. Another factor to consider is the expiration trade. Once a contract gets to the expiry date, it can be declared useless. You cannot afford to make a loss because you failed to recall the expiry date of an option. This is a risk that you cannot afford to make. You can also minimize risks by proper timing. Analyzing the trading graphs can allow you to know when to trade and when to avoid trading. This information can direct one on the best time to engage in a trade for maximum profits. As a trader, the biggest task will involve minimizing the risk to generate extra money. Know how to tackle losses. An investor has to be open to the fact that they can encounter anything while trading options. You can get a loss or a profit depending on the trade outcome. We are all expectant that we will earn profits and no one prepares us for failure.

Success is nice and good, but failure is part of the success journey. Even if you have all the knowledge in the world, you may still encounter failure. Due to the fact that no one prepares us for the possible losses that we may encounter, we end up being unable to manage when it happens. This has led to depression and ulcers in some people. It's high time that we become open to the fact that one can encounter a loss while carrying out a business or any investment. People should also invest in that which they can afford to lose. In some cases, failure is inevitable and there is nothing that we can do to prevent it. We just have to learn how to live with it. While trading, avoid having high expectations and be open to the possibility of a loss. When it strikes, you will be in a better position of recovering and moving on. Have proper knowledge of the trade market Once you decide to engage in trading option, the next major move will involve acquiring knowledge of the industry. There is a lot to be learned each day. Option trading is a diverse topic that you can barely exhaust.

As the market grows, new items are being added and introduced. This increases the information concerning option trading. The interesting thing is that it happens daily. So, you need to keep up if at all you want to be an expert trader. This knowledge has been made available in a variety of platforms. There are books, the internet, and training aimed at passing trading knowledge. The majority of the brokerage accounts are now offering training on option trading. This is a marketing strategy to allow people to trade using their account after providing them with training. I have nothing against this strategy; in fact, you should utilize it to get all the information that you need. You may not invest from their accounts, but at least you will have learned something. Do this and see the impact it will have on your trading success. Be flexible and patient While trading options you will have a need to be patient and flexible. There are moments when you may take a long time before earning a profit. As you analyze the graphs, you may discover that the conditions surrounding the trade are not favorable and hence you will delay exercising your option contract.

This may occur many times in a low and you may grow impatient. In such a situation, you would rather wait instead of making a move that can lead to a loss. On the other hand, you may have started trading with the expectation of getting quick money. You need to know that it may take some time before you start earning your returns. You will have to trust the process and wait until you get to the point of earning the huge returns. Flexibility will apply while deciding on the various option strategies to use in a given trade. You may find that there are some strategies that you are more familiar with than others. The trade market may not allow you to carry out that strategy; hence you need to be flexible such that you can use the required strategy.

Conclusion

Thank you so much for reading the *Options trading crash course Intensive Guide to Options Trading, with all the winning strategies, tips, and tricks, that will allow you to invest and make money Income by Options Trading all Step by Step. In this book, we will show you how to make money from options trading* till the end. As you can see in this book, we learned a lot when it comes to options trading. We taught you how to start your options trading business and how to get it to be profitable. One thing you have to understand one following options trading is that you need to know how all the terminologies and how the strike price works.

We have laid that out entirely in this book, so you will have no problem understanding and acting on your goals. Even though this book was very informational, we made it so that you can start taking action as soon as possible. Reading the book is excellent; however, if you want to see results, then we highly recommend that you take action as quickly as possible.

If you're going to see results, then you need to read the book and act on the situation as soon as possible before it is too late for you to make money. The thing about options trading is that it is continuously going up and down. This is why you need to act on the information provided to you so that you can make the most money from it. As always make sure that you keep reading up on options trading so that you can better your knowledge.

Description

☆ *55% OFF for BookStore NOW at $ 34,95 instead of $ 45,95!* ☆

If you are interested in learning the best advanced strategies on options trading, this is the book for you.. Start earning serious money through Options Trading.

Are you looking to make a lot of money, from options trading and investing your money? If the answer is yes to both, and then you need to read this book as soon as possible and start making money. We are going to be talking about options trading and helping you understand how to make money from trading with options. Options trading is one of the most lucrative methods to make a lot of money, as it is straightforward to get into once you understand the basics. The basics have been altered with a lot in the past years, which is why we created this book; that way, everybody knows the right answers to options trading so that they can start making money.

In this book, you will learn:

- Introduction: Talk about the book.

- Chapter 1: Options Trading 101: Talk about what options are and how they were created.

- Chapter 2: How to start options trading: Talk about the ways to get started with trading.

- Chapter 3: Short term strategy: Explain to the readers how you can make money in the short term with options trading.

- Chapter 4: Long term strategy: Talk about long term strategies with options trading.

- Chapter 5: Put them together: Explain to the readers what people who are well versed in trading do for both long term and short term

- Chapter 6: How to avoid risk: Talk about the potential risk with options trading and how you can prevent it

- Chapter 7: Advanced options trading: Talk about options trading, and how it can help you to make even more money.

- Chapter 8: Tips for success: Touch up on how to be successful with options trading

- Chapter 9: Put it all together: Give readers a full-proof way to make long term money with options trading.

- Conclusion

As you can see, we will be going through everything in this book to make sure that you are ready to start trading in the options market. Keep in mind, and this book has everything from beginners advice to advance advice, which makes this book one of the most excellent books to read on options trading. If you are looking to slowly build-up to the advanced level of options trading, then this book will help you to get there. Just make sure that you read the basics before you get into all the Advanced Techniques. And as always, don't wait for this book to go off the air. The truth is we don't know how long this book will be on the market, which is why we want you to make sure that you start utilizing that information provided to you in this book so you can be successful with options trading. If you wait another month to get this book, the chances are the prices will go up and you will be a month away from making money. Instead, if you spend the money right now, and get this book, then you will be in a much better position to making money and to do it quickly.

Buy is NOW and let your Customers get addicted to this amazing book!

CPSIA information can be obtained
at www.ICGtesting.com
Printed in the USA
BVHW070108090321
602012BV00002B/291